ORPHANS OF WAR

ORPHANS OF WAR

WORK WITH THE ABANDONED CHILDREN
OF VIETNAM 1967—1975

ROSEMARY TAYLOR

IN COLLABORATION WITH

WENDE GRANT

COLLINS
8 GRAFTON STREET, LONDON W1
1988

William Collins Sons & Co. Ltd
London · Glasgow · Sydney · Auckland
Toronto · Johannesburg

British Library Cataloguing in Publication Data
Taylor, Rosemary
Orphans of War.
1.   Orphans —— Vietnam —— History
I. Title
362.7'044   HV1300.5

ISBN 0—00—217737—4

First published in Great Britain 1988
Copyright © Rosemary Taylor and Wende Grant
Photoset in Linotron Sabon by Wyvern Typesetting Ltd, Bristol
Made and printed in Great Britain by
T. J. Press (Padstow) Ltd, Padstow, Cornwall

'. . . our work depends on us not seeing
the whole problem – we have to see the few
children in our care and limit our attention
to them . . . if we started to see what we are
not doing, we would be able to do nothing at
all. As it is, we are doing something . . .
This has the curious effect of making people
think that they can do something, too.'

Margaret Moses

Contents

PART TWO

List of Illustrations

War-torn Provincial Vietnam (opposite page 30)
1 Refugees return to Hue, after it has been recaptured from the Vietcong, March 1968. [Photo © Central Press Photos Ltd.]
2 A Chinese-born shopkeeper sits in the ruins of his former business. [Photo © Central Press Photos Ltd.]
3 Refugee children in a camp at Qui Nhon. [Photo © Three Lions Inc.]

Arrivals at the Nurseries (opposite page 31).
4 Six babies for To Am, from Soctrang. [Photo Ilse Ewald]
5 Sang, from another Saigon orphanage. Many children had been left lying without stimulation, until their muscles became atrophied from lack of use.
6 Lucy, in the nursery at Phu My. Sr Angèle is giving her an IV infusion.

Daily Life in the Nurseries (opposite pages 46 and 47)
7 Newhaven Nursery.
8 To Am (1969).
9 Hair-cutting at Phu My (1967).
10 Classroom activities at Allambie (1974).
11 New arrivals from Soctrang are held by older children at To Am (1971).
12 Potty time.
13 Thien helping himself, To Am (1971). [Photo Ilse Ewald]

Special Cases (opposite page 102)
14 Collecting children by ferry from Providence Orphanage, Culaogieng (1969). All three girls (now in Belgium) had eye problems.

ix

15 Jason, a paraplegic boy, from Sacred Heart Orphanage, Danang. He survived the C-5A crash.
16 Cuong, totally blind, from Providence Orphanage, Cantho. He died in the crash.
17 Sr Rose and Sr Raymond help a group of polio children on their way to school at Phu My.

Some Staff and Helpers (between pages 102 and 103)
18 Peter Trueman, with Margarita on her baptism day.
19 Christie Leivermann.
20 Mary Cusack.
21 Susan McDonald.
22 Ilse Ewald, with Ut, at Providence Orphanage, Cantho.
23 Anne Barry, with Jacqueline (Jade) at Allambie.
24 Peggy Hammond.
25 Sgt-Major George Miles, at To Am.
26 Sr Rose-Marie, director of Phu My. She is holding two children who are about to depart for Europe.
27 Margaret Moses. She died in the crash.
28 Dolly Bui. She too died in the C-5A crash.
29 Yvette Charamont, feeding Lara at Peter Trueman's house.
30 Mary-Nelle Gage, preparing visas and embarkation cards. [Photo Bernadette Marks]
31 Lee Makk. She died in the crash.
32 Sr Angela, at Sacred Heart Orphanage, Danang.
33 Rosemary Taylor, with Vanessa, who died a few weeks after this photograph was taken.
34 Doreen Beckett, at Allambie, with Coi (1974).
35 Birgit Blank, with twins, Sun and Flower, now in the USA. Birgit died in the C-5A crash.
36 Sr Ursula, in charge of the Good Shepherd Nursery. She, too, died in the crash.

On the Move to New Homes (opposite page 103)
37 Sr André, French Superior of Vinh Long. The two girls with bags in the cyclo are setting off to families in Switzerland (1967).
38 Travelling to Tan Son Nhut airport, on the way to Europe (September 1973).
39 This young lady is on her way in a cyclo to the airport, en route to Switzerland.

Children Then and Now (between pages 262 and 263).

66, 67 Little Bear – now Kim – held by Agnes at To Am, Christmas 1971, and in Australia, aged 15 (August 1986). [Photo Richard A. Dobson]

68, 69 Margarita (see also no. 18) dressed as a mascot, and now in the USA, aged 17 (1986).

70, 71 Sanh in his Cub Scout cap, To Am 1971, and now in Canada, a member of the Bronstein family.

72, 73 Francesca hugging her sister Sophie in Italy in 1978, first seen in To Am 1971.

74, 75 Thu Van, now Tia, at Providence Orphanage, Soctrang in 1971, and in America, 1985.

76, 77, 78 Reunion of some children adopted in Germany, Cologne 1984 [Photo Holger Schmitt]. Torge, in 1968 at St Paul's Bien Hoa, in no. 77, is in the back row of the group. Marcus and Aurelius, twins at To Am in 1972, in no. 78, are standing together, now called Matthias and Andreas, in the German group.

79, 80 Turtledove, now Anna Tiffany, in Colorado General Hospital, July 1975, is now in England. Seen with her little sister, Josephine, in 1986.

81, 82 Jacqueline, now Jade, first in Rach Gia with Lola d'Orazio, the day she arrived at Allambie, and later in the USA, aged 13.

Children of Several Nationalities (opposite page 263)

83 In Australia, Fiona, Heidi, Lisi, and Rosi (in 1986).

84 In France, Cecilia, aged 11 in 1979.

85 In England, Safi, aged 12 in 1986. She was a survivor of the crash.

86 In Germany, Kim (Brian), aged 18. [Photo Holger Schmitt]

87 In Finland, Pami (Joy), aged 14.

88 In America, Benjie, and Chad, members of different families.

PREFACE

THIS BOOK is the story of the orphans of Vietnam, thousands of whom are now growing up in adoptive homes in many different countries. Their new life was made possible through the dedication of hundreds of people around the world – people who gave of their time, love, energy, and wealth for the orphans. Some gave their lives.

We have felt it our duty to tell this story for the children themselves and for those who know them, so that they will have some truthful reference when they begin to question their origins, and search for an understanding of the events that changed their lives so radically. They will not learn from this account anything about the politics of the war in Vietnam, but they may learn something of how that war affected the lives of the people, caused a disintegration of the social structure, and filled the orphanages with abandoned infants. They will then have a clearer understanding of our motivation in sending them out of Vietnam to a new life in families abroad.

The main narrative, for which I have been responsible, links a selection of my journals and nursery records, extracts from letters to family, friends and colleagues, and general newsletters sent overseas during the years I was in Vietnam (1967–75). But just as Wende Grant's contribution to the work in Vietnam was of paramount importance to our project then and during its after-math, so too she has played a significant role in the preparation of this book. Wende contributed accounts of the beginnings of the 'Friends' groups in America – her family was one of the first to have adopted a Vietnamese orphan (ch. 3); of the eventual development into Friends For All Children (FFAC) (ch. 7); and of the registration as an adoption agency in Saigon; of her visit to Cambodia (ch. 10); and of the evacuation of the Canadian nursery from Phnom Penh (ch. 12); and of the difficult and prolonged aftermath of litigation in America (chs. 19 and 20). She has generously allowed me to use her versions, which appear at least as a basis for what is included here, and often as much more.

There is also a collage of letters, FFAC correspondence, contemporary accounts, and memoirs elicited from or offered by other colleagues. These are cut and patched together to avoid repetition (though not, I hope, to the point of distortion), or sometimes deliberately overlapped so as to build up a many-sided impression. I haven't distinguished between my own letters as opposed to diary entries where they make up the narrative, but specific extracts are dated and particular correspondence or other people's records have been more precisely signalled.

I am particularly grateful to Anne Barry, the late Sr Doreen Beckett, Mary Cusack, Sr Mary-Nelle Gage, Peggy Hammond, Christie Leivermann, Sr Susan McDonald, Elaine Moir, Ruth Routten, and to Peter Trueman (who also supplied the Chronology of the Vietnam War), for allowing me to draw on their material so freely. I have also depended on accounts and letters written by Margaret Moses, who with other staff and seventy-eight children died on the crashed C-5A as the main evacuation of orphans from Saigon began. Ilse Ewald contributed many photographs, and they have jogged our memories more vividly than any written account could do.

The typescript, originally over 700,000 words long, and including much medical and legal documentation, was first assembled in 1977, apart from the three final chapters. In late 1979, when FFAC became involved with Cambodian refugees in Thailand, we temporarily put aside the idea of commercial publication, as the urgency of present need took precedence over reflection on past action. (In 1976 we had privately published a book of photographs of the children.) It was not until 1985 that Lady Pamela Egremont, a friend since her many working visits to Saigon and Phu My Hospice, introduced me to Roger Graef, a film maker, and through his auspices the typescript found its way to the publishing house of

Collins. A special acknowledgement is due to Jacqueline Simms, who played the major editorial role in reducing and shaping the original contents to publishable proportions.

Many of the adoptive parents and the children themselves have contributed to the last chapter on 'the children now'. My only regret is that in a work of this size, I simply cannot speak of each child individually, nor can I do more than hint at the experiences and impressions of many colleagues and friends who shared very closely in our work with the children, and who would each have a new tale to tell.

ROSEMARY TAYLOR
Bangkok, May 1987

CHRONOLOGY
OF THE VIETNAM WAR

1954   **May** Surrender of French garrison at Dien Bien Phu.
        July Agreement signed at Geneva to partition Vietnam along the 17th Parallel.
1955   **May** South Vietnam formally requests the United States for instructors for their armed forces.
1956   **April** American Military Assistance Advisory Group takes over training of South Vietnamese forces. French Military High Command disbands and French troops leave South Vietnam.
1959   **May** US begins sending military advisers at the request of the South Vietnamese government.
1964   **August** Following North Vietnamese attacks on two US warships Congress adopts the Tonkin Gulf Resolution, which endorses whatever measures the President considers necessary to repel attacks on US forces and to prevent further aggression.
        December Total US strength in South Vietnam – 23,000.
1965   **March** First deployment of US combat units to South Vietnam – a Marine infantry battalion, followed in May by an airborne brigade.
        December Total US strength in South Vietnam – 181,000.
1966   **December** Total US strength in South Vietnam – 385,000.
1967   **September** General Nguyen Van Thieu elected President of South Vietnam.
        December Total US strength in South Vietnam – 486,000.
1968   **February–March** The Tet offensive erupts throughout Vietnam.

May Delegates from the United States and North Vietnam meet in Paris for peace talks.

December Total US strength in South Vietnam – 536,000 reaching a peak strength of 543,000 in early 1969.

1969 **July** Start of US withdrawal and by the end of the year troop strength is down to 474,000.

1970 **March** Attacks by South Vietnamese and US forces across Cambodian border against Communist base camps.

December Tonkin Gulf Resolution repealed and US strength in South Vietnam down to 336,000.

1971 During the year the Free World countries (Australia, New Zealand, South Korea and Thailand) announce that they will withdraw their forces from South Vietnam.

December North Vietnamese build-up in the southern part of their country.

1972 **March** North Vietnamese invasion of Quang Tri Province, eventually halted by South Vietnamese ground forces helped by US aircraft.

September Quang Tri City re-captured but most of the rest of the province remains in North Vietnamese hands.

December All US combat troops now out of South Vietnam leaving 43,500 airmen and support personnel. Bombing north of the 20th Parallel comes to an end after the North Vietnamese agree to negotiate a truce.

1973 **January** The Paris Peace Agreement is reached to end war, and is formally signed on 27th.

March Last US troops leave South Vietnam leaving only a Defence Attaché Office.

1974 **January** President Thieu claims that the war in South Vietnam has re-started.

1975 **March** North Vietnamese forces launch attacks in the Central Highlands.

April 15th North Vietnamese forces capture Xuan Loc 38 miles east of Saigon.

21st President Thieu resigns and is succeeded by General Duong Van Minh.

30th North Vietnamese troops enter Saigon and new President announces unconditional surrender.

PART ONE

Chapter 1

FIRST YEAR IN SAIGON

I ARRIVED in Saigon on 18 February 1967, billed as an educational social worker and 'the first Roman Catholic to join a refugee service team' sponsored by the Australian Council of Churches. It was intended that we should work in the temporary camps at Tuy Hoa, about 250 miles north of Saigon. I had no clear idea what I would be able to do, and, with no experience of life in a war-zone, seem to have absorbed without preconceptions the sights and sounds of war that greeted me in Saigon: the ubiquitous military presence, the armed guards at every turn, the huge coils of barbed wire barricading streets and buildings, the unlikely range of military and civilian vehicles jockeying for space in the city streets, sounds of gunfire and rocketing in the distance; and the ordinary civilians going about their business as though oblivious to it all.

On the other hand, I was amazed the first time I saw a family of seven aboard a single motorbike. I never ceased to be astonished by the whiteness of the schoolgirls' Ao-Dais,[1] considering the sordidness of their surroundings, and at how they could ride a bicycle wearing their bamboo hats – something I never managed to do. I would also wonder, for eight years, how the young women could bear to work in the heat of their schools and government offices with waist-length hair hanging around them, and in such perfect order. And I puzzled at the strange Asian logic of the traffic system: why, for instance, north-bound vehicles would fill up both sides of a two-way street, causing jams that would take hours to unravel. It baffled and often almost asphyxiated me.

[1] The Ao-Dai is a close fitting long-sleeved blouse with mandarin collar, which splits at the waist to become two panels front and back, reaching to mid-calf and worn over black or white satin trousers.

My first six weeks in Vietnam, devoted to intensive language study, were spent between books and bathroom, the inevitable dysentery proving the body to be far less adaptable than the mind. And then, in the seventh week, I was officially expelled from the team, and found myself on my own. This was certainly an inauspicious beginning.

Frustration had begun to develop amongst the team members in Saigon almost at once, as we became better able to assess the situation. There was friction with the Burmese Director of the team, Mr T., who provided no real leadership. Dr John Whitehall, there with his wife, Elsie, a kindergarten teacher, had been reassigned four times, but still had no local authorization to practise medicine. Our Director was not only unable to organize competently, but was embarrassingly discourteous to other officials, and demoralizing to some of the team members with his bullying and dictatorial ways. He would tolerate no discussion.

It was easiest for me to object and go to the defence of a colleague or a servant, since I was probably the most independent member of the group, and not planning to make a professional career in the service. Inevitably, I began to clash with him. But I wasn't alone in my reaction. We were all uncomfortable with the high-handed way the domestic staff were treated in the house (absurd demands were put on them to produce sophisticated 'cuisine': the Director's wife flew into a rage when we had chicken-noodle soup twice running!). More seriously, it seemed that church money collected to support us and our work was ill-used in helping sustain an atmosphere that was a parody of Christianity:

30 March 1967, Rosemary Taylor [RT] to Australian Council of Churches: I'm not exaggerating. Would you believe that in this time of war when everything is upside down, when the servants themselves sleep in the garage and eat off packing-cases in our backyard ... the Director and his wife [complain] because our cook never serves 'hors-d'œuvre'. . .

For a few days, John, Elsie and I went to Tuy Hoa for a preview of the situation; it is miserable enough. The camp now has about 6,000 refugees with no facilities at all beyond a fly-infested shack used as a clinic. A bamboo school has just been constructed with four classrooms. Back in Saigon, I returned to language study, and John continued studying tropical diseases and tried to collect the wherewithal to establish some kind of medical service in Tuy Hoa. Then Mr T. changed his mind and decided to send him to Cai Be instead.

Despite this small matter of administration, I am happy to be here, and look forward to commencing work in earnest in a few weeks.

But then another incident involving the servants provoked a row for which I was held responsible, and a few days later Mr T. summoned me into his office and told me he was sending me back to Australia. I refused to go, but clearly our collaboration had by now become impossible. It was eventually arranged by headquarters that I should work independently and, in May, I was transferred to the local sponsorship of Catholic Relief Services, though this relationship was also to prove short-lived. Meanwhile, however, the American CRS said they were due to embark on a refugee programme, sending out fifteen teams in the coming year. They told me I would be assigned to the first team, as soon as the programme received final approval from Washington.

In June the Whitehalls would also leave the Australian group, as they felt they were wasting their time and talents in the badly-managed local situation; and by December, the official newsletter from Asian Christian Services announced that in all, seven of the original team members had quit the group in Vietnam. My situation that May was certainly discouraging. After a sticky and difficult beginning, there I was in Vietnam two months later, mosquito-bitten and sometimes incapacitated by dysentery, with no team, no status, and no specific task. The days and nights were filled with the noise of constant shelling, low-flying helicopters, phantom jets and convoys of tanks rolling through the streets. It would be illogical – absurd, even – to choose to remain in such uncomfortable circumstances without a strong conviction that one's presence was useful. I was aware that I must have appeared somewhat of an 'adventuress', or at best an amateur, to the personnel of more established organizations. But somehow it didn't occur to me to give up. There was a sea of human need around me; I knew I had the resources to respond, though how to do so had yet to become clear.

Going to work in Vietnam was not the result of design or long-cherished ambition. In mid-1966 I was at home in Australia awaiting a permanent visa that would enable me to return to teach in Alaska. My career to date, since graduating and teaching for a couple of years in Australia, had taken me to England as a psychiatric research assistant at Littlemore Hospital, Oxford, for eighteen months, while hoping meanwhile to be granted a visa to work on the Alaskan Missions. Eventually in 1963, though still without a visa, I had gone to Alaska, where I was attached to the Jesuit Mission School near Dillingham for seven months. As an unpaid volunteer, I taught, cooked, looked after Eskimo children, and did anything that came to hand, until the Immigration Authorities caught up with me, accused me of depriving an American citizen of a job, and deported me. (Two FBI agents, who seemed rather apologetic, saw me off at Anchorage airport.) Back again in Alaska in 1965 (after a period teaching Grade 12 chemistry and algebra in Canada), I obtained a temporary visa and a teaching certificate for the school year, and worked as a member of the mission in Bethel. There I came into contact with the thousand and one problems of the disrupted Eskimo community: problems of poverty, alcoholism, promiscuity, boredom, and lack of opportunities for work or entertainment. There was no mission school in Bethel, but the children came to the centre for religious instruction and recreation. For a while I substituted at the regional high school; and I had also taken an evening course in 'Teaching Modern Mathematics', which offered three credits towards the six I would need to renew my teaching certificate.

When I went home then, it was with every intention of returning to Alaska as soon as US Immigration would allow. But months passed, and by the time the US Consul in Adelaide at last notified me that my visa was ready to be issued, I was able to thank him, but decline. By now I had become more aware of the war in Vietnam and felt the need there to be more pressing. I applied to join the team (which I had seen mentioned in the local paper), sponsored by the Australian Council of Churches, a branch of Asian Christian Services, to work in a refugee camp in Vietnam. The panel of Educational, Social Welfare, and Church dignitaries that interviewed me asked me what I thought I would be doing in Vietnam; I replied that I had no precise idea, but that I expected to observe the situation and respond appropriately. They must have accepted my

4

Alaskan experience as proof of adaptability and I was approved for the assignment in Vietnam, issued with a list of suitable clothing and supplies, and given 125 dollars with which to equip myself.

In April 1967, when it seemed as if the Council's confidence had been misplaced, I was introduced to Phu My by Anna Forder, a social worker for Catholic Relief Services (CRS). Phu My, on the outskirts of Saigon, was directed by the Sisters of St Paul de Chartres, and was a refuge for the homeless, the destitute, the incurably ill, and the dying. It was also an orphanage and centre for polio children. Situated in the Thi Nghe district, the eight-acre block fronted Huong Vong Street, which in those days smelt and looked like – and was used as – a public rubbish dump. Within the walls of Phu My was another world, clean, calm and well-ordered, where 1,500 inmates lived in the starkest simplicity. There was the plank bed, the crude utensils, and the diet mainly of rice, spinach, dried fish and bananas; there was the security of a regular regime, companionship, and the comfort of religious worship. Sr Rose-Marie (Marquis), the Swiss Superior, had already been in Vietnam for sixteen years. Before coming to Phu My she had directed the well-known Clinique St Paul in Phan-Thanh-Gian Street. Phu My was to be my home for the next eight years, and Sr Rose a faithful ally.

I began to work at Phu My on a temporary basis, helping Sr Angèle in the nursery-orphanage section, and learning a great deal from her. Soon I was giving medication and shots, putting in IV infusions, and studying pharmacology. I made the daily buckets of yoghurt, helped to feed the most difficult children, and participated in all the regular nursery chores. Sr Angèle had only a few words of English and I had my laboured Vietnamese: we communicated habitually in French, which was easiest for both of us.

To begin with, I missed my former Australian colleagues and felt rather depressed by the turn of events; my morale was certainly at a low ebb those first weeks after I had left the team. But I was soon enjoying my work, and feeling quite at home at Phu My, where I was given a room (as I described to my family in May), that

is built into the wall surrounding the grounds and so is a natural haven for wild life. I share it with many of God's lesser creatures

– dragonflies, spiders, cockroaches, lizards (good, because they eat the flies), flies, mosquitoes, rats, frogs, bats, and ants . . .

Very soon, the layman director of Catholic Relief Services, Mr Mooney, who had agreed to sponsor me in Vietnam, was due to leave, and his replacement at once made it clear he had no intention of including volunteer labour, let alone Rosemary Taylor, in his plans (although in theory I supposed I was still under the auspices of CRS until they formally severed the connection the following year). But by now I had clearly seen an opportunity of being useful, and realized I need look no further than Phu My.

While there was still a foreign military presence in Vietnam, there was considerable help forthcoming for the orphanages. Each military unit had some civic-action programme and soldiers came regularly with truckloads of food, clothing, medicines and toys. The children were sometimes partied and picnicked by the military and many of the men displayed an involvement beyond the call of duty. Some felt, particularly when children were concerned, that the programmes were the only way they could justify their presence in Vietnam, and it was a relief for their own homesickness to entertain the orphans. They also donated labour and building materials for building improvements. English was an asset at this time, and being the only English-speaking person on the premises at Phu My, I was continually called upon to interpret needs or to translate from French into English.

At the farewell party at the Continental for Mr Mooney, I met a young lieutenant from Special Forces ('Green Berets'), and mentioned our need for 1,500 sacks of cement to build a pavilion in which to house polio children and adult invalids. Penicillin was also in short supply:

30 June: Next morning he came to Phu My, picked up the list I had prepared detailing our most important medical needs, and returned in the afternoon with two truck-loads of rice, bulgur, cornmeal, clothing, health- and school-kits for the children, plus all the medication I had listed. Five hundred sacks of cement arrived the next day. The efficiency of this operation quite impressed me. I've been trying to get some cement for two

6

months from other sources, but so far have only received fervent promises.

The experience of my first boil shocked me into the use of disinfectant, as I wrote home:

9 *July*: I've just finished some laundry, squatting on my front 'patio' at Phu My. I even tackled the doormat (a sugar sack), soaking all in disinfectant which is my way of defying Asia and working off all kinds of complexes . . .

This morning I was howling with rage. Immediately after Mass, Sr Rose asked me to go to the Saigon Children's Hospital, Nhi Dong, with one of the ladies from Phu My whose eleven-year-old son, Duc, was seriously ill with haemorraghic fever. Sr Rose wanted me to enlist the aid of the British medical team based at Nhi Dong, if it would be helpful.

The boy, Duc, had been admitted to hospital yesterday evening and the mother was told to provide blood and medication before 11 a.m. today or her son would die. With Sr Rose's assistance, she obtained what was needed. We were both at the hospital when the blood was hooked up by a Vietnamese nurse who ambled in and out with no trace of concern. Two of the three children in this room were dying. The room was stinking and the furniture cruddy, but the nurse's toilet and manicure were perfect. As soon as the nurse left the room, the moment after she had fastened the needle into the boy's vein, his arm began to convulse violently.

I left the room in anguish and walked the corridor looking for help. A British doctor appeared: 'Is the boy yours?' he asked. 'No, I've never seen him before this morning,' I replied. Though it was unethical for him to interfere, Duc not being his patient, he nonetheless comforted me by checking the boy's file. There was nothing more that could be done, he said; Duc was already too far gone, his body covered with tiny sub-cutaneous blood blisters. The doctor offered the mother a supply of blood if more were needed, and his concern was some consolation to her. Even as I write this I am tied up in knots just thinking of a hospital where they won't give a blood transfusion unless one can afford to buy the blood. And when I think of the filth, the piles of refuse in the corridors, and the dying children left to the tender mercies of nurses who have the remarkable gift of perfect uninterest, I understand why Sr Angèle from Phu My never wants to send the children to hospital.

Duc was discharged the next day and died almost as soon as he got back to Phu My.

When I was in the process of hunting for cement and iron rebar [supports] for the polio pavilion, I first made the acquaintance of Barbara Baden, a USAID nurse-adviser, working in the Giadinh area. She had been sent with a team of colleagues to investigate Phu My's need for the new building. I had already had numerous interviews with different people, and showed them the plans for a plain building that would provide basic shelter; each time I was referred to someone else:

> 9 *July*: I thought I had struck the jack-pot the other day when two engineers came along, with a nurse and a doctor who had been working in this area. The nurse, Barbara Baden, had told the two engineers, who were sceptical, of our need for 1,500 bags of cement (that's only for half the building). Well, I produced the blueprints once more, and they saw the estimate was an understatement . . . As they seemed pleased with the project, I pressed on, and asked about the rebar that we needed. 'Sure, no problem,' they replied, but I would have to contact the Provincial Representative and make a formal request, etc. They say it will be here within a week, but I become less credulous as time goes on.

When I wasn't acting as 'building adviser', I was in the crèche, helping look after dozens of sick children at Phu My. Each morning we had to bandage savage skin eruptions on the younger babies. Very occasionally, we received important visitors:

> 26 *July*: Last week we had another visit from Mme Thieu [wife of the President] with a retinue of four other women . . . Very cynically, I suspect these visits are opportunely made before the forthcoming elections as good campaign policy.

> 3 *August*: On Tuesday, Sr Angèle went to Bien Hoa, and I was left in charge of the crèche for the day. First I prepared the yoghurt (two buckets full) and puréed food for the babies, then went to the pharmacy next door to get some medication for the

dressings. I returned a few minutes later to find that two-year-old Kim Lien had fallen from her crib and gashed open her forehead. For the next twenty minutes, while someone else applied pressure to staunch the bleeding, I searched for the suture clips and applicator, turning all the cupboards inside out. The babies needing dressings for boils and other skin infections had to be abandoned while we scarred Kim Lien for life probably, with about eight suture clips, and bandaged her up . . . She seems to be in no pain now.

30 August: I'm on call all night, and a group of children will track from the crèche over to my room at the bottom of the garden, at any hour of the night, to tell me that a baby is sick, which usually means a high fever. Last night I went over at 8.45 to check Oanh and bandage up his ear and head. As soon as I appeared with first aid equipment, all the older children besieged me with their little sores and wounds. So I set up clinic and hacked away at hair clotted with blood and dried mounds of infection, mostly scouring the wounds with Phisohex antibacterial lotion and then bandaging. After an hour of this unscheduled clinic, I turned to the original task of bandaging Oanh's head and ear, but the baby was asleep and as his sleep was worth more than the bandages, I let it go and returned to my room at 9.45. Then at 12.30, there was a knocking at the door. Phuc and Ngoc had fevers so off I went again and spent until 2 a.m. trying to reduce their fever.

The supplies problem continued, and during the 'siesta' lull, I would continue my visits to Province and District Chiefs, in pursuit of building materials; the rest of the time, I would be on duty in the crèche, at odd intervals of the day and night:

8 October: Last Tuesday night I was called at midnight because three-month-old Marguerite was very low. Marguerite weighing $4\frac{1}{2}$ lb had just been brought back from the orphanage at Bien Hoa. She was in a state of serious malnutrition with bloated belly and fleshless limbs. Sr Angèle had also come down. As Marguerite was badly dehydrated, we prepared an intravenous infusion but did not have it working until 2.30 a.m. For the rest of the night I sat by her crib to supervise the infusion, checking for signs of exhaustion or infiltration. Marguerite pulled through the night but now she has bronchial pneumonia and is very weak.

At 8 a.m. I went to my room and flopped on the bed for a short nap but at 9.30 I was called again. This time it was Sr Aimée from Bien Hoa Orphanage. Her wall had been knocked down by a military jeep a few nights before, and she was on her way to the 'claims office' in Saigon. She needed me to interpret as she spoke only French.

The Military civic-action programme provided occasional medical teams. These were usually not very successful at Phu My chiefly because the patients were long-term chronic sufferers, or terminal cases, and a casual visiting physician was in no position to make any useful contribution beyond the collection of medication he would bring with him. Part of my job was to try and find medical help for the patients:

8 October: We have many episodes of doctors promising regular visits and then fading out of the picture. One episode began a couple of months ago when some of our US Air Force benefactors arrived with a surgeon and great plans for setting up a 'surgery'. Two months went by with no sign from our surgeon or the physician we had been promised. Last week, the same lieutenant turned up, but this time he had a fledgling general practitioner in tow and no mention of the surgeon. He also had a truckload of mouthwash (!) [breath sweetener only], which had been sent for Phu My (probably a forced withdrawal from the US market, or a tax-deduction for some business). I conducted the GP around the hospital and took him to some of our elderly patients who were eaten away with bedsores and diabetic ulcers: this to him was a waste of time – nothing much to be done. Moreover, the people back in the US didn't want pictures of this sort of thing, he said; they liked to see photos of children. 'Well, what sort of things do you want to do at the Tuesday clinic?' I asked. I was still under the impression they wanted some surgery. I was disappointed when the doctor replied: 'I'll fix up the children with 102° temperatures and skin rashes.' 'But,' I protested, 'our children have temperatures of 104° and we can deal with this ourselves. Moreover, they don't wait for Tuesday to develop fevers.'

The weekly clinic was established at Phu My, but the medical team varied rather wildly:

10 November: Last week's was composed of two corpsmen (medically trained but not doctors), who did nothing; and two Air Force nurses, one of whom was visiting for the first time and seemed dumbfounded by the proceedings.

Sr Odile, bright and businesslike, ushered in the first patient, questioned him in Vietnamese, translated his reply into French, and then I took over and turned the French into English. Then, I questioned the patient in French and while Sr Odile translated my questions into Vietnamese, I translated my French into English so that the nurse would know what I had asked. Back came the patient's reply in Vietnamese, transmitted in French by Sr Odile; I got it back into English. Everyone was talking at once; it was bedlam. Then, Sr Odile sent the patient out and hauled in a new one while I protested that we hadn't finished with the first patient. I tried to rouse the corpsman to make an examination. But he, looking rather washed out, said he would leave the examining to the nurse, who knew more about it than he did anyway; which was true. And so the nurse was examining and diagnosing and keeping her records, while I was suggesting medications (according to what I knew was available), and keeping my records a step ahead of her so that she could copy from me later.

This went on for two hours. Then, when the last patient told us he had trembling in his stomach at night and the nurse suggested a 'midnight snack', I broke down and in a moment we were all doubled up with laughter, including the patient, who was in no real pain. For the first time a corpsman actually roused himself to activity and reached for his movie-camera to film the whole absurd scene. (The tummy tremblings were ordinary symptoms of opium withdrawal, as I found out later from Sr Odile.)

The remedies were simple, mostly Phisohex, Bacitracin, Kaopectate, Maalox, aspirin, or some cough elixir, depending on whether the patient indicated discomfort in the region of the skin, bowels, stomach, head or chest. If the medicine dispensed was of dubious benefit, the show at least provided some welcome diversion for the patients and, as such, was a genuine panacea.

The occasional visiting dental team had somewhat greater success. There was little chance that any of the Phu My inmates would ever visit a regular dentist, and so everybody wanted to avail himself of the opportunity to have painful teeth extracted. Nothing more complex than extractions could be tackled at these outdoor dental clinics. The military dental teams had a field-day when they came to Phu My. For a time there was also a weekly eye clinic:

> *19 November*: I've just discovered a most dedicated American ophthalmologist from the 24th Evacuation Hospital, who travels fifteen miles to Saigon each week, and sets up clinic in a local Vietnamese hospital quite close to Phu My, in Giadinh. He has been operating on two of our Phu My patients every week, and I am always there for the operations. Last week he saw eighteen patients and had five surgeries without a break . . .

This was Dr Jon Tierney, who had been introduced to us by Barbara Baden. When he applied for an extension of his tour in Vietnam, I wrote, on behalf of his patients at Phu My in particular, in support of his application to the US Army. ⟨ received a reply from General Westmoreland. But Jon did not receive an extension, and if he was replaced, as was promised, we never heard from his replacement.

In this haphazard way I meandered around the complex military support system, discovering how I could best put to profit the supplies and services available. I soon learnt that procedure and protocol ultimately counted for nothing: it was merely a polite way of passing the buck. What mattered most was the good will of a few individuals and that could bring impressive results. I spent the first six years in Vietnam without official status, and relied heavily on the personal good will of friends who had professional skills, services or supplies available to them.

While I was working in Phu My nursery, I met a Swiss nurse, Yvonne L., from the organization Terre des Hommes, which was then mainly involved in a medical programme. They sent to Europe those children in need of complex medical treatment not available in Vietnam, and then supervised completion of the treatment when the children returned. Yvonne was also involved in arranging the adoption of a few of the orphan children into European families. I was delighted to learn that some of the children I had been looking after in the nursery would not waste their childhood in an orphanage, but would go to families in Belgium and Luxemburg, and that there would be others destined for Switzerland, France and Germany. For a limited number of children, at least, the problem of abandonment could be solved by placing them in adoptive families abroad.

29 *October*: Lately, I have been very busy with adoptions, helping the Swiss representative of Terre des Hommes to get the children away. Last Thursday we set out for Vinh Long, by local civilian transportation, in order to bring back four orphans who were due to depart on Saturday. For once I was thoroughly scared, not by the possibility of a Viet Cong encounter, but by the crazy driving. The bus was propelled at 50 m.p.h. over treacherous roads, all mud from recent rains, with swampy fields on either side. Once the bus was fired upon and pulled up. They were only friendly forces, having a bit of sport I suppose. After a few minutes of strained silence, our trigger-happy friends swaggered up to the bus and stood guard while the passengers descended and relieved themselves by the roadside. As the descent seemed optional, Yvonne and I stayed put.

At the end of 1967, Yvonne had to leave Vietnam and she asked me to be responsible for the departure of several dozen children whose adoptions were still in progress. With my deep conviction in the rightness of this programme, I agreed. Before she left, Yvonne introduced me to some of the provincial orphanages where the children were waiting. We hitchhiked on military planes and jeeps, or took civilian cyclos and Lambrettas. Yvonne informed Switzerland, France, Belgium and Germany that I would continue with her work, and asked them to send me an 'order of mission' enabling me to act on their behalf. Her parting reminder to me was a warning to keep a copy of everything I wrote and a note of every piastre I spent; I never forgot that advice.

From then on, my position changed considerably:

26 *December*: Theoretically, I am still working in the crèche at Phu My and conducting the usual clinics, but the adoption work is taking up more and more of my time. I have been invested with authority to act on behalf of Terre des Hommes Germany and I

have also received a letter from TdH France, hoping that 'our collaboration will be fruitful'. I shall continue processing the papers for the children going to Switzerland until such time as they send their own representative.

On Saturday, 23 December, we had a group of eleven children ready to leave for Europe. I had been reduced to tears of frustration many times in those last days as we struggled to obtain the travel documents for the children. Then, on departure day, just one hour before take-off, while we were at the airport, we received a cable through Air France telling us not to send Kim Lien since her entry visa for Luxemburg had not yet been issued. Kim Lien is a delicious, intelligent little girl of two years and everybody's favourite (the same child we had to suture the day she fell from her crib). Now she will have to wait for the next group of children, who will be leaving in January. It was a great disappointment to Sr Angèle to see Kim Lien return to the crèche that night.

Another of our babies has died; Lucy, I had called her. She was abandoned at birth and we received her the next day. The night of the 12th/13th I kept vigil with her and spent five hours setting up for an intravenous infusion. This was the first time I had been alone giving an infusion, and I needed hours to search out various bits of the apparatus which would fit together. We did not have any compact units, but only an ill-matched collection of tubing, needles and bottles, some French and some American. Also, the child was so small, and the veins so constricted, that it was difficult to find a vein strong enough to hold the needle. When a vein was entered it would clot up the needle almost immediately. Finally, I succeeded and the infusion continued for three hours before it was dislodged.

I spent two nights and three days without going near my bed. On the third night I was physically incapable of continuing but I offered to keep vigil as I knew Sr Angèle was exhausted; my involvement in adoption formalities had left her on her own during the day. But when she offered to do night duty herself, I had to accept as I was literally fighting off unconsciousness. At 5 a.m. next morning she called me; Lucy was in a hopeless condition. She died at 8 a.m., only three months old.

Yesterday, Christmas, the Air Force came to entertain the

children with gifts, hot dogs and a trip to the zoo. They also brought soap and candy for all the other inmates of Phu My.

In the morning, the choir from the International Protestant Church came carol singing. It was great entertainment for the patients and I'm sure the choristers must have enjoyed the appreciation of their audience.

The departure of the adopted children left more room in the orphanages and more places for transient families in need of temporary shelter. At Phu My, Sr Rose did all she could to prevent the splitting-up of families whenever possible, by giving work to a mother to enable her to support her children. By now I had visited a dozen other orphanages in Saigon and in the provinces and begun to appreciate the dimensions of the problem of abandoned and orphan children. Nothing in my previous experience or reading had prepared me for this. I was coming into contact with hundreds of newborn babies with no identity and no prospects. There were healthy and handicapped babies; the fully Vietnamese and the mixed-race; the legitimate and the illegitimate. Poverty, illegitimacy, birth defects, and the fact that the children were never 'wanted', would account for most of the abandonments, but there were also a few orphaned through the death of the mother, or abandoned by a wealthier family because of an inauspicious birthdate.

Many of the orphanages were run by Vietnamese Catholic Sisters, who were mostly doing the best they could under the worst conditions in a situation that was never meant to be. The offspring of men arrive one at a time for a reason. These babies came by dozens each month to the already overcrowded orphanages. They were never the centre of anyone's universe and never received the nurturing warmth of parental love. They often lacked the minimum necessary to animal existence. How much more did they lack the affection and stimulation needed to promote their human development. My instinctive reaction was to resist this destruction of personality and work towards getting as many of these babies as possible back into the mainstream of human development. To give them caring parents was the first step:

30 January 1968: Last Thursday we sent thirty-six children to Belgium, four to Switzerland on Friday, and eight to France on

Saturday. The group of thirty-six was sheer folly but the director of Terre des Hommes from Belgium, who was escorting the children, insisted that they all leave together, and that they be dressed in their European snowsuits as they were collected from their various orphanages, that is, while still in Saigon's tropical heat. This arrangement lacked even a modicum of common sense; it was bedlam even before the flight started. Most of the children were howling and they had all done pi-pi or ka-ka, and hadn't eaten for seven hours by the time we eventually boarded them. Nor did they have any in-flight change of clothing . . .

Between 23 December and the end of March 1968, sixty-two children left for their new homes in Europe, despite the prolonged disruption caused by the North Vietnamese offensive on the night of Tet, 30 January, the Vietnamese New Year. I had been offered weekend hospitality in the house of some friends, near 3rd Field Hospital, Tan Son Nhut, and was there when the North Vietnamese surprise attack began under cover of the noise of firecrackers that night. A strict curfew was imposed and I wasn't able to return to Phu My for a week. Luckily, I had my little portable typewriter with me and distracted myself recording events and writing home:

3 February 1968: The Viet Cong had supposedly taken the street not a hundred yards distant from the house. The next night I was alone in the house. The first burst of machine-gunning in the alley sent me scuttling upstairs in search of a wardrobe big enough to hide in. But once I wrapped myself in a helmet and flak jacket that I found, I reckoned I would suffocate in the wardrobe so I abandoned that idea. Up on the terrace it was no better; all the roof tops seemed to be spitting sniper fire at anything that moved. Finally, I appropriated a bedroom on the middle floor as the safest place to spend the night. Thinking some sort of drink might help me sleep I found some Scotch and mixed it with warm, canned quinine water for want of anything else. With the electricity cut, there was no tap water available. A few mouthfuls of this disgusting brew convinced me once again that the cure was worse than the complaint.

Last night, finding the confinement intolerable, I walked down the alley and crossed over here to the hospital. I'm here again tonight, sitting in the emergency reception and waiting for the ambulances bringing casualties. I am helping in a very insignificant way but the least activity is salvation. Many of the patients have been mobilized and they are on guard duty in their blue pyjamas, flak jackets and helmets.

I'll get a few hours' sleep tonight as I did last night, stretched out on the lawn in front of the hospital chapel. A short time ago there was sniper fire and a five-minute alert. Lights went out and the men grabbed for their weapons. I ducked down on my stretcher, zipped on my flak jacket and waited. Nothing more.

After being stranded for a week at Tan Son Nhut, the curfew was lifted for a few hours and I set off back to Phu My:

18 February 1968: I found a ride as far as Saigon but no further. The streets were deserted – no sign of taxis. I asked at the US Embassy for a Military Police car to take me the remaining mile but they said the whole area was off-limits for them. My frustration was overwhelming. I hurled my bag on the empty road and yelled with all my strength to ease my feelings. Then I picked up the bag and walked a few blocks to the motherhouse of the Sisters of St Paul de Chartres (St Enfance). Soon after, the convent car drove me to Phu My. The place has suffered no damage though neighbouring areas have been destroyed. Every night since, the bombing and the fighting have continued in this area. Last night seemed worse than anything to date, and at 2 a.m. I decided to clean up my room for the rest of the night as sleep was not to be considered.

Food is a problem for all of Saigon and all the orphanages are suffering from a milk shortage. The last UNICEF shipment was never delivered and we have had nothing to replace it. Refugees, who have lost their homes in the recent fighting, can be numbered by the tens of thousands. I have seen acres and acres in the city itself, reduced to rubble, especially over in Cholon, Ba Queo, Thi Nghe and Go Vap. In the school next door to Phu My, there are 4,000 homeless within a hundred yards of the burnt-out wreckage of their homes.

It was almost impossible to find a plane that would fly me to the Provinces, to collect more children, but at last, after weeks of fruitless searching, I had the chance to get out on a Vietnamese military helicopter to Soctrang in Ba Xuyen province:

28 February 1968, at Vinh Long: The trip back with three toddlers was not so simple. I went from one airport to another, hitching rides on different planes . . . One of the children vomited on each flight, all over me, the bags and herself. Arriving at Vinh Long, the plane stopped for three minutes only to unload us and to wipe up the mess from the floor, and then took off. Carrying Hanh and two bags while the other two trailed barefooted over the steel tarmac, we wound our way in and out of barricades, helicopter stalls and military paraphernalia looking for someone to help get me to St Paul's Orphanage where I had to pick up several more children.

On base we were given a jeep and an armed escort to drive us through town, and what a grim scene it was! The city has suffered great destruction and the Cathedral grounds housed thousands of refugees. We drove through streets of razed houses and rubble.

The orphanage was still standing, though considerably battered. Sr André (the superior) told me of her struggle to convince the 'friendly forces' that there were no Viet Cong in the compound. Still, they were gunned from every side and there are holes all over the walls and roof. Poor Sr André is distraught with anxiety for the children. She keeps saying how happy she is that fourteen of them have already gone to France and have escaped this recent hell.

Today is Ash Wednesday, and the whole country is covered in ashes.

1 March 1968: I reached Saigon at 6 p.m. yesterday, which meant I had the five children at the Vinh Long airport for ten hours before we found a plane. We were finally put on a small unpressurized cargo plane, a Caribou, jammed in between some large crates. Ascent and descent was so rapid that the sudden changes in pressure and inertia flattened us all. The baby was terrified and the oldest girl vomited. Even I felt uncomfortable.

When we arrived at Tan Son Nhut airport I phoned the Air Force detachment that helps us so much and they sent a van with armed guards to take us to Phu My. The poor lads were very jittery driving downtown.

In Saigon alone, there are an estimated 300,000 people made homeless by the recent offensive, and they are camping out in eighty-one refugee centres, schools, hospitals, churches and orphanages. Since we are now approaching the peak period of the annual cholera and plague epidemic, the deteriorating sanitary conditions are really serious. Great tame rats browse through the rubbish that litters every street and there are dead rats appliquéd at intervals along the roads and footpaths.

This last outbreak of fighting has brought a steady stream of refugees, the sick and orphans to the gates of Phu My. We have newborn babies coming every day. One poor little girl, one of the happiest babies I've seen in a long time, has shrapnel wounds in her arms and legs and is bandaged from head to toe.

For some time after the Tet offensive, movement within Saigon was even more restricted. Rolls of barbed wire barred the route at every turn. The police headquarters on Vo Tanh Street were heavily guarded. I had to go there each day because at that time the children still needed police clearances before the Ministry would issue the passports. Getting past the guards and barbed wire was a daily test of patience and ingenuity.

In the last days before Easter I was preparing travel documentation for seventeen children. I was to escort the children myself and applied for my own exit visa. It was refused because it turned out I did not have, in the first place, any residence authorization. This was the first time I realized that I should have renewed my residence authorization, when I had been less than fifteen months in the country. Before I could leave, I had to have permission to stay! And so, with the children's departure already scheduled, I had suddenly to start stumbling my way through the formalities for regularizing my own status. I finally obtained the exit authorization with the residence permit still pending. This would at least enable me to return to Vietnam within one month.

Huong, aged one-and-a-half years, whose documentation was complete, and who was all ready to join her adoptive parents in Switzerland on this trip, came down with what the orphanage described as a sudden toxicosis and was sent to Nhi Dong Hospital. As soon as I discovered what had happened, I rushed to the hospital and found her unattended. She had an IV drip still in place, but the bottle was empty. Nobody was bothering with this orphan child whose life or death seemed so insignificant. The sight of a foreigner attracted the usual throng of curious onlookers and as Huong acquired a new importance a nurse appeared and began to readjust the IV. But Huong died that same night without regaining consciousness. (Our relations with this hospital were to prove consistently disastrous. Again and again, children sent with minor conditions died from some other unspecified or unrelated illness with no explanations offered.)

On 6 April 1968 we left without Huong. Two air hostesses helped me with the children, aged between three months and eight years, and I set up some guidelines for escorts and for Air France on convoy procedures that would involve the least trauma for the children, the airline personnel, the escorts, and the other passengers. After delivering the children I reported to the Air France directorate in Paris, and we concluded an agreement on the conduct of future convoys, and the areas of responsibility.

In Europe on that trip, I was also able to contact the various national headquarters of Terre des Hommes, in order to discuss our policies and procedures, and to help promote a better understanding of the orphan situation in Vietnam.

Chapter 2

TO AM NURSERY:
FIRST ADOPTIONS
May 1968–January 1970

IN THE BRUSSELS headquarters of Terre des Hommes I met Rosa Tintore, a Spanish nurse, who, sponsored by TdH Belgium, was about to come to Vietnam to work in one of Fr Olivier's Redemptorist orphanages. By 6 May, I was back in Saigon, to find Phu My busier than ever:

> *11 June 1968*: We've had another orphanage from Cholon evacuated in with us so that our population has trebled and we have three or four babies in each bed (placed sideways). We don't know how long this will last, but a few days ago an orphanage in Cholon was hit by a rocket and there were many dead and wounded.

On 18 June I had to make a second rapid trip to Europe to leave one child in Paris and eight more in Geneva; I slept one night in Geneva and returned to Saigon the next morning.

Rosa Tintore arrived in this same month, and spent some weeks working with seventy or so children under three years, half of them newborn babies, living in four small rooms of a gardenless villa behind the market in Truong Minh Giang Street. The mortality amongst the babies was high, but more babies flooded in to take their places. Rosa, with years of experience in public health and pediatric service in Third World countries, set to work with great enthusiasm. But much of the good she did was undone by the untrained local Vietnamese staff who could not understand the need for the better child care she proposed. They were mostly poor women of the neighbourhood, with no knowledge of nutrition,

21

hygiene or child development, who merely adapted to the hopeless-
ness of the situation and continued to do things as they had always
done them. It was not surprising that they should resent a foreigner
with her new ways and seemingly bizarre ideas.

The Australian Army civic-action team was supplying Fr
Olivier's orphanage regularly with all the babyfood necessary for
an excellent diet. Unbeknown to them, the US Army was supplying
the same orphanage. The teams came on different days of the week
and never met up. Rosa, however, provided the missing link. She
was baffled by the disappearance of these supplies and the unvarying diet of rice with its splattering of carrot specks; genuinely
concerned, she reported the disappearance of the babyfood to Fr
Olivier, the orphanage director. According to Rosa's own colourful
version of the episode, she was accused of being a 'visitation from
hell'! It seems that Fr Olivier himself was disposing of the supplies
to finance the purchase of greater quantities of less expensive food,
since he was responsible for feeding hundreds of other orphans in
other orphanages. He quite rightly reasoned that it was better for all
the children to receive a little benefit, rather than for some to be
regaled while others went hungry.

At this point Rosa and I decided to open our own nursery where
we could give the intensive care needed for the survival of these
abandoned newborn babies, and where Rosa could implement
standards of hygiene and child care without the frustrations inevitable as a foreign intruder in an already established orphanage.
While I continued to live at Phu My, we rented a room in a run-
down building in a rat-infested alley in Phu Nhuan. (Tests later
showed that the water supply on the premises had sixteen different
types of harmful bacteria.) The inauguration of the nursery, which
we named To Am – Warm Nest – took place in early August 1968
and was attended by Sr Rose from Phu My and another sister from
Tu Du, the Saigon Maternity, as well as by representatives from the
Ministry of Welfare and a number of the Australian and American
army boys. Rosa was in charge. The rent was paid by Terre des
Hommes Belgium to the owner of the building who lived in Europe;
the thirty-five baby beds were bought by the Australian Army; the
US Navy donated the refrigerator and the Army trucked in the
drinking water; packages from friends abroad supplied all the linen
needed and donations from friends both in the country and abroad

enabled us to meet current expenses. The children in the nursery came from other orphanages or directly from Tu Du. They were all abandoned children and would all, in these early years of the nursery, eventually go into adoptive families abroad.

4 *August 1968*: I have just come back from two extensive trips to the provinces. The first to Danang, Hoi An and Hue, and the second down to the Delta region, to Soctrang, Vinh Long, Sadec and Cantho. I hop from plane to plane depending on what's available: Caribou, helicopters, Beachcraft. In all the orphanages of the Sisters of St Paul de Chartres and the Sisters of Providence, I have met with welcome. In the provinces there are many abandoned children needing adoptive homes, and for the most part the sisters are happy to co-operate in an adoption plan.

In Sadec, I had to collect a baby who was soon to go to her family in France. She is only five-months-old and weighs about 6 lb. She survived an epidemic which killed all but two of the tiny babies in the orphanage, and the thick mop of black hair she had at birth has now fallen out through sickness. She had been baptized Cecilia and Sister had asked me to be her godmother, when I had first located her about two months ago.

When I brought Cecilia up from Sadec yesterday, I took her to the new nursery where she is being fed every quarter hour at the moment. Within a month she ought to be in good condition. She has a strong personality already apparent and a ravishingly beautiful smile.

Rosa Tintore was a most competent nurse and administrator. She had specialized in Public Health and Tropical Diseases and had diplomas from Spain, Belgium and Switzerland. Moreover, she was vivacious and charming, and the US and Australian civic-action teams could not do enough for her. They were delighted to see their assistance translated into such immediate improvement in the lot of the orphans. Rosa's nursery was spotless and cheerful. She had the babies dressed in little white suits from Spain, insisting that her children would not be treated like orphans. But she was soon forced to face the reality that 80 per cent of the nursery supplies would be filched by the local staff, who couldn't see the point of orphans being looked after with such consideration, or having finery that was unavailable to their own poor families.

Rosa and I took turns to accompany children going abroad; I was spending more time on the paperwork of adoptions:

25 August 1968: I have many impending departures this coming month and so there are complications in the routine: medical examinations, vaccinations, 'crash' building-up programmes, obtaining the exit-tax exemptions, having expired visas re-validated, finding suitable escorts, cabling parents, arranging transportation, and packing for convoys. There is also much anxiety for the state of health of the tiny babies, as I daren't send them on such a long journey unless they are in reasonably good condition. I am hoping that Rosa will accompany this next convoy as that would relieve me considerably.

While Rosa and the new nursery were reasons for rejoicing, and great sources of encouragement to me, it was, nonetheless, made clear that in certain official circles I did not head the popularity polls. In August, I received a letter from the Director of Catholic Relief Services in Saigon, informing me that 'after careful investigation and consideration ... as of 1 September 1968 CRS-USCC Vietnam severs all responsibilities and relationships with you and your activities within the Republic of Vietnam'. In fact, the careful investigation had not included granting me an interview; the Director said he would speak with me only when I had a social work diploma equivalent to his own. I had never associated my activities with the CRS programme, but I had been receiving mail at their address. This was now forbidden. But, though irritating, it was no serious setback.

10 September 1968: We currently have a new problem concerning exit tax which amounts to about 160 dollars a person. Until recently, we were systematically given a tax exemption for the orphans, but two weeks ago I was asked by a department head in the Ministry of Finance to send his two sons to Europe for education under the Terre des Hommes medical scheme ... I refused unequivocally. It was more than just coincidence that our tax dispensations have now been delayed ...

17 October 1968 (letter home): Don't send up that white lace dress. Can you imagine me wearing white lace when I'm splashing through mud and garbage on my motorbike, or tearing through the country in military cargo planes. I eventually manage to get what I want without having to seduce any of the officials. I get by on sheer persistence and the worthiness of the cause. I am so well-known in the Ministry that I am almost part of the furniture there, and certainly just about as seductive.

25 November 1968: On 10 November, Timmy and Steven, our first two babies for the US, were escorted to their homes in Colorado by the US Consul himself (this was a personal gesture, not official, of course). These adoptions were a tremendous amount of work, as I had to discover the procedure step by step. Now I have about fifteen more American adoptions in progress, and about 200 for European countries. So far this year 150 children have gone to their new families.

Medical assistance for To Am came from 3rd Field Military Hospital at Tan Son Nhut, the Australian Army Clinic at the 'Free World' Headquarters and from the British Medical Team based at Nhi Dong Children's Hospital.

7 December 1968: Rosa has just detected our first case of typhoid. Three Vietnamese doctors had looked at the child and scoffed at her diagnosis, saying it was merely bronchitis or some other such infection. Rosa insisted it was typhoid and took the child to the Pasteur Institute for blood tests. She was right.

Then we needed typhoid tests on all the babies. The blood had to be drawn, slides made and all rushed within the space of an hour or so to a laboratory on the other side of Saigon. We had no transportation of our own, so as usual the military came to our assistance and had a jeep ready and waiting at the nursery door. I held the babies while Rosa drew the blood and expertly prepared the slides with great economy of movement. The last baby was difficult, and I was rigid with nervousness as Rosa had to go into the jugular vein, while I held the baby upside down and steadied over the corner of the table.

Rosa has impressive expertise as a diagnostician. Again and again, subsequent laboratory results prove her initial diagnosis correct, when such a diagnosis has not occurred to another doctor. Our first case of diphtheria was a shock, but Rosa detected the condition in the early stages, was able to obtain the antitoxin needed from the Pasteur Institute and nursed the child back to health, isolating her in her own bedroom.

I was scheduled to go to Europe with sixteen children last Saturday but withdrew two days before departure. I had too many other children to prepare so Rosa went in my place.

On departure day one of the children was discovered to have typhoid, so Rosa had to leave her behind. The Belgian parents were bitterly disappointed. This was the fifth child they had been expecting and each time something (three times death) had prevented them receiving the child. However, this little girl will be well enough to go with me in a couple of weeks . . .

27 December 1968, in England: This time I brought over fifteen children, twelve of whom were under two years. At 5 a.m. in Nice I gave the first four babies to their adoptive parents. Especially moving was the handing over of my godchild Cecilia, whom we had just discovered to be a polio victim. Her left leg was paralysed and her left arm partly affected. I had written express to warn the parents just one week before but to my joy they cabled me to 'bring Cecilia immediately'.

In Paris, the children for France and Germany were taken off by the hostesses, and the rest of us were taken directly to the Geneva plane which had been held up on our account. The flight was just long enough to dress the last two babies in their arrival finery. One, a darling mite of three months, must have weighed all of 6 lb. I left another six children in Geneva, managed to shower myself at the airport, and then flew directly to London with the last baby of six months, Bach Yen-Theresa, our first child placed in England.

6 February 1969, Rosa Tintore, Saigon, to RT temporarily in Australia: Many things have happened here since your departure. First, our fight against the rats in the house has killed twenty-five in ten days. Then the water: we had to put a new pipeline from the well to the house. The Australian soldiers worked like madmen to complete the job. Unfortunately, the well has now dried up and I have been without a drop of water for the last two days. However, they are only the minor problems.

Now with Tet, everything is paralysed, so don't return before 8 March . . .

When I got back to Saigon, I found 116 pieces of mail accumulated on my desk. In my absence, the regulations for getting on local planes around the country had been tightened up, and I found it hard to book myself on flights; this was a real handicap for my work.

The health of the children was always a significant variable to consider in making travel arrangements to send them abroad. It was quite astonishing how many children showed the first symptoms of chickenpox on the morning or eve of their departure. Of course, any spotted disease was fearfully regarded as 'smallpox' by over-cautious health officers in the country of destination.

20 April 1969: Another of our little three-year-old girls, who was due to go to Switzerland tomorrow, has come down with typhoid and can't go. Imagine how I panicked at this new outbreak.

Now that I had been alerted to the symptoms, I recognized them in another child I had just brought down from Danang, and took the child to Nhi Dong Hospital. I asked the British medical team to do a blood test for typhoid. The child had it, indeed, and the doctor confessed her surprise, saying she would never have thought of typhoid.

All the other children had to be tested and two more with positive indications were hospitalized for isolation purposes.

I escorted five children to New York and Montreal on 30 April, and on 17 May, another eleven children to Europe. In the Stuttgart railway station at midnight, as I was waiting to board the train for Belgium, my purse was stolen with every penny I possessed, including a large donation I had just received for the nursery. I howled for the first fifteen minutes in the train, and the conductor was so astonished and worried that he brought back one of his English-speaking colleagues to determine the cause of my distress.

I travelled frequently to the provinces, locating children who were abandoned in orphanages and needed adoptive homes, as well as children who were handicapped or in need of special medical care. Children who were ready to go to their adoptive families would be brought to Saigon for the final departure formalities, where they would be cared for temporarily in To Am, Phu My or some other nursery or foster home, depending where a space could be found.

27

I learnt by sad experience that many of the small babies would not survive the lengthy adoption formalities. Between one visit to an orphanage and the next, many of the babies would have died. If they were to survive, I realized that we would have to encourage in them the 'will' to live, by giving them more personal attention than was available in the overcrowded orphanages; this, in addition to an improved diet and medical supervision. We needed a larger facility in Saigon, to care for more children. Sometimes we had to break the news to a family that the child they had been offered had contracted polio or died from measles complications. Polio was rampant, especially in the Delta area, and even though we had quantities of vaccine sent from Germany and France and attempted to vaccinate the children systematically the effectiveness of the programme was limited. It was tragic to see the number of lives being wrecked by a disease as unnecessary as polio.

The adoption procedure, as it stood, was not beneficial to the children; it was a long drawn-out legal process totally unrelated to the individual needs of the child. The prospective parents were assessed automatically according to age, number of years married, and presence of other children born of the marriage. If they did not fulfil the conditions, they were automatically granted a waiver after a few months' waiting. The child was assessed by the birth and release certificates, mere formulas. During the long procedure the child existed only on paper and the courts never once alluded to his or her state of health or development. The only course to take in the interests of the children was to present the facts to the highest authorities and appeal to their logic and compassion to change the system to fit the need.

Acting on advice from the Ministry of Interior, I petitioned the Prime Minister to permit the orphans to leave for their adoptive homes as soon as possible, particularly in view of the health hazards of the orphanages. I wrote a long, impassioned, and detailed letter, addressed personally to the Prime Minister, which immediately ran into difficulties. At the Post Office, the clerk stared at the envelope suspiciously, considered it outside his competence, and refused to accept it. He called a superior officer to handle the situation. Later, I learnt that this letter aroused antagonism in the Ministry of Social Welfare; according to them I had committed an unpardonable breach of protocol in addressing myself directly to the Prime

Minister and they were most annoyed when my letter was passed on to their department.

22 June 1969: Went to Danang for almost one week, to check on the children and to help the servicemen who are adopting from Sacred Heart Orphanage.

Just a few weeks ago I was at the Apostolic Delegation in Saigon to voice my grievance about Go Vap Orphanage. At this time there were between twenty and thirty admissions a month and as many deaths. I had checked their statistics which were posted up on the office door.

Yesterday, I went again to Go Vap to collect three of my children who had been assigned to adoptive families in Switzerland, by a direct authorization from the Archbishop of Saigon. Go Vap had said they would need his permission, probably thinking I would never go as far as the Archbishop. I went directly. Monsignor Nguyen van Binh received me without any prior appointment and very graciously authorized the adoptions, in writing. The children were in pitiful condition. One child had been in the infirmary for the past month and was covered with evil-smelling discharge from her ears. Sister tried to excuse the child's condition by saying they weren't all nurses and hence could not clean the ears. The child is over two years old, and can't even sit up unaided. I'm awaiting Rosa's return. She is in Spain at the moment, but I'm expecting her before mid-July. We have had lots of support promised us for the nursery, but we are still trying to clear up problems concerning ownership of the house.

About now we won a victory in a struggle with the New Zealand government, which had refused to allow the entry of baby Su-Anh, whose passport I had had ready since before Christmas. I wrote to explain the embarrassing task I would have in returning Su-Anh's passport to the Ministry of the Interior and informing the Vietnamese government of New Zealand's refusal to allow the entry of a single orphan baby. As I expected, New Zealand Immigration revoked their decision, and issued Su-Anh with her entry visa, warning me, however, that it should not be considered as establishing a precedent. I vowed to spare New Zealand any further political embarrassment; and Su-Anh was in fact the only Vietnamese child we sent there.

25 July 1969: Two weeks ago the Regional Director of US Immigration was visiting in Saigon. He invited me to dine with him and the Consul-General and a couple of Vice-Consuls so that we could iron out some of our common problems. He mentioned he was going to My Tho next day, and I promptly reserved a seat in the car since I had to collect some babies from My Tho Orphanage. So Mr P. travelled back to Saigon with a six-week-old baby – Michelle – in his arms and I had two more. As we arrived in Saigon too late for me to find more suitable accommodation, I bedded them for the night in the house of Peter Trueman [assistant Defence Attaché at the British Embassy], in empty dresser drawers with airmail copies of the London *Times* bunched up to provide a mattress of sorts.

Last weekend I was in Danang to collect five children who will be departing in a few days. I've also finally met the Danang Vice-Consul, with whom I have been pen-pals for some time. Since I'm involved in many US adoptions and since the Embassy here refers adoption queries to me, I convinced the Consul-General that he ought to help me, with, for instance, plane reservations for in-country travel, especially to Danang. Yesterday, he located a businessman who would act as escort for a seven-month-old baby going to the US. The baby will travel first class . . .

Transportation was authorized by the Australian Air Force, on a chartered Qantas flight, for two more children, and Barbara Baden duly escorted Sophie to Sydney, and Su-Anh on to Auckland. The Australian Forces (like the American) were of service to us in a thousand ways, with transportation, maintenance and supply. We were particularly grateful for the parcel post – a direct, free-of-charge service between Australia and the nursery door.

Peter Trueman's empty dresser drawers were just one example of his support:

1 August 1969: The 'Brits' here are a brave lot. Lt. Col. Peter Trueman is one of our greatest supporters. He is a splendid fellow and always at our disposal in any need. His resourcefulness and good will are endless and it seems he is constantly defending our reputations against slander and calumny.

The Air Attaché flies his own plane all over Indo-China. It is a 1945 model, I think, and they always take along the mechanic

War-torn Provincial Vietnam. 1 Refugees return to Hue, after it has been recaptured from the Vietcong, March 1968. **2** A Chinese-born shopkeeper sits in the ruins of his former business. **3** Refugee children in a camp at Qui Nhon.

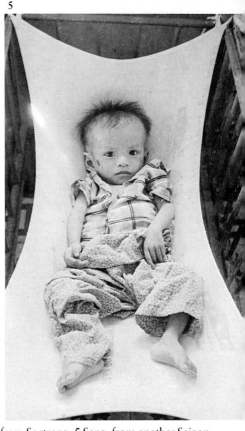

Arrivals at the Nurseries. 4 Six babies for To Am, from Soctrang. **5** Sang, from another Saigon orphanage. Many children had been left lying without stimulation until their muscles became atrophied from lack of use. **6** Lucy, in the nursery at Phu My. Sr Angèle is giving her an IV infusion.

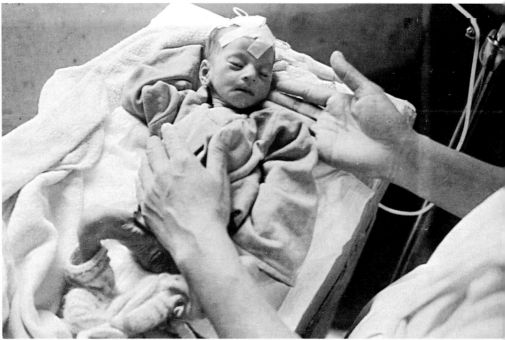

with his full kit of rubber bands, sticking-plaster and some beer bottles full of extra fuel. There are seats for two passengers and they offered to take me to Danang a few weeks ago, with the Ambassador, as they knew it was one of my regular routes. On that particular occasion I had to decline.

Peter swears that the last time they were in Danang, they couldn't start the plane, so they had to pile out and turn the propeller by hand. He said all the Americans rushed out on to the field with cameras, killing themselves with laughter . . .

The whole war seems like a monstrous farce – all the loss of life has been so futile.

On 2 August 1969 Margarita Baden, Barbara's adopted daughter, was baptized at Queen of Peace Church. Monsignor Alberto Tricarico, Counsellor at the Apostolic Delegation, conferred the sacrament, with Fr Crawford assisting. Harold Christie from the US Embassy and I were godparents. It was a joyful occasion and we celebrated with a party afterwards on Fr Crawford's terrace. The baptism of the 'exquisite Margarita' is one of the events recalled by Peter Trueman. He remembers, too, 'a hilarious morning when we took five would-be American citizens to the US Embassy in Thong Nhat so that their ethnic background could be determined. Their average age was six months':

> Rosemary and I carried them there in shopping bags and sat them on a pretty Vice-Consul's desk for examination. In this case American bureaucracy was more apparent than real and was conducted with humour and humanity. Our protégés were all given excellent pedigrees – a touch of Thai here, some Filipino there maybe and this one has certainly a Korean father. Complete agreement was reached in five minutes which was somewhat swifter than the local track record. It may have helped the youngsters in later life.

And, more grimly, Peter Trueman recalls 'driving to My Tho in the Mekong Delta with Rosemary and Barbara Baden to collect five children who were to be adopted in Europe – (Barbara, a nurse in a cancer hospital, and the kindest and most warm-hearted person I have ever met)':

> On our arrival at the orphanage we were told, blandly, that all

our babies were dead but what matter, the Vietnamese sister said, there are plenty more! This calm acceptance of, or indifference to, death was perhaps the most difficult aspect of Vietnamese attitudes to come to terms with. There was no good reason for it. At that time Vietnam touched the conscience of the world and there was no shortage of food, clothing or shelter. With certain shining exceptions, the missing ingredient seemed to be love and care. A concrete example: in this particular hospital there was row after row of white painted metal cots each with their tiny occupants. Periodically, a feeding bottle would be thrust into a mouth; the mite would manage one or two sucks and then the bottle would fall away with no one to retrieve it. So the weak perished. It was as if birth control was achieved after the event rather than before it.

2 October 1969, RT: I've just returned from a week in the provinces with Rosa, visiting Providence Orphanages in Soctrang, Cantho, Sadec, Baclieu and Culaogieng. I have at least a hundred more orphans needing adoptive homes and could have any number more, but I cannot handle any greater number at the moment. There are endless newborn babies, stacked in cardboard boxes (condensed milk boxes) when the cribs are filled.

Our transportation was local: vehicles like unsprung carts attached to the back of Honda motorbikes, over roads pitted with canyons every foot of the way. For part of the route to Culaogieng, we had to use a boat along the canals of the Mekong because the orphanage is not accessible by road in certain seasons. There are over 300 children in the orphanage . . . I shall attempt to have them sponsored.

Next Monday we shall be moving To Am to a new, more sanitary location [Nhat Linh] where the property will still be rented, but where at least we shall have a decent water and electrical supply. We had to pay a year's rent in advance, 3,600 dollars (US) at the official exchange rate.

27 October 1969: The struggle continues with the Ministry. I thought I had won a victory the other day when the Director told me, in front of the Superior of the Providence Orphanages, that he would grant the children their visas before the adoption papers were complete . . . He did grant ten visas, and refused all the rest. (He apologized later and showed me a communiqué from the Prime Minister, obliging him to follow the old policy.)

Since yesterday, the cost of living has risen drastically. Petrol has doubled in price overnight, but that won't break me as my mobylette uses less than two gallons a week.

On 17 December I took another convoy of eight babies to America via Honolulu. I wrote to my family, while still in New Jersey, and described the trip:

1 January 1970: We checked in seventy-three minutes before take-off but Pan Am took over forty minutes to process our tickets which left inadequate time for passing the immigration police. We were rushed to the plane a few minutes before take-off. They would not permit the 'non-passengers' carrying the babies to board. There we were with eight babies and thirteen bags and someone was yelling at us to get off as the engines were about to start. This was the first time I have ever seen Peter [Trueman] trembling with anger. I stood there in the centre of the plane and reasoned audibly that if Pan Am allowed a check-in time of one hour, then they ought to have adequate groundstaff to cope. And I informed them that if they insisted on closing the doors at that moment, then they would have seven extra passengers to Honolulu. The sympathetic hostess on board later made a full report of the incident.

The changeover in Honolulu was an equal fiasco. Although Pan Am had supposedly been alerted, they were once again unable to cope with eight children. They put us on the plane after all the other passengers had boarded (contrary to our usual manner of boarding) and they had the children scattered in odd seats around the plane (some held by passengers) instead of keeping us in one block. I had to leave the plane to search for the passports, and came back to find they had put two soldiers in two more of our seats. Again, I had to protest before a full plane, and insist that we have at least the eight seats we had paid for. They compromised by giving us one more seat saying that they would work it out after take-off.

Thus, I began the second part of that unforgettable trip. I had asked for back seats near the toilets and they had sandwiched us in the middle of the plane between the other passengers. The diarrhoea started and it had never been worse. I had to carry the dripping children back through the crowded plane as meals were being served. I would discard the clothes in the bathroom and the next child would be ready. The stench was awful. I had no seat myself and had to stand between the seats in a contorted posture in order to feed the babies. The situation was so nightmarish that I broke down and cried at one point but kept my head bent low between the seats so the other passengers would not see me.

By the time we reached San Francisco (where I left two children), Pan Am headquarters in New York had been alerted about the wretched treatment accorded us. They assigned a special stewardess to help me for the remainder of the trip. At her kind insistence, I slept a little between San Francisco and New York while she cared for the remaining six children.

That night at Kennedy airport I met for the first time Connie Boll, and also John Wetterer, both of whom would become very involved with supporting our nurseries over the next years. John introduced himself and asked if I could help his aunt adopt a little boy, Hoa, whom John had met and befriended during his recent military tour of duty in Vietnam. He gave me details of Hoa's orphanage, and I promised to see what I could do. Later, he not only acquired Hoa as a cousin, but three sons of his own from Sacred Heart Orphanage, Danang. Each time he visited, Sr Angèle expressed her satisfaction by bestowing on him a new son. She did not seem to consider John's bachelor status any obstacle.

Chapter 3

THE FOREIGN ADOPTION –

a 'difficult form of pregnancy'

By NOW the growing number of United States adoptions was involving me in extensive personal correspondence with each family, with separate State Welfare Departments, and with the Immigration Service. Eventually, Wende Grant in Boulder, Colorado, because of her willingness and obvious competency, became our principal liaison with the States and adoption applicants were referred to her for initial information and assistance. The Grants had already worked their own way through a Vietnamese adoption and ,had received one-year-old Diahan Thi back in April 1965. Community interest was aroused and Wende was called upon to share her experience with individual families and with organizations. Consciousness of the plight of the orphans grew as servicemen returned from Vietnam and related their experiences of the orphanages. In 1967 Friends of the Children of Viet Nam (FCVN)[1] was incorporated for the purposes of assisting orphanages in Vietnam by sending funds and supplies. Wende Grant was a member of the original Board of Directors. This was the beginning of the proliferation of the 'Friends' groups.

> *Wende Grant writes*: At a meeting of FCVN in 1967, a new member, just returned from Vietnam, suggested sending funds and supplies to an Australian woman who lived and worked in Phu My Orphanage, Saigon. Her name was Rosemary Taylor

---

[1] FCVN: later this group split up (see ch. 7) and the branch associated with Rosemary Taylor and dealing with adoptions re-formed and re-registered in Saigon as Friends For All Children (FFAC). The closeness of names was later to cause some confusion, when both organizations were arranging the adoption of Vietnamese orphans.

and she was arranging some inter-country adoptions. We entered into contact with Rosemary who expressed her willingness to place some children with families in the USA. My function at this time was to assist prospective parents with their documentation. The arrival of each child stimulated public interest and more people became involved in the collecting and shipping of supplies for use in the orphanages. Rosemary didn't know it, and I'm not at all sure she would have wanted it, but many of us made a firm decision that we were working for Rosemary Taylor and her programme to save children in Vietnam.

Although Wende Grant had been assisting families for some time, it was in autumn 1969 that she expressed their desire to take 'just one more' Vietnamese orphan into their own family. A second letter reiterated her hope for a baby girl and said that she had already proceeded with the Colorado requirements for a home-study. Some weeks later I could write as follows:

8 December 1969, RT to WG: Here is a photo of the child I have chosen for you: 'Elaine' [Lara] in Cantho Orphanage. I am waiting on her birth certificate to know her correct Vietnamese name. I shall send copies of the birth and release certificates when they are available. She is a few months old.

Let me have your dossier as soon as you can. I enclose a list of documents needed for the lawyer and a model of a power of attorney.

Christmas greetings to all the family.

18 December 1969, WG to RT: We have had 'Elaine's' picture for five days and already feel she is part of the family ... We should be approved by the State of Colorado within a few days and be ready to file our application for a visa with the Immigration and Naturalisation Service as soon as we receive the baby's birth certificate and release.

When I returned to Saigon after my Christmas convoy, I found Wende's next letters:

6 January 1970, WG to RT: I enclose our papers for the lawyer. Once I have the birth and release certificates from you, Immigration can complete their investigation in six weeks ... I went over the file of Thi [Diahan's] adoption and found that after receiving the picture of her on 28 December, everything was completed by 22 February. In starting this adoption I promised myself that I would not become anxious. We went through all of this before . . . so know what delays can be anticipated.

Happy New Year.

26 January, WG: . . . perhaps we are all suffering from the symptoms of this most difficult form of pregnancy – the foreign adoption. We call one another frequently to ask 'Have you heard anything?'. . . It is almost too much that we must satisfy state, national and foreign requirements when all we want is our babies.

3 February, RT: Here is some news that applies to the Colorado families . . . they will now have to wait for the end of the Vietnamese adoption formalities before I can get the passport.

I saw Sr Anicet from Cantho a few days ago. Please write to her directly if you want news of your baby as she is still there. Her official name is Nguyen Thi Nhu Y; her documents are in preparation, but I must confess I am astonished at the rapidity of Thi's adoption. This time you will have a much longer wait . . . Please try to be patient.

9 February, RT: Here is the release certificate for your daughter.

16 February, RT: Here are three copies of your daughter's birth certificate and several certified translations.

14 February, WG: We have received your letters of the 3rd and 9th. The news of the delay imposed by the government there is very discouraging. I'm enclosing a bank draft to help with the cost of the milk . . . We are pleased to get the release and learn how old our baby is.

24 February, RT: Forgive my incredulity about the speed of Thi's adoption. The situation is different now because there are many hundreds of adoptions taking place here in Saigon and only one JP who signs a maximum of six or seven every week. To hasten your dossier might mean retarding some other dossier – I'm sure you'll appreciate this.

I received your last documents yesterday, and the lawyer will have the translations by the end of the week. In fairness to him you must start counting from that point.

4 March, WG: Last Thursday Duane and I filed the visa application at the Immigration office in Denver. There is little we can do now except wait. From your letter of 24 February, it seems it will take over a year . . .

Our snapshot of Lara Pauli is getting dog-eared from handling.

11 March, RT: . . . Not a year – more like six months from now. I'm handcarrying the dossier, to cut off days and weeks in each of the 'ten thousand' departments involved.

Last week in Cantho I saw your daughter. She was recovering from measles and naturally wasn't feeling her best, but her beauty shone through!

A baby had arrived for another family in Colorado:

9 April, WG: Everyone remotely connected with adopted Vietnamese children has spent the morning on the phone . . . Having one baby arrive makes the rest of us start thinking and scheming again about ways our children might come sooner . . .

9 April, RT: Here is some good news. Your adoption contract was to be signed on 17 May but the Judge, on request, moved it up to 17 April. Unless there is some extraordinary delay you ought to have your child by July.

The children from Cantho must be brought to Saigon for an interview at the US Consulate. This is the last formality required for the approval of the Immigration petition. But until I can open another nursery I'm afraid Lara will have to stay at Cantho.

As far as time permitted, I kept close to the dossiers and made personal contacts with the officials and clerks involved. I never criticized or demanded service, but tried by a friendly attitude to promote in them a sense of accomplishment – that their prompt attention would be benefiting orphan children. Occasionally, I encountered lack of interest and even resistance from petty officials, but I also met with genuine concern and helpfulness at all levels of the bureaucratic structure – from officials in the Peace Court, Court of First Instance, Ministry of Interior, Ministry of Justice, Office of the Secretary General, Ministry of Finance and National Police.

They realized that my only motive was the welfare of the children, and that I was receiving no payment for my efforts. Many were willing to co-operate in what they saw to be a sincere attempt to help their destitute children. I expressed my gratitude on behalf of the children verbally, and never used any sort of 'bribe' to obtain a favour (unless the thought of being rid of me was motive enough to tempt an immediate signature from some tormented man).

14 April, WG: My first reaction was to whoop for joy and my second to wonder why they must delay from 17 April to July. But truly, I am not complaining, I am very thankful for the two month advance in the date I can expect our Lara Pauli Elaine Nhu Y. It is very exciting. Thank you.

20 April, RT: Although the contract was signed on 17 April, the adoption must then be ratified at the Court of First Instance. I know all the families are longing for their children, and I am longing to send them, but there will be no more miracles. I've just heard that one of the Directors in the Ministry of Interior has been relegated to a function where he will have no more contact with foreigners. This is a blow. Perhaps he has jeopardized his own position through his humane concern.

The babies are dying on all sides. This morning a six-month-old baby at Phu My came down with meningitis, after measles complications. Yvette [Charamont, who arrived in March] carried the mite off to hospital, giving her an intravenous infusion en route. The Adventist Hospital wouldn't accept the baby, and poor Yvette was left standing out in the filthy street in the intense noonday heat, trying to hail a taxi to return to Phu My. She had the baby in one arm and the bottle of intravenous fluid elevated in the other, trying to prevent the baby's death through dehydration. And the damned Ministry of Interior enforces these diabolically conceived laws. The baby will probably die, though Yvette is down in the nursery now fighting for its life.

Barbara Baden left Vietnam on 6 May 1970 with her adopted daughter, my godchild, Margarita. Barbara's USAID apartment had always been a focal point of hospitality; she was gracious and welcoming to everyone, no matter how inopportune the hour. Highly regarded by her Vietnamese colleagues in the hospitals where she had worked as an adviser for several years, she was probably one of the best 'ambassadors' in the USAID ranks, always projecting an attitude of the highest professional competency together with a genuine concern.

Margarita had gone to her new home; the correspondence with Wende over Lara's adoption pressed doggedly on:

6 May, WG: With the recent escalation of the war, I wonder more and more if this will affect our adoption.

The situation here in the States is getting critical. The economic picture grows more bleak by the day – more inflation, growing unemployment, steadily dropping stockmarket – and the internal social and political conflict increases. Four students were shot to death Monday for protesting against the war on their campus. Some universities have closed for the rest of the semester to head off trouble . . . If nothing changes here, we are heading for a crisis that can affect our policy in Indochina. Whether this bodes good or evil for the Vietnamese, I couldn't guess now. I just wish I could get our baby over here with us.

10 May, RT: I enclose Lara's medical report and a letter to the State Welfare Department, which is self-explanatory.

Your daughter is a delightful child and now in To Am nursery. She seems quite robust apart from what appears to be a slight muscle defect in her left leg. I took photos yesterday and shall send them as soon as my film is developed. I shall also send the X-rays of Lara's legs in which no abnormality could be detected.

9 June, RT: Lara charmed the Vice-Consul when she went for her consular interview. She seemed very self-confident. She sat all by herself in the office chair, and smiled continually as if she knew she ought to be putting on a good show.

The box of cereal, milk and clothes arrived today. Many thanks.

11 June, WG: I am enclosing a bank draft for any last minute needs Lara might have for her trip.

Last Sunday we had another families-with-Vietnamese-children picnic. There were nine families: six already have children, three of us are expecting our second, and three are awaiting the first . . .

Just seven more weeks till end of July. I don't think I have ever wished away a summer as I have this year. Our family doctor has examined the X-rays you sent and feels there is some suspicion of a dislocated hip joint, but is going to consult with a specialist as soon as she arrives.

15 June, WG: Your letter of 9 June arrived today. I'm sending the ticket for Lara immediately. I called Immigration and the petition is approved and being sent out tomorrow.

20 July, RT: I know these last weeks [after various postponed dates] have been painful for you, and for me, too. I am planning to bring your daughter on 8 August, arriving in Los Angeles on Pan Am 2 at 8.25 p.m. I shall spend the night in the airport hotel before continuing with the other children to New York.

I am somewhat worried. As Lara gets older, her leg problem becomes noticeable. I sent you a report from the pediatrician at the Children's Hospital – he couldn't put his finger on any specific problem. Now, today, I had her examined by a Swiss doctor, who thinks there is some spasticity in the legs. Lara sits up perfectly; she can move her legs and they have normal shape and bulk, but she cannot stand up . . . I don't want to alarm you unnecessarily, but I feel a responsibility to let you know what he suspected – that the child may be a permanent invalid and may never be able to walk . . . it is difficult to determine the nature of the complaint or give any prognoses in so young a child. Are you able to go ahead with this?

29 July, cable from Colorado: BRING LARA – Wende.

1 August 1970, RT: Good news . . . this morning Lara stood up, holding on to the end of her bed. I'm sure the Swiss doctor erred in his judgement. Lara can pull herself into a kneeling position holding on to the bed end, and she can keep standing if she is helped into this position. It seems to me that one leg is quite normal and the other will definitely respond to therapy. I was elated this morning and wanted to cable you, but there was too long a queue at the post office.

The last few days I've been feeding Lara myself whenever I'm at the nursery at mealtime. She eats very easily, like a little lady, and is usually sweet-tempered. I've been telling her about your telegram as I feed her, and she seems to understand and smiles beatifically as I say 'Mommy says "BRING LARA"'.

On 8 August I left Vietnam with the children, and in San Francisco five of them, including Lara Grant, were given to their adoptive parents. I spent a sleepless night with the remaining four in a nearby hotel, and the next morning continued to New York unassisted, after a hectic departure from San Francisco air terminal. As I was stumbling along with babies and baggage, four-year-old Hoa pulled out all stops with a display of cantankerousness, and refused to be cajoled. I tried to be nonchalant, pretending to ignore him as he trailed obstinately in the rear. I did, of course, have one eye firmly fixed on him, but this was not evident to scandalized onlookers, who felt it their duty to point out to me that 'my son' was far behind and that I would lose him if I didn't watch out . . . In fact, I half hoped I *would* lose Hoa at that point . . .

All the children reached their intended destinations, and I returned once again to Saigon shortly after.

Chapter 4

THE NEW TO AM NURSERY
March 1970–February 1971

WHEN ROSA TINTORE left in February 1970, after eighteen months in Vietnam, To Am was taken over by a Belgian nurse, Anne de Stoexhe. Terre des Hommes in several European countries contributed towards the rent, equipment, and wages of the local staff. However, this nursery in Nhat Linh (the second site) was small, and already inadequate for the ever-growing need.

In March, Yvette Charamont had arrived unannounced at Phu My. She expressed enthusiasm at the idea of helping me start up a new nursery, and while we were looking for a suitable location, she worked with Sr Angèle in the crèche at Phu My.

> *13 April 1970*: Yvette has fallen from heaven. She is dedicated and competent, with extensive nursing experience. We have already planned to open our second house. We have lost so many babies the last weeks in other orphanages, that we think it worth any amount to open another nursery in Saigon. Sisters in the provincial orphanages are begging us to do so. Only this afternoon we heard of three more toddlers who have come down with polio; they had supposedly been vaccinated.
>
> We have decided to take over Peter Trueman's house when he leaves in June. The British Embassy intend terminating their lease.

> *17 June*: Peter's landlord [Vietnam's Foreign Minister] won't let us have the house for the children. We were very disappointed, though now we have found a better and bigger house, excellently situated.

Because we can't pay eighteen months' rent in advance, the landlord is making us pay twelve months at a rate of 700 dollars a month instead of 650. But if we pay eighteen months' rent, it will leave nothing for running expenses . . .

We need another nurse to live in the house with Yvette. It astonishes me that there are not more volunteers for this 'chance of a lifetime' job . . .

Next Thursday we shall give a farewell party for Peter – in his own house, of course. We have invited the British and US Consuls, the Anglican and Catholic priests, the secretary to the US Ambassador, and members of the Australian Army civic-action team, amongst others. Yvette will prepare her special Indian curry, which seems to consist of 'mutton' and 'saffron' but as we have neither she will substitute 'chicken' and 'curry-powder' . . .

14 July 1970: Although we have paid for the house we haven't yet moved in, as the contract is not yet signed.

Terre des Hommes France are sending us a little Renault van, which will be precious now that all our friends with cars have left the country. The van is already en route and Yvette is trying to clear tax papers before it arrives.

At last, on 23 July 1970, we were able to sign the lease and move into the new nursery. Beneath the grease and grime, we could see the splendid potential of the house. The main building had three storeys: the third floor consisted of one large airy room which became a nursery with a small pharmacy and bathroom attached. A staircase led to the roof where the babies could sun themselves early in the morning, before the heat became too fierce. The three smaller rooms on the second floor served as bedrooms for Yvette and myself, and isolation rooms for premature and newborn babies, and sick babies. Down below was a large living room and pantry. Behind the main building there was another block with five rooms upstairs, at first occupied by resident Vietnamese staff, and downstairs a kitchen, storeroom and laundry, and a bedroom for older children. During the next four years, nearly all the rooms would be converted for the use of the babies, and improved extensively.

The name To Am was transferred permanently to this new

nursery, though Anne de Stoexhe continued to look after a small number of our children in the Nhat Linh site.

The first four children came to the new To Am on 25 July 1970, brought by Dr Wayne McKinney, the American doctor who was being sponsored by An Lac Inc. Dr McKinney had already gained considerable notoriety in Saigon for his dedication to the orphans. He was uncompromisingly outspoken, and would not hesitate to state on a death certificate 'careless nursing' as a cause of a baby's death. Closely acquainted with the condition of Saigon orphanages, and with the growing burden being placed on them, Dr McKinney encouraged us with the To Am project, and would bring us abandoned babies in need of special care. When World Vision later opened a nursery, he used To Am as a model to show what could be done.

4 September 1970: 12.00 p.m. One hour ago Lang died. She had been born 9 May in the Saigon Maternity and abandoned. Because of her low birth weight of 1,750 kg, Sr Paul had kept her in an incubator until one week ago, then sent her to us with three other babies. We knew that she was not well and tonight she could drink very little. I thought I would feed her throughout the night, a few drops of liquid on a spoon every fifteen minutes so she would not dehydrate. I propped her in her carrycot right next to me on the bed where I was working; I could hear her breathing. Suddenly, I was shocked by an awareness of silence and looked at Lang. She was dead. I called Yvette who was in the next room. Despite all our efforts we could not revive little Lang. I am heartsick.

29 September 1970: Dr McKinney has just made his evening visit. This time he brought his dental instruments, i.e. pliers, to pull a molar from one of our eight-year-old girls as it was badly decayed and causing much pain. There was no anaesthetic of course. After the extraction, the doctor made a quick getaway. Now Yvette and I are both in a state of shock because he pulled a flawless molar and left the problem tooth with its gaping cavity. It's hurting me just to think about it though Anh has recovered amazingly well. But soon she will be undeceived as her bad tooth begins to ache once more.

We received seven more children today from the provinces, and all the girls have hair infested with lice. Yvette has been powdering them with DDT trying to get rid of the insects, but the million eggs have to be picked out by hand.

It is now the morning after a very broken night. One baby who arrived yesterday is feverish and will need tests done. Another baby looks as if she must die today; she is covered in great ugly ulcers and, as she weighs only 5 lb, she hasn't much resistance. We've no more injectable penicillin. We have to scrounge every little bit of medicine. Germany has sent us several large shipments, but penicillin goes so quickly.

As I type this, I have one arm around a tiny mite who has just wandered in for some comfort. Sr Marie Marthe from Soctrang asked me to bring Mai to Saigon because in the orphanage she was picked upon by the women helpers, and was terribly unhappy. She is a precious little creature of two years. She is standing beside me with a hunk of bread and Vegemite (sent from Australia) and is so happy to be able to rub her grubby little Vegemite hands on some welcome knee and not be slapped and sent away.

Newsletter, October 1970: We have forty-five children in the house now, and thirty-seven of these are babies ... more are arriving each week. The logistics involved have been absorbing all our time this last month: hiring staff, food-marketing, acquisition of more furniture, exploration of possible sources of baby-food, milk and other necessities.

Until a few days ago we had been going to market every couple of days and hauling vegetables back on my motorcycle. One morning I taxied to the Saigon market, instead of the local market, armed with bigger bags and more money, hoping for better bargains. I reached for my purse to pay for a pumpkin and was stunned to find the nylon bag had been slashed open and the purse gone. The loss paralysed me for the rest of the morning ... but the babies still had to be fed. I'd lost about 100 dollars, and I was grateful that I had already purchased the mosquito netting before going to the food market. After that I kept to the local markets.

Now we have acquired a car, a bright blue Renault sent by

Daily Life in the Nurseries.

7 Newhaven Nursery.
8 To Am (1969).

8

7

9

10

11

9 Hair-cutting at Phu My (1967).
10 Classroom activities at Allambie (1974).
11 New arrivals from Soctrang are held by
  older children at To Am (1971).
12 Potty time.
13 Thieu helping himself, To Am (1971).

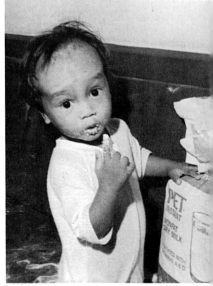

12

13

Terre des Hommes France, and released from the port after one month of exasperating conflict with local bureaucracy and inter-ministerial lack of co-operation. The credit for the release of the car belongs to Yvette. She was fed up from months of 'taxi-ing' from orphanage to hospitals with sick babies, from standing in the filthy streets waiting for cyclos, or carrying babies, or corpses, in shopping bags on the back of my motorcycle.

With the present population of the nursery, plus five live-in Vietnamese staff, three 'dailies', Yvette and myself, we have almost reached temporary saturation. My room, in which I camp at night, has been gradually turned into an isolation unit for the premature and newborn babies. I have six with me at the moment, and although I am out most of the day, I consider them my responsibility from the evening meal until after baths next morning. Yvette lavishes her special talent on the sick babies isolated in the room next door. So our nights seem to be broken into half-hour dozes ... Initially, I didn't intend to become so involved in the daily management of the house, but the project seems to require the constant attention of both of us. Yvette is responsible for the daily care of the babies, while I'm concerned with sources of supply, income, and all adoption formalities.

The house at its present capacity is costing us about 1,500 dollars a month, including staff salaries, utilities, fresh veg-etables, rice, nursery and kitchen equipment. For milk, baby cereal, toilet articles, clothes, linen and disposable diapers, we have been dependent on donations and we hope to be able to continue without having to add these extra costs to our budget.

Financially, we are dependent on no one organization. This helps us to retain our independence and to keep running the nursery on a completely international basis. It also enables us to live simply and to eliminate most 'operational' costs.

Help has come to us from many quarters: Terre des Hommes France have sent the car, and a regular supply of an excellent baby formula. Germany have been sending us shipments of medication and instruments. Small groups in Australia and New Zealand have been keeping us supplied with baby-food, cereal, linen, and toiletries. An Australian rubber company donated all our mattresses. Occasional or regular money contributions have been coming from Australia and America. Here, in the country, we have friends both military and civilian, who will shop for us at the 'PX' [post exchange], or 'appropriate' for our use 'surplus commodities', cleaning equipment, paint, refrigerators, parachutes (for shade), and a supply of fresh whole milk for the older children. The Australian Signals Corps delivers packages regularly from the AFPO [Armed Forces Post Office], and they barter an occasional sack of captured rice for us, from the Thai forces, in exchange for a case of beer. Because we are able to use cheap military postal channels, we are, fortunately, able to receive substantial donated supplies from the USA and Australia.

We have one American Sergeant Major, George Miles – indispensable to any nursery – who comes almost every evening to empty the garbage, hand-wash dirty diapers, unclog drains, paint, saw, hammer, haul, wire and find a solution or the right equipment for every need. 'Miles will fix it' is a refrain with which we mutually encourage each other in the daily disasters. He also scrounges surplus food, furniture and office supplies and arranges military transport for us to the provincial orphanages.

Dr McKinney provides daily medical supervision. He, too, is adept at appropriating supplies for us. Thanks to him, our older children have now a choice of three desserts – butterscotch pudding, plum pudding, and date roll – to supplement their unvarying rice.

We tried not to keep the older children too long at To Am. Sanh, aged five, was an exception. He came in September 1970 when the Sisters at Soctrang noticed his unusual pallor and lethargy, and asked us to take him to Saigon for medical attention. Thalassemia was diagnosed and soon after Sanh's spleen was removed at Grall Hospital in an attempt to slow down the degeneration in his condition. The surgery and regular blood transfusions brought some slight improvement of a temporary nature. As his friends left one by one for their families abroad, Sanh became sadder. He would ask if he also had a family, and when would he join them? He knew he had been waiting longer than any of the other children. We asked an American family to 'sponsor' Sanh. They wrote to him, and sent him photos and small gifts, and his world brightened as he spoke of his 'mummy and daddy'. He received a Cub Scout cap and kerchief which he wore with pride. It then occurred to us that there must be a family somewhere who would be prepared to accept Sanh and bring a little happiness into his life by giving him what he most longed for: his own family.

I explained the situation to the organization Families For Children in Canada. The Bronsteins, who were co-founders of FFC and already the adoptive parents of Tam Lien and Tran, responded with a prompt acceptance. We sought an immediate exit visa on medical grounds, and thanks to special letters of support from the Canadian Prime Minister and the Health Minister, which Naomi Bronstein herself brought to Saigon, Sanh obtained his visa and went to join his new family in Canada fifteen months after he had come to To Am.

In November I flew to Danang to collect eight children due to leave on the next convoy abroad. On the return journey we were in an unpressurized military cargo plane with no seating suitable for small children. This time we not only made stops in Nha Trang and Qui Nhon, but were also routed through Vung Tau. Between Vung Tau and Saigon we flew through an electrical storm. The plane was fiercely buffeted and the children, flung out of their seats, were vomiting and yelling. I was nauseated, and had only one pair of hands for all the children. I quickly restrapped the oldest boy of four years tightly into his seat, then stretched myself full-length across the seat pinning down with my body four other children. I clung on tightly with one arm, and with the other tried to control the three babies in boxes on the floor. The plane shuddered and vibrated so badly that lightning could be seen through cracks in the seams. That it didn't disintegrate seemed to me no mean miracle.

At first To Am took in children of all ages and the older children would help feed the younger children. Mealtime was a circus, since the children had to be fed, bathed and pottied in the same large room. Rice would be spattered on furniture or flung in soggy messes on the well-irrigated floor. Potties would be worn as hats with imaginable consequences. Most of the children seemed at least to be enjoying themselves. But the house was not really suitable for this mixed community. There were no beds big enough for the older children, so they slept on the floor, with one military-khaki towel to be used as suited the comfort of each child. Since we received twelve large sticks of bread a day from some Catholic Relief flour programme, the older children ate bread at two meals a day. For the small babies, the bread was soaked in milk and served as a sort of mush. There was certainly no extravagance in the diet but at least the best quality milk formula was provided for the babies. For six months Guigoz Company in Saigon delivered six cases of milk a month to To Am. This may have been a gift or it may have been paid for in France by Terre des Hommes. It was certainly the most expensive milk on the market and was well-tolerated by the babies.

Some of the army surplus commodities were suitable for the older children. There was a plentiful supply of 100 lb sacks of powdered milk, but this was not very popular for drinking. Meat was scarce. I would hunt the 'black-market' street stalls for a 16 oz can of army issue beef-and-gravy, which cost 500 piastres (3 dollars), and would give the older children a dob of it on their rice, and add some to the puréed vegetables of the babies. The can would last for two days with careful economizing. We would also buy plenty of cheap fresh vegetables and bananas from the market.

World Vision gave us a large supply of Gerber baby food, but as most of it was puréed prunes it was impossible to give it to the babies who had no need at all for the laxative effect of prunes. Happily, the foreign staff found the prunes a welcome diversion from bread and bananas and for the next few years, ice-cold puréed prunes became a significant element in our diet.

Nursery care was undoubtedly an improvement over the orphanages, but still inferior in most cases to private foster care. We were always seeking suitable foster homes for as many children as possible, particularly for those children who were developing very poorly and who needed an immense amount of personal attention to coax them out of their physical and psychological decline. At one time we had over thirty children in foster homes (mainly of people from the British, American, Australian and Dutch Embassies or employees of Shell, Esso and IBM). Deanna Dirks Dubinsky, whose husband was a pilot with Air America, fostered nine of our children between 1970 and 1974, and eventually adopted two as a beginning of their own family. Deanna describes her first experience (when she was still single) of fostering a baby:

On 15 July (1970) just before evening, Rosemary came riding up in a pedicab, carrying a pathetic bundle which she handed over to me. Sasha was four months old and weighed less than 4 lb. Rosemary told me that she was very sick, and that if she should die during the night I was not to blame myself. Even though I was inexperienced, she felt I could take better care of her than wherever she had come from. I was given a bag with bottles, formula, diapers and some clothes before Rosemary took off again. The transfer took less than fifteen minutes, and left me in a state of shock.

I hardly knew where to begin. Sasha could barely drink an ounce of formula at a time, and this could take an hour or longer. She did not know how to suck on a bottle . . . The first few days passed in a blur but the nights I remember very clearly. The shelling and rumblings of war served as a constant reminder that this was a far from normal situation. Several times bombs went off just down the street from where I was. And through all this night-life, a pathetic thin wail of a cry weaving in and out. It tore at my heart and yet exasperated me, too, since I didn't know how to stop her crying.

During the next two months Sasha grew stronger only to fall ill again, with a terrible case of diarrhoea. The few pounds she had managed to gain evaporated before my eyes. Nothing I did would control the diarrhoea. The 3rd Field and then Adventist Hospitals refused to admit her . . . Her condition was desperate when my landlady advised me to try the French Hospital (Grall) downtown. I called an army officer I knew (from the Demolition Explosive Ordnance) and asked him to drive us there. Late that night we went roaring down in his jeep and checked Sasha into the Grall, where she was immediately given intravenous fluid. I hired a girl at the hospital to stay with her twenty-four hours a day, and provided the formula and medication prescribed. She stayed in hospital two weeks.

When Sasha came home again she immediately started to thrive for the first time. Five months after coming to me, she left with Rosemary, to join her family in Luxemburg. She was now a plump and smiling 12 lb baby. I hated to see her go, but it was an experience I would never have forgone.

On 17 December 1970 I took Sasha and several other children to Europe. A couple of weeks later, this time while Yvette was away taking a convoy to France, we heard that there was an epidemic of viral meningitis in a nearby orphanage in Truong Minh Giang Street:

7 January 1971: They have lost a third of their children in the space of ten days. Suddenly we lost four-year-old Do before we recognized it for what it was, and our desolation turned to panic at the idea of an epidemic. Six-year-old Khan was in full crisis, but we were able to treat him in time, and he pulled through. We had to tape him to the couch in the living room and sit holding his leg all night so that he wouldn't dislodge the intravenous infusion with its vital medication.

... Yvette is always expressing her nostalgia for India and trying to return there, so she may not be in Vietnam for much longer. I shall be in need of a nurse to carry on here.

6 February, 2.30 a.m.: Somewhere between one sleepless night and the next, I have been to Europe with a group of babies going to their adoptive homes. As soon as I can send off the next group to Europe and several to the US, I must go home to Australia for a few weeks, to try to recruit some volunteers to help me. We are badly in need of more personnel.

Little Tuyen next door is yelling for her bottle; she starts up every two hours like a fire-brigade siren. I'm just wondering at this point if it's worthwhile going to bed at all, or whether I'm conscious enough to continue with my basket of correspondence – it's a clothes basket . . .

Chapter 5

GROWING RESPONSIBILITIES
Allambie and Newhaven Nurseries

YVETTE'S EVENTUAL DEPARTURE in April 1971 saw the end of an era. Since the opening of the third To Am, I had been sleeping in the new nursery in order to share the chores with Yvette, and using my room at Phu My as an office by day. We had also alternated as escorts for convoys, so that when one of us was abroad, the other had full responsibility for the nursery. Between December and February each of us had made three trips to Europe. Obviously, it could not continue like this. More helpers were needed to share the growing responsibilities.

In March I returned to Australia to look for some volunteer nurses. To help with the administrative burden, I hoped to enlist an old friend, Margaret Moses. Margaret's organizational talents, her eloquence, her humour, and her very good French would be a real asset, but I particularly wanted someone with whom I had a solidly based rapport, on whom I could depend completely, and who would stay for as long as necessary, providing a stable nucleus for the expanding work. Margaret would be perfect, and I was presumptuous enough to ask her to resign from the education department and join me as a volunteer. She agreed.

Carmel Curtain, a mothercraft nurse from Melbourne, and Judy Seward RN, from Adelaide, also volunteered to join us. Terre des Hommes Germany had promised another nurse to replace Yvette, and shortly afterwards Ilse Ewald appeared unannounced. (By chance we were playing a cassette of Beethoven's Ninth Symphony when Ilse walked in. She later admitted how much this music had calmed her initial trepidation at joining a group of 'foreigners', and made her feel quite at home.)

53

I had planned to move back to sleep in my room at Phu My, but stayed on at To Am to bridge a crisis with our Vietnamese staff. The help of the local Vietnamese was of course vital to us; without them we could not have functioned or added to our nurseries. By the end of our stay in Saigon, when there were never more than two or three foreign staff running each nursery, we would have about 400 Vietnamese helpers, working in shifts. It was difficult, particularly in these early years, to find local staff who were willing to implement our ideas of child care; they could not easily accept that mere orphan children deserved such consideration while their own children or siblings had even less. At this point, however, we felt obliged to dismiss half of the helpers, and to seek more willing workers; meanwhile the foreign staff coped with the many extra tasks involved in caring for the children and doing the household chores.

Ilse very soon assumed all the nursing responsibilities at To Am and, as light relief, she reorganized the house, built furniture, redecorated, and spent many nocturnal hours mending my motorbike, which seemed to have defied every mechanic in town. Ilse had previously been on the German hospital ship in Danang, the *Helgoland*, and she was familiar with the Vietnamese scene. She was not only a highly qualified nurse but had also trained in hospital administration. Her talents were legion, and her compassion for the children so excessive that she drove herself to exhaustion. She had no regular bedroom and would just throw herself fully clothed on the couch in the living room, for a couple of hours of interrupted sleep. Half the room was converted into an intensive-care emergency room, so that at every moment she would be close to the babies most in need:

13 June 1971: Ilse is another gift from heaven. She is a most experienced nurse and has an extraordinary capacity for work. She has been up night after night, with no more than two or three hours of broken sleep. In this weather the babies' lungs are in a terrifying condition: they are so close to pneumonia all the time. The lungs fill up with fluid and we have to suction it out. We have had the oxygen cylinders in constant use the past weeks. When the babies are too premature, there is almost no hope of success.

Last week I went to Danang and brought back twelve children, eight of whom were babies, and two toddlers. They nearly all have boils (staph infections) and badly congested lungs.

Ilse escorted a group of children to Europe a couple of weeks ago and brought back some Quintovirelon vaccine (diphtheria, whooping cough, tetanus, polio and measles all in one). She also brought back other useful items, such as scrubbing brushes, brooms, paint, tools, contact paper, strawberries, roses and champagne (carefully stowed in the portable icebox with the vaccine).

Marg was ill for a few days in hospital. We feared hepatitis, but since the doctor seemed rather vague on the matter, she had herself discharged and has been going like wild-fire ever since. With her deep wells of patience she is particularly good at the PR work, which was never my forte.

Judy joined Carmel setting up a nursery at Sancta Maria Orphanage, but they felt frustrated by the Director, who seemed to regard the new nursery only as a status symbol; it was continually invaded by curious visitors who distracted the nurses from their routine. By July we decided to open another new house, where Carmel and Judy could function freely. The new house, on Ngo Tung Chau Street, Giadinh, was named 'Allambie' – an Australian aboriginal word meaning 'rest a while'.

The older children from To Am moved over to the more spacious Allambie. Wendy Burdon, a mothercraft nurse from England, came to join the team there. She was sponsored by Project Vietnam Orphans, in co-operation with which we subsequently made a number of adoptive placements in the UK.

15 July 1971, to American Embassy, Saigon: Requesting the following item be placed in the next edition of the Embassy Bulletin:

WANTED:
Nursery/Household Equipment
A group of volunteer social workers
operating two sixty-bed nurseries providing gratuitous care to orphans and assisting in their adoption abroad, urgently
need donation of washing machine,

refrigerator and other nursery/household
equipment. Contact Rosemary Taylor or
Margaret Moses, PTT 24671.

1 August 1971: Next week, our 'maintenance man', Sgt-Maj.
George Miles, will return to the US. We had a foretaste of life
without him when he was on leave recently and our pump broke
down. We started out by carrying 40 lb buckets of water up two
flights of stairs to the nursery in order to bath the children. Later
in the evening, we consulted a phone list and tried to find some
man we knew who might have an idea of how to mend a pump.
Most of our Embassy friends had limited talents in the field of
applied science. Finally, we phoned Dora at the US Embassy,
who promised to contact their maintenance department early
next morning. The men worked all next day, and as they were
about to knock off before the new pump was installed, I invited
them at least to help us carry water upstairs to the third floor
before they left. The boss decided to press on and complete the
installation that night. But that was only the beginning. The new
pump was too powerful for the old water pipes which started to
fall apart at the seams. New piping had to be run from the lower
reservoir in the laundry to the upper reservoir on the roof. They
then discovered that the pump would drain this lower reservoir
in two minutes flat and because there was no automatic cut-off,
the pump would burn itself out if left on for more than two
minutes. Their next job was to put in wider piping from the
mains to the lower reservoir so it would fill as fast as the pump
drained it. They then fitted automatic cut-offs both on the inflow
pipe and on the pump.

Margaret coped with most of this as she is responsible for
maintenance.

While there was a US military presence in Vietnam we were
authorized to send children being adopted by military families on
military transportation. The complicated procedures were first
handled by Sgt-Maj. George Miles, but later had to be taken over by
the military chaplains. They would complete the paperwork, make
the necessary contacts, and take it upon themselves to bludgeon
some innocent into acting as an escort for the 'military dependent'.

They also helped with transportation problems within Vietnam, whether they involved children or supplies.

While Ilse Ewald was absent escorting children to Europe in early August, Margaret and I held on grimly. The morning George Miles, his tour of duty in Vietnam finished, was due to escort two 'military dependent' children back to America, one of them, Son, with his jet black skin, broke out in chickenpox. It was too late to cancel his travel. We tried to camouflage his spots with powder, then took him to the airport with his face well-hidden. We passed Son and Mai-Linh over the barrier at the last minute, and advised Miles to keep Son's face concealed as much as possible. Arriving in Anchorage, Alaska, Miles took the two children through Immigration and Health inspection; the officials saw the spots and suspected small-pox! Miles explained it was only chickenpox, but nine doctors in all were unable to verify this. Miles was taken off the plane and isolated in a trailer with the two toddlers. Food was left outside the trailer. For three days they remained in isolation until biopsies were sent to the Infectious Disease Hospital in Maryland and the results came back – chickenpox.

I had gone down with some sort of dysentery and felt worse than I had ever felt in my life. But as I was responsible for giving the babies their daily medication and shots, I would drag myself to the nursery several times a day, and then return to Phu My to collapse on the bed. I was trying to hide from Margaret the fact that I felt so ill, hoping she would think me simply bad-tempered. When Ilse returned from Europe, she saw that I was dangerously dehydrated and over the next several days she gave me 10 litres of IV fluid.

It was Sunday and Marg, Ilse and I were at To Am. We thought about preparing some food and hunted in the cupboards. There was canned spinach, canned tomatoes and eggs – ingredients enough for an omelette. We all participated in the mixing, and the result was a khaki-coloured mess that remains vivid in my memory. It smelled good enough and I was determined to eat something. A couple of spoonfuls and I collapsed again on the couch. Next day we got ourselves tickets on Air America and flew to Danang.

21 *September, RT*: Last week Ilse and I went to Danang to bring back fourteen children. I did not think I would survive the plane trip as I felt so weak and nauseated. While we were there I had a

complete check-up on the German hospital boat. Gardia Lamblia, what might have been a sequel to amoebic dysentery, and a low potassium level were the only irregularities detected at that stage. After that the problem cleared up speedily. I think the freedom from the tension that gnaws at one continually in Saigon may have contributed to my recovery. Ilse had good friends on the boat amongst the doctors and nurses and we came back not only loaded with children, but also with medicines, black German bread, wine, chocolate and assorted goodies.

Back in Saigon, Marg met us at the airport, and on the way back to the nursery, she gave a resumé of the crises that had occurred in our absence: Huong and Hoa, three-year-olds, got into the fridge and had perhaps consumed twenty-seven anti-typhoid vaccination tablets. We could not be sure. They were rushed to the hospital but apparently showed no ill-effects. There had been an 'alert' in Saigon and we were thereby deprived of the valuable carting and carrying assistance of our military friends.

Our laundry situation is grim. It is the rainy season and almost impossible to dry anything outdoors. We've used all our reserve supplies of linen and the lines are filled up with soggy clothes day after day, smelling rather evil. We would appreciate a couple of simple washing-machines and dryers.

On 1 October 1971 I left Saigon with a group of thirteen children, eight for Europe and five for the USA.

At about this time the Ministry of Welfare was expressing exaggerated concern for the fate of the orphans who had gone abroad for adoption. I felt that this concern was misplaced given the lack of interest taken in some of the children still in the country. Not only were children languishing in orphanages, but others were sold or rented-out for begging purposes right in the city of Saigon, on the very doorstep of the Ministry.

One day I came across a beggar woman who had stationed herself in Kennedy Square, in front of the Central Post Office. On her lap she had a small child with a dirty piece of gauze taped to his face. I stopped to look at the child, drew back the gauze, and saw the rot of noma already advanced. The boy had been in hospital, but the old woman, far too old to be his mother, needed him to beg so she had asked for his discharge. She showed me the discharge slip. I was upset, and asked the woman to accompany me, with the child, to the Ministry on the other side of the square. Over at the Ministry, office workers flocked around to stare, but the situation lacked a precedent and they did not know what action to take. Eventually, someone called Caritas Centre, and I was invited to bring the child around. When they saw the noma was still in the active stage, they regretfully refused to admit him. I took the woman and child back to To Am until I could find another solution.

Margaret and Ilse called Joyce Horn at the Barsky Plastic Surgery Unit, but they, too, had a policy not to accept active noma. In the end they made an exception for Hung, as there was no other hope for him. We took Hung to Barsky, and lest the woman be tempted to snatch him back before completion of the treatment, Margaret, Ilse and I emptied our pockets and gave her all the money we had (7,000 piastres) so that she would leave the boy in hospital. We told her to come back later and we would give her more money; she came back once and we kept our promise.

The Welfare Department had been powerless to intervene on behalf of this child, though they had established that Hung was not related to the woman in any way. We could not see that he was less worthy of their concern than the children who had gone to families abroad.

On one of our trips to the Delta, in October 1971, we found a little girl, Ut, at Providence Orphanage, Cantho. Ut was about four-years-old, weighed 15 lb and had a chest rattle that could be heard from across the large room that she shared with thirty other children. We brought her back to Saigon in our Renault, with eight other children who were either seated in plastic carrycots, or were strung up in hammocks across the van. It was a trip that fixed itself in my memory. At 4.00 p.m. we drove on to the ferry to cross the Mekong at Cantho, calculating that we would make it to the second ferry outside Vinh Long and be well-advanced on the road to Saigon before nightfall. We were anxious to avoid night driving along these unlit roads given the added hazards caused by rain and flooding.

On the ferry, as usual, our van was surrounded by curious pedestrians who pressed their faces tightly against the window panes. We could see nothing but these faces. The heat was stifling but it would be useless to open the windows. After we had been there for about half an hour, the crowd dispersed and we were beckoned to drive off. I presumed that there had been a breakdown of this ferry and that we would have to take another. As we drove back on to the landing, Ilse and I signalled that we had an emergency load and that we wanted to go immediately on to the adjacent ferry, and not take a place in the queue standing far back on the roadway. The traffic director allowed us to do as we wished, so we boarded ferry no. 2 immediately. This ferry crossed and discharged us on the other side and we drove off in great relief. It took us several minutes to begin to suspect what had happened. We drove straight into the bus terminal square of Cantho and were faced with the indisputable evidence of our stupidity; we were back where we started. The first ferry had been crossing the river all the time we thought we were stationary, and on alighting from the first ferry, we had crossed back again in the second ferry . . . We set out again to cross this particular part of the river for the fourth time in a few hours, and managed to make it to the next river crossing outside Vinh Long before the darkness and rain descended. Ilse, of course, was at the wheel (she did all the driving in the provinces). I was twisted around, trying to minister to the children behind, steadying the hammocks as we bumped over the rutted road in torrential rain and otherwise straining to help Ilse detect the yellow line, faintly visible in our headlights, which was the only indication that we were still on the road. In order to keep Ilse alert I kept handing her cups of cold coffee laced with effervescent vitamin C tablets: it tasted awful.

Next day in Saigon, Ut was taken to Grall Hospital where massive TB involvement was confirmed. She had only a small portion of one lung still functioning, and was hospitalized immediately. Within a few months Ut had doubled her weight, but in April her heart showed signs of severe strain. The French pediatrician, who was treating her with such dedication, begged us to obtain some special medication which was available only in France. We cabled Mme Gallozzi in Paris; she had the medication on the next Air France flight to Saigon. But the authorities at Saigon Airport ignored the clear instructions on the package and sent it back to Paris. By the time it arrived again the following week, little Ut was dead. We were all deeply upset, especially the pediatrician who had invested so much professionally and emotionally in her treatment.

Some of the most significant medical contributions to the orphan children were undoubtedly made by the French doctors at Grall, the former French Military Hospital and one of Saigon's best facilities. It was a French doctor who first diagnosed pneumocystis carinii in a dead orphan baby in 1970. Most of the surgery on the Phu My polio children was also performed by a French orthopaedic surgeon at Grall.

Margaret found herself in the role of medical interpreter between the French-speaking doctors and our English-speaking nurses. She would later report with wry humour on her initial circumlocutory attempts to describe conditions such as undescended testicles, umbilical hernias, etc.

Louise had come to us on 2 July from Providence Orphanage, Soctrang. That day we had packed eleven children into cardboard boxes, three babies to a box, and carried them back to Saigon in a helicopter graciously lent to us by a Vietnamese general. She developed beautifully once at To Am; she fed heartily and gained weight steadily. She was a great personality in the 'pig-pen' room. She had her own crib and her own musical mobile which she would attend to with fascination. Then on 3 September, two months after arrival, her breathing became difficult and she showed intermittent signs of cyanosis.[1] Ilse diagnosed inflammation of the glottis which was gradually closing off the air passage. A visiting doctor made a similar diagnosis but said there was nothing he could do. So we hovered over the child for the next three days, Ilse using all her skill to restore breath to little Louise. The oxygen cylinder emptied and we needed another brought down from the second floor. It was impossible for any of us to carry a large oxygen cylinder down two flights of stairs so Margaret raced to the US Ambassador's house, round the corner from the nursery, and asked the marine guards for help. They came immediately and carried the cylinder downstairs. Meanwhile, I had been holding Louise while Ilse was adjusting a portable emergency cylinder. Louise's faint breath stopped alto-gether. Ilse rapidly laid the child flat on the floor and began to resuscitate her. Louise revived. That was noon on 5 September. She continued to maintain a tenuous grip on life until late afternoon and

---

[1] Cyanosis: a bluish-purple discoloration of the skin and mucous membranes usually resulting from a deficiency of oxygen in the blood.

then as her breath grew less and less perceptible we used every means available to increase her oxygen supply. For half an hour we laboured to revive this child we all loved so much, but she was slipping from us. Then we knew it was all over and that further effort would be useless. Louise was dead on the floor and we were kneeling beside the tiny corpse emotionally and physically exhausted.

Little Bear took the place of Louise, for the N. family in Australia. Although we had previously succeeded in sending Sophie to the state of New South Wales back in 1969, and Fiona Be to South Australia in January 1972, Little Bear was our first child for the state of Victoria. Immigration would not issue a visa without approval from the International Social Services as it was the only agency judged to be competent in this field. In fact, ISS refused categorically to participate. Seven other agencies were then declared competent, but were unwilling to become involved. Little Bear had her passport in December but as Christmas approached, Australia kept its doors firmly barred against this tiny 'yellow-peril'. Finally, Methodist Child Care's Director, Graeme Gregory, saw through the political and racial obscurity which hung as a cloud over the Victorian authorities, and consented to handle the case. Little Bear arrived home on 6 February 1972, escorted by one of her godmothers, Sr Monica Marks from Adelaide. I was her other godmother by proxy, and she was baptized 'Kim'.

This was only the beginning of the struggle with Victorian authorities. There were five more adoptions for Australia (four for Victoria) nearing completion in Saigon and the families had been fighting for months to obtain the welfare approval needed for the entry visas to be issued. Elaine Moir had initiated these adoptions the previous year when she had visited Saigon and located the children in different orphanages. Some of the children were now being cared for in our nurseries. For months, the battle raged between the adoptive parents, the Victorian Minister of Welfare, the Director of ISS, the Minister of Immigration, the press, Elaine Moir and other concerned individuals. The Opposition party naturally made political capital of the issue, and the Federal and State governments were accused of callously passing the buck in the issue of the adoption of five Vietnamese waifs.

The five children had completed adoption papers and passports, and were ready to join their families, but the Australian Embassy was not authorized to issue entry visas. Elaine Moir was determined to get the children to their families and the Victorian welfare authorities were adamant in their opposition. Elaine came to Saigon; she obtained some good quality white envelopes, stuffed them with adoption papers and birth certificates, sealed them and addressed the envelopes to the Australian Immigration Authorities. She placed the envelopes in each passport and set off with the five children for Australia. When questioned at the airline check-in, in Saigon and again in Singapore, concerning entry visas for the children, Elaine indicated the sealed envelopes. No one thought to pursue the matter further.

The arrival in Australia of the 'smuggled waifs' without visas caused a nation-wide stir. The 'cloak and dagger secret flight' made headlines in every state newspaper; Elaine was either the heroine or the villain of the day depending on one's viewpoint. Her own account is brisk:

When the plane arrived in Sydney I waited until all the other passengers had got off, and then I marched down with the children. BOAC officials and crew helped me carry the babies. We were in an area separated from everyone else. I knew the only way to finish the job was to get the babies into their mothers' arms so I quickly walked outside, handed over the babies, and returned to immigration.

I put the passports on the counter in front of the immigration official and watched him anxiously as he went through the documents. He went right through them all and then started again. He said, 'There don't seem to be visas here for their entry.' I simply said, 'They have none.' He picked up the passports and said sternly, 'Come with me.' I followed him through to an office and was offered a cup of coffee. I was told they were phoning Canberra. The passports were returned to me after about two hours, with thirty-day visas in them. I asked him why thirty days. The official said, 'That should give you time to sort out your problems with the Social Welfare Department.'

The problems were sorted out, and the children stayed.

Elaine Moir is without doubt the person who contributed most, in Australia at that time, to an increased awareness of inter-country adoption, and the plight of innumerable abandoned children in some neighbouring Asian countries. It was her personal initiative that pioneered the way and her determination that overcame all obstacles in the end.

In March 1972 rioting out in the Giadinh area had forced us to relocate Allambie in a much less attractive but more accessible building, in Hien Vuong Street, just a block away from To Am. Tim Seward, Judy's brother, joined the team for some months and worked as carpenter, builder, plumber, and mechanic. He built a toilet system, a wading pool, furniture, and play equipment for the children. He, like Sgt-Maj. George Miles, had exactly the talents needed.

Sr Anicet had moved from Providence Orphanage, Cantho, up to the Highlands, near Kontum, where she was working with the Montagnard people. Wende Grant wrote to her with news of Lara's progress, and corresponded with us during 1972, about her work with FCVN, and soon about her own family's wish to adopt a third Vietnamese child. This was Thu Van (Tia), a crippled child from the Providence Orphanage at Ba Xuyen, who had been brought to FCVN's attention by a Maj. Joe Pinaud.

4 *August 1972, RT to WG:* The lawyer has your dossier, and I shall be able to make application for [Tia]'s passport within a week.

25 *August, RT to WG:* Come by all means. You will be able to escort back your own daughter and the M. children for Colorado. Accommodation in the nursery will be impossible as it is chock-a-block with babies everywhere ...

Just yesterday Sr Sylvie brought more babies from one of the remotest provincial orphanages ... babies needing surgery for cleft palates. One poor little mite had a huge growth attached to his back, balloon-shaped and half the size of the baby. We hope it can be removed and the baby saved.

Wende Grant made her first trip to Vietnam in September 1972, with another member of FCVN, and while they were there they visited orphanages in the Saigon area and, in Wende's words, they were 'left with an overwhelming rage at the waste of children's lives':

64

In those dirty, crowded and understaffed institutions, tiny babies lost weight and died. Illness was untreated and pain ignored. Beautiful little children seeking attention and love and receiving neither, withdrew into twilight worlds of their own. Lacking stimulation, bright young minds slowed in their development and eventually were judged retarded. War, poverty and custom had combined to condemn thousands of innocent children to a sub-human existence, and often to death.

In contrast, the three nurseries offered nutritious food, medical care, love and concern. Infants were held while being fed. Toddlers were encouraged to walk and play. Older children drew pictures, had playground equipment, learned songs and discovered that the nurses and child-care workers were interested in the individual children they cared for. The emotionally disturbed, the retarded and the physically handicapped children received medical care and therapy. Their improvement in many cases was miraculous. Most encouraging was knowing that the nurseries were half-way stations for children on their way to families of their own.

On our return home our efforts on behalf of Vietnamese children redoubled. The FCVN group collected more funds and supplies. There were more members, more publicity, and more prospective adoptive families.

Advising adoptive families and co-ordinating their cases was a full-time job by the fall of 1972. Rosemary sent pictures and descriptions of available children. The children were offered to families already approved for adoption from Vietnam, who had sent completed dossiers to Rosemary in Saigon. By supervising the preliminary steps we were saving time for Rosemary, and preventing unnecessary delays in processing the adoptions.

We learned from each adoption. The Colorado State Department of Social Services continued to advise us on inter-state placement procedures as we offered children to families outside Colorado. Once we helped find another home for a failed adoption. By early 1973 we had helped place some fifty children and were functioning more as an adoption agency than as an adoptive parent group.

The growing publicity that Wende mentions had its unfortunate side, too, as can be seen in the following circular letter I sent that autumn:

23 October 1972, Saigon, RT to WG, NBC newsmen, etc.: I must tell you of a recent event which has upset us very much. A few weeks ago we were pestered by some NBC newsmen who wished to photograph a certain child. We refused permission. Our policy is not to give interviews to newsmen unless we have some definite purpose to be served.

The NBC newsmen, however, were undeterred and ambushed us at the airport as we were trying to send off a group of children. Our usual procedure is to handle the formalities as quietly and calmly as possible, both for the good of the children and the good of the project.

Last week the departure was a disaster due to the brutality of these NBC cameramen.

We fought physically and verbally to keep them off. We were helped by a concerned American passenger, who was badly bruised and lost his passport in the fray. He was frankly ashamed of the behaviour of his fellow countrymen and did all he could to protect us.

The struggle was both undignified and exhausting. I myself was in tears. The babies were carried on to the plane in great disorder and we were not even able to get them strapped into their seats before having to leave the plane. Ilse, the escort, was in pieces and – we were told later – that she cried for the first part of the trip, so unnerved was she by the experience. In order to avoid a possible repetition of the scene in New York, she insisted on changing her schedule in Paris and was prepared to stay over-night with the eight children if necessary.

To aggravate us, the NBC crew trained their cameras on us as we were leaving the airport in disarray. We stopped to talk with a representative of the US Embassy security who had come to try and help us, and they again trained their cameras on us. When we were in the bus coming back from the plane across the tarmac, and trembling with anger, they shoved their microphone right in our faces. What human decency was there in such an action?

. . . Please inform prospective parents of our attitude to news coverage while the children are in our care. We will not prostitute the children for political sensationalism . . .

In November 1972 we opened another nursery, Newhaven, at 31 Phan Dinh Phung Street. Newhaven would take the older babies and toddlers from To Am, and relieve the congestion at both To Am and Allambie where the children were often having to spend between six and twelve months before their adoption papers could be completed. Terre des Hommes France had agreed to assume some regular financial responsibility for the rent and upkeep of Newhaven:

14 November 1972, RT to WG: Thanks to the recent financial support we have been receiving, we are now able to have a permanent night-duty nurse in each room. We have also converted a back room for the newborns, and put in an air-conditioner. In this way we can isolate the newborn from the sick, who still occupy the other half of our salon so that they can be under constant supervision. Ilse brought back a baby weighing less than 2 lb; she borrowed an incubator, but as it isn't in working order, she improvised with a small electric blanket around the baby. Miraculously, the child is still living and gaining weight steadily, but still a long way from being out of danger.

Anne Dolan, a children's nurse (who had come to Saigon with the English Ockenden group), was by now in charge of Allambie.

During the next few weeks, Wende remained a focal point for our news, though she had fallen ill with hepatitis after getting back from Vietnam in September and was only just recovering.

2 December 1972, WG to Sr Sylvie and Sr Marie-Marthe: Thu Van [Tia] is a wonderful little girl and we are delighted to have her for our own. She is very intelligent and is learning English with surprising speed. She taught her father to count to ten in Vietnamese and when he did it correctly she said, 'Good girl, Daddy'!

So far she has been having physical therapy every day for several weeks and is making progress. This week she goes to see the orthopaedic surgeon again and he will decide if she must have surgery and when. In any event, the doctor assured us that she will be able to walk. Right after she arrived we had to have all her baby teeth removed. The dentist has put in retaining wires to maintain the proper shape of her mouth until her second teeth come through. It hurt me terribly to put that little girl through such fear and pain, but now her mouth is free from infection.

12 December, Anne Dolan to WG: We have just had a very timely Canadian airlift so the children will have a good Christmas. We are making stockings for them all, filled with small cars, dolls and candy. We have painted a crib scene and hope to get a large tree. Nine more children came in from Danang today so we are really crowded with over sixty children at Allambie.

I've started the children on a fresh food diet. So far we've had no diarrhoea from the beef stews, scrambled eggs and whole milk (when the boys next door manage to steal some for us), pork, etc. We are hoping the skin conditions will improve and gradually, when finances permit, we shall get the children off all the 'stodge' they usually eat. We now buy meat in bulk and store it in the freezers.

26 December 1972, Anne Dolan to WG: We had an exhausting Christmas with over seventy children, and just Christie Leivermann, a recently arrived nurse from Minnesota, and I to cope, but the children really enjoyed themselves. Some US Embassy people came on Christmas day with gifts and gave the kids, of all things, apricot juice and loads of candy. We have used over half a gallon of Kaopectate trying to stop the diarrhoea.

25 December 1972, RT to WG: ... your cheque for 3,630 dollars is already spent, though not yet cashed. Our hospital bill this month was almost 800 dollars, partly due to the need of a private isolation room for measles cases. A Soctrang baby brought measles into the house and we've had to isolate a few children in hospital. We do have a 'one shot' vaccine, but it is for babies over eight months. The 'three shot' vaccine can be given earlier but some of the children haven't completed the course. Moreover, two of the babies with completed vaccinations have just contracted measles ...

In the last two months we have had to find accommodation for 111 new children. On 12 December, a group of twenty-nine orphans flew down from Sacred Heart Orphanage in Danang; they are awaiting departure for the USA, France, Canada, and Germany.

Children and families were 'matched' in different ways. Sometimes I sent information on a certain child to the agency abroad and they made the choice of a suitable family. Sometimes I received the parents' dossier in Saigon, with the request that I choose a child. The system varied from country to country. If a child were handicapped in any way, we tried to describe the case as clearly as possible, so the parents would not over-estimate their ability to cope. We were unable to place children with families expressing racial discrimination, or those wanting the guarantee of a healthy baby.

The Paris Peace Agreement was signed while I was in Australia for a few weeks' leave:

24 January 1973, Anne Dolan to WG: An historic day! Have listened to President Nixon's speech. Now we are wondering what will happen to us. We'll wait and see.

Christie and I are a bit disenchanted with Vietnam. Christie went out and was stoned – and we've both had one infection after another. Now I have conjunctivitis in both eyes; she has it only in one eye. We also have constant strep throats and flu. Then I burnt my left arm with cooking oil . . .

Marg heard from Wende that typhoid had been detected in one of the babies recently arrived in the States:

25 January 1973, MM to WG: Thanks for the unwelcome news. It coincided with an epidemic here and with one in Danang. It hit a number of our babies between 2 and 4 lb. Ilse seems to have it under control since Sunday, but no one yet has any positive confirmation of what it was.

Marie-Therese: Basically, and perhaps brutally, the facts: the child is struggling with a number of problems, principally pneumonia and otitis[1] (both bilateral). The doctor feared, initially, that she might have a heart condition: she is at the moment too ill to test. In any case, she is going to the Barsky Unit this weekend as she has a bad necrosis[2] on her left leg – a small wonder there is so little muscle there for injections. Tell the

---

[1] Otitis: a painful inflammation of the ear leading to impaired hearing.
[2] Necrosis: death of one or more of the body's cells, usually in a localized area, resulting from an interruption of the blood supply.

adoptive family to keep faith and courage. I shall send another progress report next week. She is a lovely little girl.

Families receiving children from To Am or Newhaven should be alerted to the fact that the children have all been exposed to measles. Did you know that the gamma globulin from Canada was lost?

Before Wende read this letter, Marg had already received my expulsion order from the Ministry of Interior in Saigon.

Chapter 6

ON THE BRINK OF EXPULSION

Registration as an Adoption Agency in Saigon
January 1973–October 1973

DURING 1972 Congressional and public pressure forced USAID to turn its attention to the adoption scene in Vietnam. Although we were still operating in Saigon without an officially registered name, we were responsible for the only significant adoption programme in existence.[1] Our work was already well enough known for the US Senate Committee on Labor and Public Welfare to write to me, on 27 August 1971, to ask for my comments on a draft of the legislation to further inter-country adoption. In Saigon we operated three nurseries, or half-way houses, with a local staff of a hundred, and we had placed over 500 children in adoptive homes during the year 1972, working in liaison with professional agencies in most countries, and in particular with Terre des Hommes in Switzerland, Germany, France, Belgium, and Luxemburg.

From 1968 to 1972 we had managed to place a total of 1,132 orphans. Caritas Nutrition Centre arranged a small number of private adoptions, and their statistics were not available to USAID. World Vision also arranged a few adoptions, in 1971 and 1972 – twenty-five in all, according to their own statistics. International Social Services was responsible for twenty-six adoptions over the five-year period prior to 1972; and then there were, inevitably, a small number of private adoptions arranged by direct contact between family, orphanage, and lawyer. Holt Adoption Agency was not yet operating in Vietnam; and the Catholic Relief Services

---

[1] Ambassador Bunker, on 31 October 1972, had cabled the US Secretary of State: 'Suggest Congressman contact Miss Rosemary Taylor, To Am Nursery, 64A Doan thi Diem, Saigon, for information on finding adoptable child in Vietnam. Miss Taylor is outstanding authority on Vietnamese adoptions.'

(in that five-year period) processed six adoptions on an unofficial basis. The figures were to be presented in a misleading light at the hearing of 11 May 1973, a year later, of a Senate Judiciary Sub-committee on problems connected with refugees, chaired by Senator Edward Kennedy, which seemed to want to imply that, thanks to the USAID grant of 100,000 dollars, ISS had processed the majority of adoptions from Vietnam.

Before this hearing, in January, while I was at home in Australia, the office of the Social Welfare Adviser to the US Mission and the Government of Vietnam, perhaps realizing that USAID had no controlling influence whatsoever in this area of child welfare at that time, telephoned the Ministry of Social Welfare (where USAID obviously called the tune), and told them that this was the time to refuse my latest residence application, which had been pending for some months. We received this information courtesy of a well-placed ally in USAID. On 28 January 1973, the Ministry of Interior, following the instruction of the Ministry of Social Welfare, issued an order of expulsion giving me eight days to leave the country. No reason was given and no interrogation conducted, but it seems that as an Australian unassociated with USAID, I had become an embarrassment. Margaret Moses telephoned the news to me in Adelaide, and I flew back to Saigon before the expiry of the eight days' grace.

The US Consul immediately began an active investigation into the matter. He obtained a stay of expulsion order by phoning the National Police and requesting them to suspend further action until they received a written communication from him. The Police were gracious and treated the situation with good humour when I was summoned for an interview some days later. It was conceded that a 'lack of official affiliation' was the chief reason for the proposed expulsion, and there would be no reason not to rescind the order were I to register our Saigon operation under the auspices of some licensed adoption agency. The US Embassy backed my application for temporary residence, pending proper registration of our activities. As far back as February 1972, the Consul-General, Mr Robert Lewis, had written to the Minister of Interior in Saigon, in support of my request for a multiple exit–re-entry visa:

Miss Taylor has been instrumental in placing numerous war

orphans with European and American families. Her work in this regard has earned her considerable renown and respect, and her reputation and personal qualities are of the highest calibre.

The Australian Embassy had no desire to be involved at this point and in no way encouraged inter-country adoption. Since I was an Australian citizen, however, the Embassy was asked to furnish a document in support of my application for residence and the consequent reversal of the expulsion this entailed. The Australian Consul, on 8 February, graciously signalled the feelings of his department with a message that was memorable for its brevity and non-commitment:

> This is to certify that as far as the Australian Embassy in Saigon is aware it sees no objection to Miss Rosemary Taylor remaining in Vietnam.

When it was known that we needed an official name in order to continue the work we had been doing without one, Margaret went immediately to the USA, and asked Wende Grant to become licensed in Colorado as a child placement agency, and then to come to Vietnam to register locally. Wende did just that. (Although our operation was in all respects multinational, with no political affiliation, a US registration had to be obtained if only because the US Embassy was willing to give the necessary diplomatic support in Saigon.)

Let Wende Grant now describe developments in Colorado and the registration of FCVN:

> By September 1972, Friends of the Children of Viet Nam had divided into two functions. Most of the members devoted themselves to the collection of funds and supplies for Vietnam. A smaller group assisted prospective parents with adoption procedures, and it was the members of this latter group who presented the request for a licence to the Colorado State Department of Social Services. Thanks to the personal involvement of John Califf, Director of Social Services for the Lutheran Service Society of Colorado, the licence was granted in March 1973. A few days later, Margaret Moses, John Califf, and I [WG] left for Saigon, carrying a slim purple folder containing our new licence,

John's social work diploma, and a hastily typed copy of agency policies and procedures. With that we intended to prove our experience and dependability to the Vietnamese Ministry of Social Welfare and Land Reform.

We deliberately started our campaign for registration at the USAID office. The official said he had no influence over the Vietnamese Ministry, but he asked how long we intended staying in Vietnam. 'As long as it takes to register', was our reply.

From USAID we went to the Consular Section of the US Embassy, where Rosemary Taylor and her work with adoptions was well-known. We left feeling we could expect some assistance from the Embassy.

The Ministry was next. We spoke to the person on the lowest rung of the welfare ladder who could speak English. He served tea and suggested we seek an appointment with someone with more authority as he himself had no power to register us.

The days developed a pattern. Margaret, John and I saw someone at USAID, at the Embassy, and at the Ministry. If possible, we saw someone whose position was a step higher than the one of the preceding day; the same pat speeches were given. The responses remained fairly constant. On the fifth day our regular USAID contact was absent, and we talked instead to Hugh O'Neil. He was friendly and efficient. He suggested we prepare a contract and submit it to the Ministry, and he gave us a copy of a contract to use as a model. In two days we submitted our proposed contract. Margaret had written it in English, and Bui van To translated it into Vietnamese. The American Consul, Mr Naran Ivanchukov, wrote on 24 March to Dr Phieu, the Minister, in support of the application:

> ... In my dealings with Rosemary Taylor over several years, I have found her to be single-minded in her devotion to the welfare of Vietnamese orphans.
>
> Miss Taylor is a woman of great integrity, good character and the highest moral standards.
>
> I strongly recommend your kind endorsement of Rosemary Taylor's remarkable work so that with your approval it may continue.

The round of meetings resumed to discuss the specific contract. In the third week of our stay in Saigon, the US Ambassador's office requested that I go there for a meeting. The Ambassador was not there. His secretary asked if we were licensed and if we were competent. Someone asked if we had paid any bribes in trying to become registered. I answered 'yes' to the first questions, 'no' to the last. That was all, but I felt at last that Rosemary Taylor would continue her work in Vietnam.

During that six weeks' stay in Vietnam, I became more aware of what the day-to-day work in the nurseries involved. On 4 March 1973, for example, while the authorities were concerning themselves over names, titles and licences, eleven more abandoned scraps of humanity arrived at To Am, from Providence Orphanage in the Delta: Mercy, Constantin, Fortitude, Fidelity, Barnabus, Loyola, Excelsior, Justin, Courage, Patience and Esperantha. Mercy, a newborn black boy missing an ear, survived one day. Esperantha was a fragile four-month-old, who weighed less than 5 lb and looked like an old woman. The Vietnamese staff called her 'Ba Noi', meaning 'grandmother' or 'old lady'. Her face expressed worry and fear; her head had been shaved for the insertion of IV needles. Ilse Ewald worked over the child trying to keep her alive. The poor infant was so ugly and had so little chance that we all felt great pity. Unless she was tied to an IV bottle, I held her and talked to her between the ritualistic meetings about the contract. During the weeks we remained in Vietnam, Esperantha blossomed visibly. [WG]

Wende Grant and John Califf returned to the States, all necessary formalities accomplished, leaving us to await the outcome in Saigon. Meanwhile, despite the precarious status of my own dossier, I had continued working on the children's dossiers. Back in February, there was an additional problem over US entry visas. Some states had complained to the Embassy about a few children who had been let in on 'non-preference' visas before Christmas. We were being told that we must wait for the approval of the I-600 in nearly every case.[1]

---

[1] The I-600 was a petition to obtain immediate relative status for the adoptive child and thereby permit the child to enter the USA with a preferential status, and not have to wait as an ordinary immigrant for a quota number. Each family had the right to file only two I-600 petitions; a third foreign adopted child had to wait its turn on the immigration quota. Occasionally, the quota numbers were current, and a non-preference quota visa could be issued more promptly than a non-quota visa which needed several months to process the I-600. The debate was whether or not the orphans should be allowed to use up the quota numbers unnecessarily.

2 May 1973, RT to WG: Currently, we have an epidemic that is striking not only the nursery but the babies we have placed in foster homes. They are being brought back to the nursery by the foster parents with the same symptoms: sudden swelling and hardening of the abdomen, causing pressure on the lungs and impeded breathing. It must be a type of intestinal infection. We have lost several babies recently from this unnamed illness. Those sent to the clinic have also died. A few have pulled through, and now we hope no more will be lost.

At this time we had no facilities for regular autopsies. The babies were buried with no verification of the doctor's stated cause of death, and, therefore, a very limited possibility of learning from these deaths.

If the child died in hospital, we would go and collect the tiny corpse and bring it back to the nursery, where Ilse would wrap it in a clean sheet or blanket and put the corpse in an empty milk carton. Marg would help tape up the carton and would drive to one of the orphanages that had its own burial ground. This uncelebrated ending to a life that had never been lived weighed heavily on us all. Ilse would be physically and emotionally exhausted and very depressed for each life lost; I was deeply frustrated by the inadequacy of the facilities available. For Margaret, the death of each nameless mite was an event of cosmic significance, and the ineluctable futility of it all weighed on her cumulatively. Occasionally she would have to shut herself away in her room for several days – struggling to make sense of it all, and to seek some hope that would give her the courage to continue.

The diplomatic struggle over our contract continued:

2 May 1973, RT to WG: I have just come back from the farewell reception for Ambassador Bunker. I was the only person in the whole assembly who seemed to be wearing a 'business suit', which I naturally presumed to be 'working clothes' ... Every other woman there had on a long dress – with the exception of Laurie Peters, US Vice-Consul, who had on a short black dress, but very elegant. So there I was. I shook hands with Ambassador Bunker and thanked him for all his efforts on our behalf ... afterwards Laurie introduced me to Ambassador Whitehouse who was, in fact, the person responsible for the intervention in our affairs. Then I spied Dr Phieu, the Minister of Welfare, and introduced Laurie to him. She played her part beautifully and asked Phieu if our contract would be signed soon, saying how 'she and Ambassador Whitehouse had been discussing it' and would be very happy to know that it was signed. Phieu said he thought the report from Washington had only come through two days ago. I couldn't resist the chance to mention that Dr Anh was deliberately creating obstacles.

On the whole, the reception was a great opportunity ... Ambassador Whitehouse remarked that we seemed to have more friends than anyone else in Vietnam. He was referring to a telephone call he had received from the States. I don't know the details, but you probably do.

9 May, RT to WG: Still no contract signed. Mr Hien blames Miss Quoi and says she is obstructionist. Miss Quoi pretends to be thinking of our interests, and says Hien has the dossier; Hien says Quoi has it. Please try cabling the Embassy and the Ministry of Social Welfare from over there. I'm worried in case it is not signed before Naran Ivanchukov (Consul) leaves. He is our principal support in this affair.

On 10 May I wrote to Dr Phieu asking if he could possibly intervene personally so that our contract could be signed, and our situation regularized.

But there were always other more modest problems to distract us:

> DIEN LUC
> Repairs, Installations, Maintenance,
> Electricity and Refrigeration
> 52 bis Cach Mang, Saigon
> 9 May 1973 To Whom It May Concern
>
> Please be informed that your washing machine
> (Simpson 220 volts) no more economically repair-
> able. Every part in this machine are worn out. This is
> the last repair.
>
> > Respectfully yours,
> > Thomas Khoi

In addition, our third nursery, Newhaven, was not yet well-organized. It lacked firm direction, and some of the local staff took advantage of this. There had been break-ins on one or two nights and the circumstances and staff reaction made it obvious that there had been collusion between the robbers and some nursery staff:

24 *May 1973, RT to WG*: I called by Newhaven on Saturday morning and they told me of the night robberies and other problems. We had to set to work immediately. We sent some of the older children to Allambie to reduce the work load. Then we were obliged to dismiss the entire staff but three. This meant interviewing and choosing a whole new staff, and a guard to protect the house. It was a traumatic experience for us all but from now on I am sure the situation will improve immensely and the children will receive better care. Bui van To was a great help to us throughout the operation, and took on the responsibility of explaining to the old staff exactly why they had to be dismissed. He also helped interview the new applicants and spoke to them explaining our expectations and the attitude they ought to have towards the children.

That month Sr Susan McDonald RN, a Sister of Loretto from Colorado, arrived in Saigon and took over the complete management of Newhaven. Sang, a Vietnamese who had been in the nursery since its beginning, became Susan's administrative assistant; I remember Sang as being an extraordinarily beautiful and competent girl, who was held in unusual respect by the other local staff. Peggy Hammond joined Susan in July 1973. A physical therapist, she was a necessary addition to the staff since the nurseries were taking in an increasing number of physically handicapped children, particularly victims of cerebral palsy and polio. In April we had brought back from Baclieu, Françoise, Van Gogh, El-Greco, Pascale and Agnes, and again in July we had collected another group of children from Vinh Binh including Andrew, Amanda, Isaac, Trudi, Lazarus and Damian. All these children had severe problems of motor development and most of them were to improve considerably with therapy. We planned to start a small-scale polio centre and introduce some therapy for handicapped children waiting to join their adoptive families, and hoped that the Rehabilitation Centre close to To Am would assist our nurses.

25 May 1973, RT to WG: Dr Anh's latest, via Laurie Peters, is that the contract will be signed. Mr Hien asked me to submit a list of all our activities in Vietnam. I did, but I kept it brief.

Sr Rose told me to beware of Miss Quoi, who is gunning for me. This is undoubtedly partly due to a letter I wrote to the Minister a few days ago [10 May] mentioning Quoi's obstructionist tactics.

Incidentally, six of us now have courtesy visas for three months from the Ministry of Foreign Affairs with multiple exit-re-entry. As it is, we are now caught up in a violent cycle of expiry-and-renewal, trying to synchronize all the different expiry dates of contract, residence visa, nursery registration, etc. It is totally impractical but the Ministry doesn't seem to appreciate the unreasonableness of the situation.

On 5 June 1973 the agreement was signed by the Minister of Welfare, Dr Tran Nguon Phieu, permitting me to remain in Vietnam and continue our work. I travelled with the document to Colorado, where it was signed by Wende Grant, for FCVN.

The programme was now officially registered with the Ministry of Social Welfare, whose supervisory role consisted of receiving a report each trimester, and filing it appropriately. These reports, including lists of the children who had gone abroad, lists of the staff employed, and the vehicles belonging to the organization, with identifying information, went mostly unread. The Ministry continued to importune us at odd hours of the day for figures relating to children in the nurseries and children who had already left. We would refer them to our quarterly report and were increasingly irritated to learn that they were unaware that we had even submitted a report.

Lydia Brackney, who had joined us part-time, was chiefly responsible for the burden of reporting that marked the difference between our past and present status. (Lydia's husband Tom worked with the USAID agriculture development programme). With her extensive experience of bureaucratic humbug and her secretarial talents, Lydia was able to churn out systematically these masterpieces in the specious art of saying nothing – always in six copies – without losing her sense of humour.

1 July 1973, RT to WG: Ilse and I went to Cantho yesterday and Sr Eugenie gave us photos of twelve older boys (between five and eight years) she would like to be placed. She already has birth certificates for most of them but some of the ages appear a little inaccurate. All the children attend school.

6 July 1973: Here is a photo of the boy Cong and his complete medical record. He comes from Providence Orphanage, Cantho. Last year, when we saw the state of his chest deformity, we thought there would be no hope for the child. However, he has now improved considerably and we want to find him a family. His pigeon-chested deformity was due to retraction caused by his TB condition (according to the doctor who examined him). Our pediatrician says the condition is no longer contagious, but we are starting him again on medication according to the doctor's prescription.

Baby Carmel had just come into the nursery with a severe case of diarrhoea and dehydration, and Ilse had her admitted to Hoan My Clinic as a protection for the other children. At 4 a.m. the next morning, the Clinic ambulance broke curfew and brought the baby back to To Am. The doctors feared the child had cholera and were unwilling to put the other Clinic patients at risk: the risk to our other eighty children did not concern them. The Clinic had kept the child in isolation overnight and apparently had given no medication nor intravenous fluid. Ilse was appalled. She immediately drew a sample of blood to send to the Pasteur Institute and set up an IV infusion. By the time the negative results came back a few days later Carmel was dead. Treatment had been started too late.

One outcome of the Kennedy Senate Hearing, mentioned earlier, was that in July 1973, USAID sponsored a meeting in Washington to discuss 'Placement and Adoption of Vietnamese Children in American Homes'. The aim was to come up with specific recommendations to guide the US government in its efforts on behalf of Vietnamese children, particularly inter-country adoption for hard-to-place children. FCVN (as we still were) was represented at the meeting by Wende Grant and Margaret Moses. It was interesting to learn that, as former Social Welfare Adviser to the US Mission and the government of Vietnam, Mr G. Munro from Saigon listed among his achievements that the 'Ministry has taken a very active role in inter-country adoption first in inducing the registration of Miss Rosemary Taylor's activities.'

The need for a concerted effort to meet the needs of an estimated 500 black children was the principal theme underlying the two-day conference, and Dr Dumpson (who had reported to the Kennedy Hearing) recommended a 'consortium of agencies which would provide a thrust towards the black child'. FCVN, the most experienced of the adoption agencies in Vietnam, and Holt, with its vast experience of Korean adoptions, resisted the idea of a 'consortium'.

The result of the Washington all-expenses-paid conference was the establishment of another subcommittee that planned to meet as soon as possible 'to draw up the frames of reference for the purposed effort'.[1] While the 'references' were being 'framed' in higher places, Margaret and Wende flew back to Boulder, where they did a load of laundry, collected Wende's husband, and flew on to Saigon.

In Saigon they attended the wedding of Anne Dolan (former Director of Allambie) and Gerry McCrudden of the British Embassy. Gerry had demonstrated his mettle by fostering a number of Allambie children and Anne recognized his worth! The Nuptial Mass was celebrated in Queen of Peace Church and the reception held at the Ambassador's residence. Duane Grant went on a trip to the provinces with Tom Brackney, missing the wedding, but returning with a new seven-year-old son, Vinh. Sr Sylvie and Sr Marie-Marthe of Providence Orphanage, Soctrang, had been delighted to meet the father of their Tia, and had expressed their pleasure by offering this new gift – a bright-eyed little boy who captured Duane's heart at first sight. Back in Saigon, Vinh was introduced to his new mother. When the Grants returned to the US, Vinh had to

---

[1] Three months later, the establishment of an Interagency Vietnamese Adoption Committee was 'unanimously approved by representatives of fourteen organizations which met on October 3'. The objectives and functions of IVAC (we learnt) were as follows: to locate and provide Black adoptive homes for the estimated 500 abandoned Black-fathered Vietnamese orphans; to determine the nature and extent of problems of these children; to enter into purchase of service agreements with the adoption agencies, recognized by the Government of Vietnam and the Ministry of Social Welfare to expedite the required adoption services; to enter into purchase of service agreements with licensed adoption agencies in the US to locate adoptive homes in the Black community and provide other pre- and post-adoptive supportive services; and to monitor and evaluate accomplishment of the goals and objectives of the projects.

stay behind for processing. He joined the lists of children jostling for space with the others in my correspondence with Wende:

23 August 1973, RT to WG: Pierre: the little boy with the huge umbilical hernia that I proposed recently – Ilse indicated first that his age was between eight and ten months. The doctor mentions on his report that the boy is three years. Until I can further clarify this point, let's say the boy is somewhere between one and three years as a compromise.

13 September 1973: I hope to send Pierre on a parole visa, as soon as you find a family for him. His hernia needs immediate attention. We are afraid of complications should it burst over here; as you see from the photo, it is enormous. We have to keep it bandaged every day. Otherwise, the little boy is well. I think we ought to fix his age at one-and-a-half years.

I look forward to my late-October trip to the US. I hope to make a cross-country tour carrying a plastic mug for donations. We have just found two new houses and the new Allambie will cost 1,500 dollars a month, just for rent. The house does have some good points, but I'm having nightmares about the swimming pool and all the glass doors: if our kids don't drown themselves in the pool, they will surely decapitate themselves smashing through the glass. Misery!

15 September 1973: Vinh: I enclose the birth certificate for him. Sorry about the winter birthday, but Sister came up with this.

Air France Convoys: I give all the addresses to Air France and they are supposed to notify the parents. Also, I try to send an East Coast convoy list to John Wetterer in New York, and he makes it his business to notify the parents as Air France often seem to fall down on the job. Moreover, when I have enough notice, as I will this time, I send out letters myself, announcing the arrival directly to the parents.

Passports: I have forty of them for the US – just waiting for the entry visas. I told Laurie Peters that we have no more room in our office for the pile of passports.

Welcome to the new adoption staff members. We are immensely grateful to all of you for your dedication and hard work.

20 September 1973: Non-Preference Visas: Laurie Peters has just explained why this unexpected long wait for those children who needed non-preference visas [see footnote, p. 75]. Evidently, some years ago a certain large number of intending immigrants were deleted from the list, because they did not qualify according to the opinion then in vogue. Well, a case was made of it, and much later, i.e. now, it has been decided that all these people have to be reinstated on the immigrant quota list. This means a sudden backlog of thousands of people, and a long delay for all our non-preference cases . . .

Each year I helped process a handful of adoptions for British families. One day in September 1973 the British Consul let me view a document that had just come into his possession. It was a copy of a communication between the Home Office and the Foreign Office expressing alarm that, although it was only September, already thirteen visas had been requested that year for Vietnamese orphans. The letter explained that while the British government, for reasons of political expediency, had been prepared to admit a certain number of orphans each year, there was a limit to their tolerance. As long as the number had not exceeded ten or twelve a year, they saw no reason to be alarmed. But now thirteen children, with three months of the year still to go, were more than they could contemplate with equanimity. I was mentioned by name as the person responsible for undermining Britain's delicate racial balance. (In fact, I had been responsible for only seven of those thirteen visas.) The Embassy was rather embarrassed by this communication, as they had been interested in promoting adoptions. Several of the Embassy families, including the Ambassador, Brook Richards, were fostering our orphans pending their departure abroad.

I could only gasp in astonishment at this inter-ministerial memo. For a while after this, I appealed to the patriotism of new applicants, and begged them not to push Britain over the brink. Some months later there was a change of government and the official policy reverted to its previous quiet tolerance.

Mary-Nelle Gage, a Sister of Loretto, and Elaine Norris RN, arrived in Saigon about this time. Elaine was to nurse at To Am, as Ilse and Birgit were transferring to a new intensive care nursery, Hy

Vong. Mary-Nelle, living at Newhaven, would share the increasing burden of general administration for the entire programme. Margaret's directive to the nursery staff, of September 1973, sorts out priorities:

As far as possible no one should quit before the end of October. The exception is Ilse, who must take leave in order to operate our new clinic-nursery, Hy Vong, at maximum potential. The clinic will be operational from 1 November for intensive care, including dehydration, pneumonia, isolation of contagious conditions of potentially fatal proportions, short-term supervision of malnutrition cases, preliminary screening of all babies coming in from the provinces, and emergency care. The clinic will be equipped with an ambulance.

The children will be sent on to the other houses as soon as feasible. Allambie 3 will take any incoming children of advanced age, intelligence or fighting skill, who have come merely for transit purposes ... The children in intensive care at To Am should be isolated at the clinic. Results of at least one autopsy urgently needed to confirm diagnosis of pneumocystis carinii[1] as cause of present mortality rate at To Am. No funerals until after an autopsy. Grall Hospital does the best research on this killer, and will send the biopsy to France.

For general information, Grall reports local infant fatalities at their installations are caused by bronchitis virus, pneumocystis carinii, and haemorrhagic fever. Adventist Hospital confirms the last of these. Laboratory equipment at SDA currently under review by doctors.

2 October 1973, RT to WG: I think I need to sleep. I've been trying to get all my work ahead of date to carry through the time I shall be in America. The last two days I have been writing out at least 10,000 dollars worth of cheques and leaving them in the cheque book, because there are no piastres in the bank to cover them. One is for a recent hospital bill of approximately 2,500

---

[1] Pneumocystis carinii is a form of parasitical pneumonia which does not respond to the usual antibiotics, and which cannot be detected by X-ray or by any other specific clinical symptoms, other than a general failure to thrive, until the disease is so far advanced that the child may be only a few hours from death. It is a condition associated with orphanages and with babies whose resistance is lowered due to artificial feeding. The immuno-globulins are depressed to a critical point in a baby born prematurely and fed without the maternal antibody protection.

dollars; another 1,500 for boarding babies at the Clinique St Paul.

I was getting ready to leave for the States on 19 October, where I had been invited to speak at a much-heralded conference of Friends of the Children of Viet Nam. Less than a fortnight before I was due to depart, I was very disconcerted to receive, out of the blue, notice of resignation from all the adoption staff of FCVN in America (except one, who remained so that we could continue to conduct a legal correspondence). There was no time to consider the issues involved until I got to Colorado, so meanwhile I worked on at the dossiers already in hand, but proposed no new children.

Chapter 7

FRIENDS FOR ALL CHILDREN
(FFAC)
by Wende Grant

FROM ITS BEGINNING, the main thrust of Friends of the Children of Viet Nam was life support, through raising funds and equipment. Tons of medicines, formula, and clothing were shipped to orphanages in the provinces of Vietnam, as well as to the nurseries in Saigon. Adoption of a few orphans was the logical outcome of the tremendous effort to help save the lives of children suffering from the devastating results of a war that seemed to have no end. By fall 1972, as we have seen, the need to separate the life support and adoption functions had become increasingly apparent. It was important that parents be treated consistently, and that correct information be relayed efficiently to Saigon. Our small adoption staff round myself, Sue Dosh and Lani Tolman, began to build a dialogue and reliable reputation with state departments of welfare, private adoption agencies, the US Department of Immigration and other government officials.

By March 1973, when FCVN was licensed by the State Department of Social Services in Colorado, and had signed its contract with the Vietnamese government, the adoption staff had expanded and had developed the required social work procedures of the fledgling agency. As the agency continued to separate the adoption function from the life support group of FCVN, tensions grew. Many members resented not being able to share the adoption process as they had in the past. Correspondence among families, social workers, the adoption agency, Immigration, our Saigon office, the government, was no longer public information. Receiving photos and information about available children and offering them to the families was handled confidentially, in accordance with basic professional social work standards. These procedures were born out of necessity, but were responsible for many hard feelings.

In addition, the adoption staff requested its own bank account for adoption-related expenses. They needed to be able to reimburse their own mounting expenses, forward legal fees to Saigon, and purchase air fares. This was denied by the FCVN Board. The adoption staff became increasingly unhappy with the book-keeping procedures of FCVN; in the fall of 1972 an annual audit had been requested by two members of the Executive Committee, in keeping with Colorado law, but was not finally completed until summer 1973, when it revealed that hundreds of dollars were not properly accounted for.

When Rosemary brought the final registration documents to Colorado in June 1973, for FCVN to sign, the President of FCVN made a commitment of one million dollars to support her pro-gramme in Vietnam. The adoption staff, feeling that this pledge was rash, was worried that Rosemary would depend on it, and later that fall Rosemary did indeed open two more nurseries (Hy Vong and Allambie 3) and requested 10,000 dollars to meet the expenses. FCVN forwarded an amount between 4,000 and 5,000 dollars, mostly taken from prepaid air fares from families adopting chil-dren. The adoption staff were aghast upon learning this, and once again insisted that they be allowed a separate bank account.

By the end of the summer, the strain on most members of the adoption staff was taking its toll. Accusations were rampant. The pressure was debilitating to everyone. In October 1973 the adop-tion staff resigned from FCVN, and awaited Rosemary Taylor's imminent visit to the States (to a conference that in the event came to little).

Rosemary, alarmed by the unprofessionalism of some of FCVN's members, encouraged the adoption group to reincorporate and relicense themselves in the State of Colorado, this time with the name Friends For All Children (FFAC). The name was chosen to retain the associations with FCVN so that they could continue to place children under Rosemary Taylor's contract in Vietnam. But with the eventual complete separation from FCVN and the pro-liferation of 'Friends' adoptive parents groups, the choice of name proved in retrospect to be more and more unfortunate. At the time of the split, attorneys for both FCVN and FFAC issued an agreement which stated that FFAC would handle adoptions and FCVN continue to raise life-support funds and would not enter into adoptions; but later FCVN changed its mind.

In December 1973 the original FCVN Board sent a message to the Ministry of Social Welfare in Saigon indicating that Rosemary Taylor was no longer affiliated with them and could not operate under 'their' contract. Since the entire programme in Vietnam had been started and maintained by Rosemary, and the contract had been negotiated specifically so that she could continue officially in Vietnam, this was astounding. The following February, 1974, I [Wende Grant] duly travelled to Saigon again, and renegotiated a new two-year agreement with the Vietnamese government, in the new name. This time Friends For All Children was also given the right to hold guardianship and to release children for adoption, an authority that was to become invaluable.

In Colorado, the relief from internal fighting was immediate, and the new FFAC staff was happy to devote its full energies to the ever-increasing workload. For the first time, they were able to function professionally without pressure from FCVN Board members.

The goals and philosophy regarding the placement of children in adoptive homes remained constant. The functioning of the staff and agency evolved as the status of the organization changed. From operating as a group of adoptive parents offering advice on the adoption of Vietnamese orphans, the original members of the staff progressed to organizing a separate corporation functioning as a child welfare organization.

The full extent of the responsibility of such an agency became clear to FFAC when they were notified of their first placement breakdown. A seriously handicapped, six-year-old girl had been rejected by her adoptive family after a year in their home. The family had suffered severe trauma: it was understandable that they could not provide for the child's needs. With no prospective families in process, who were able to accept a child needing such extensive care, the staff investigated the costs of providing for the child until her adulthood; the figures were frightening. Through other agencies, an excellent adoptive home was eventually found for this child, and the placement was successful. But the FFAC staff had thereafter to be more critical in their evaluation of families.

There were other failed placements due to the divorce of parents, serious illness in the family, or the inability of parents to accept and meet the needs of children. The adoptive parents in most cases had not accurately enough assessed their own situation and expectations. The children were all successfully re-placed with new families. It became obvious that the handling of the few placements that fail is one of the primary reasons that child-placing agencies are necessary to adoptions.

Once we had licensed as an agency, the workload increased dramatically. We were placing about twenty-five children a month, but processing an average of 600 enquiries. The paperwork was formidable. New adoption workers volunteered; a book-keeper and another secretary were added. Still, the adoption staff, nearly all married with children, found it was taking each of them six to eight hours a day to complete the tasks required on their cases. We were more than fortunate in having volunteer staff members who were extraordinarily dedicated and conscientious. Though a few felt the pressure of work too great and left the agency, most were able to stay until after the April 1975 airlift, completing the work for the children and their adoptive families.   [wG]

Chapter 8

INTERNATIONAL RELATIONS

THE FIRST ORGANIZATION with which I had been associated in inter-country adoption in 1967 was Terre des Hommes (in Switzerland, Germany, France, Belgium, Scandinavia and Canada). I was impressed with the charter of this organization and agreed to assist them on a completely voluntary basis in their efforts to place orphaned children in adoptive families. I had a separate 'Order of Mission' from each country. But when we began to process the adoption of children going to the United States, there was a fear in Europe lest children destined for the USA and countries where Terre des Hommes had no base might, nevertheless, be benefiting from the association with the name, which the Vietnamese authorities used to pigeonhole many orphan activities.

While Belgium, France and Switzerland were taking petty action to prevent American-destined children from profiting from the TdH name, their Europe-destined children were, ironically, being partly supported by donations from USA and other non-TdH countries, and all their in-country long-distance transport was by courtesy of the USA. Belgium and France did contribute financially to the upkeep of the nurseries, but with the same anxiety lest their money might be helping children going to other countries. Germany did not succumb to this anxiety: they continued to support the children regardless of their destinations. Switzerland, the most paranoid of all about its identity, contributed nothing at all towards the support of the more than 200 children we sent to that country, except for the payment, on request, of *one* milk bill, amounting to a couple of hundred dollars. They seemed to have no realistic concept of what was involved in caring for the children before their departure, nor had they any eagerness to participate. Still, we were quite satisfied with the quality of the adoptive placements in Switzerland and that was of paramount importance. We recognized, too, that TdH Switzerland's medical programme probably absorbed all their overseas' budget.

All we ever requested, as a 'fee' for an adoption, was barely enough to cover the most obvious procedural costs. (Lawyers' fees were mainly paid directly to the lawyer and were fixed by him.)

20 October 1970, Saigon: RT to Terre des Hommes France: Since 20 April 1969, I have not sent any account of our expenses here. My notebook with details of each expenditure was stolen in the market and so I have decided to calculate according to the number of children who have left for France in these last eighteen months. I estimate for each child:

French Entry Visa	960 p	[later 852 p]
Tax on Airticket	60 p	
Photocopy	125 p	
Local transport	300 p	
Stationery (folders, etc.)	100 p	
Postage	50 p	
Vaccination book	20 p	
Photos	500 p	
average total	2,061 piastres or 10 US dollars (according to the average exchange rate during this period)	

Since there were thirty-two children who left for France [named], you owe us 320 dollars.

I would also like to add the 4,000 piastres (= 14 dollars now) for the Residence tax for Yvette [Charamont].

In March 1972, when I sent the next account to France, I was obliged to raise the fees to 15 dollars a child, since prices had risen considerably, particularly the entry visa, photos and transportation.

When we were in contact with individual families, which involved much extra correspondence and more complicated visa processing, we requested 20–25 dollars to help cover 'expenses'. That was the maximum. Our ability to ask so little was, of course, predicated on the supposition that donations would continue to come from many sources to help with the total cost of caring for any child.

Terre des Hommes had been founded in Switzerland and even though there were legitimate autonomous foundations in other countries, and an International Federation, Switzerland tried to ignore the legitimacy of these groups and, eventually, complicated our relations with the authorities in Saigon by writing a series of letters to the Ministries attempting to discredit them. It wasn't entirely possible to ignore this inter-country bickering when it affected our work in Vietnam. Seven-year-old Thao, his broken leg in plaster, had to remain in hospital for several days beyond his official discharge date because a delegate of Terre des Hommes Belgium had just convinced Grall Hospital not to give free hospitalization to non-TdH children; it was unacceptable to him that miscellaneous orphans should enjoy the same benefits. We either had to pay Thao's hospital bill or produce proof that he was destined for Belgium. We could do neither immediately. Ironically, Thao was in fact going to a TdH Belgium family, but it took several days to work out what proof we could give of this beyond our own 'word'.

We continued in a close but fluctuating association with Terre des Hommes from 1967 until 1975. In 1972, we severed contact with the Belgian branch because of the strain imposed by unsatisfactory communications. Moreover, since Belgium was receiving a considerable number of children from Korea within two to three months, the families found it difficult to accept the nine- to twelve-month wait for a Vietnamese child.

In 1973 we stopped processing adoptions for Switzerland. Communication with the adoption section of Terre des Hommes Switzerland was always excellent, but the repeated interference of the 'founder', and his paranoid accusations that we were using the TdH stamp on the dossiers of US-bound children, became more than we were willing to support. Liaison was re-established with Switzerland in 1974 when the adoption Director asked me if I would resume adoption work on their behalf and promised me there would be no more harassment.

Relatively civil, though increasingly tenuous, relations were retained with France. But finally Margaret Moses and I were forced to admit that the usefulness of the relationship scarcely warranted the exhausting expenditure of psychological energy needed to maintain it. Changes of administration in France brought into power new personnel whose basis of reality simply did not coincide with ours. TdH France and Germany had promised to help support Newhaven and make it their special project, and the French did continue to assist (while arguing petty details such as the name of the house) despite the fact that the French nurse lasted only a very short time and the management was taken over by an American.

With Germany we remained in close and fruitful association until the end. In Germany the adoption programme was organized with characteristic thoroughness; TdH Germany supplied the nurseries with important drugs and vaccines and some regular financial support. They were also ready to give immediate financial assistance in any emergency. But their most significant contribution was their sponsorship of the three nurses, Ilse Ewald, Birgit Blank, and Linda Mayers.

In January 1974 Margaret was escort for seven children going to France. Once in Europe, she set about contacting our support groups in Germany, France and Belgium.

20 January 1974, Wiesbaden, Germany, MM to WG: Minnie Gallozzi and a group of adoptive families in France and Belgium are with us, concentrating their efforts on food and medication. The Air France free freight allowance circuit is still open and Minnie is getting almost a ton a month through now. The subsidy on Newhaven terminates February: Terre des Hommes France insist that they cannot finance US adoptive parents ... They proposed other ways of raising money. When they had all aired their views, I was still silent and staring at the rain. Couldn't be bothered commenting.

Came to Germany, asked for 6,000 dollars to pay the To Am rent in March and for a guarantee of 2,000 DM per month. After two weeks of philosophy, politics and metaphysics in France, it came as something of a shock when Margot Weyer simply made the request at the TdH Germany Board meeting, and they said 'Let us know if there is anything else'.

25 January 1974, Berlin, MM to RT: You will know by now that TdH Germany has sent the rent for To Am (6,000 dollars) and that the monthly guarantee is 800 dollars. Germany is a little tired of France, but is not raising a furore about it.

7 February 1974, Letter from MM to WG, from Paris: I'm heading for Saigon tomorrow ... Did you know that the US Charter of the Rights of the Child (1959) states, as first priority, the right of the child to a name and a nationality and thereinafter (oops) rambles into a sermon about women and children leaving first when the ship goes down, so to speak, and eulogizes to the effect that a child must, of course, have its mother around. No doubt, at the time, there must have been some reason for this. But isn't it time something was done about the situation of abandoned children, like 'P.S.: it would appear logical, if hardly convenient, that a kid, once it had gone through the hell of being born, and even if its mother went down with the ship or off with the captain, that the above-mentioned kid should breathe on regardless.' I am a little enervated, and I feel I may be being a little obscure. What I meant to say was that this charter does NOT list as a priority *for any child*, not even an abandoned one (the case does not exist in the text) *the right to breathe once born.* Our operation birthright is obviously more royalist than the King. WELL, I was a little shocked. It would seem elementary ...

In Berlin, Magdalena Weinmann was responsible for establishing and maintaining Freunde de durch Rosemary J. Taylor Betreuten Waisenkinder E.V. Her organization was painstaking and her financial support came regularly. The cheques from Berlin always seemed to arrive when finances were at rock bottom; in 1974, fourteen cheques arrived, totalling 26,360 US dollars, giving 16,537,800 piastres. Original hospital, milk, food, pharmaceutical and utility bills were sent to Berlin to indicate how the money was spent. When we needed supplies of penicillin, or Quintovirelon vaccine, or any other medication available in Germany, we would alert Berlin and could be confident that the supplies would be waiting for the next escort to collect.

Inge and Rainer Mackensen (Berlin) were responsible for the organization of another group of regular contributors.

Minnie Gallozzi-Ulmann, founder of Les Amis des Enfants,

provided the most valuable French connection – she intercepted the shipments coming from the USA, Canada, Germany and Belgium, and succeeded in transferring them to the Saigon-bound plane – a feat requiring dedication, a fine sense of drama and steamroller persuasion tactics. Minnie was regularly on hand to assist with the arrival of convoys and the link-up with connecting flights. Les Amis des Enfants was active in adoption work and many of the children who were adopted through Les Amis passed through the nurseries, as did the children being processed by the French group Rayon du Soleil.

Song (Life) was established in Belgium in 1974 thanks particularly to Emil and Colette Pire, Sr Columbe Laloux and a small group of dedicated supporters. They sent us considerable quantities of medicine as well as financial aid. They were also running a sponsorship programme for some of the long-term nursery residents and this was particularly appreciated.

We placed children in Canada through Terre des Hommes (Director – Mrs Charlotte Pire) and through Families For Children (Directors – Naomi Bronstein and Sandra Simpson). FFC, besides their adoption programme, also organized several Canadian Air Force airlifts and sent the nurseries large shipments of supplies. Particularly valuable was the IV fluid which was difficult to obtain in large quantities by any other route. Naomi and Herbie Bronstein were to a large extent responsible for these airlifts. Naomi did not hesitate to go to the Prime Minister himself if she could not succeed at lower echelons.

In Australia we had many personal friends and family members who helped on an individual basis. Certain schools also collected for us and packages were sent by special permission through the military postal system, while it lasted. We were quite dependent on these supplies, especially the Farex baby cereal and the Lactogen milk. One loyal supporter in Adelaide collected each pay-day for years from all her colleagues in the taxation department; then she shopped at weekends for food 'specials' in the supermarkets.

In Melbourne, Elaine Moir organized Vietnam Sponsors and the Vietnamese Orphans Medical Fund, groups which collected large quantities of supplies for orphanages and our nurseries. They also raised funds for orthopaedic and eye surgery for orphans in need – either sending a surgeon to Vietnam or bringing the child to

Australia. Most of the money raised from private donations was used to purchase and to ship to Vietnam approximately 22 tons of food, medical supplies, clothing, nursery equipment and toys. Elaine also established a Milk Fund, which paid all our milk bills for eighteen months. In late 1974, Margaret described the prevailing milk situation:

Before the withdrawal of the Australian Military Forces from December 1971 to March 1972, we informed some friends in the state of Victoria that we would lose our regular supply of milk (previously donated by World Vision, Saigon) within six weeks. The six weeks' extra time had to be given us to allow us to find an alternative supplier; to get the milk, probably a different formula, to Saigon; and to change the formula gradually ... Suddenly, large supplies of a formula called Lactogen, manufactured by Nestlé, started coming in. The Australian Military Forces flew in these supplies postage free. In the months between December and May, enough milk came in to last until the next September.

Then, hearing the milk supply would run out, the group in Victoria approached the milk company and asked for a donation of milk to be sent ocean freight to Saigon or an order for Saigon to donate a certain quantity of milk. The milk company felt unable to comply with this enormous request and said that the volunteer group would have to pay for the milk.

Every year in Australia there is a horse race meeting of preternatural importance known as the Melbourne Cup. Every Australian stops what he is doing to listen to the Cup. Elaine Moir and our other friends in Victoria solved our milk problems by putting an article in a Melbourne paper asking the public to give 5 per cent of what they were going to bet on the horses to Nestlé's Milk Company to buy milk for the orphans in Vietnam.

Within three days, the Company protested that it was holding 25,000 Australian dollars for milk for Vietnamese orphans, and asked for donations to stop. They also requested that funds be transferred into a trust fund for the specified purpose of the donation. A trust was duly set up, and upon presentation of a receipted bill for milk purchased in Saigon, our dollar account was reimbursed monthly by bank transfer.

With this fund, we were able to function until February of 1974, when the account emptied. By this time, the group in Australia had committed themselves to medical projects in Vietnam. At the moment, milk is costing about 5,000 US dollars a month, the largest single expense of the operation after Vietnamese staff salaries. There are 500 children, most of them infants; more infants than any other institute, foreign or national, is handling. Milk is costing about 10 dollars a month per child.

The Vietnamese Orphan Fund was incorporated in Australia in May 1974. A 'Sponsor a Cot' scheme was organized where the sponsors contributed monthly to the support of whichever baby would be occupying the cot, and received photos from time to time. The response was most generous. Brian and Susi McGowran (who are the adoptive parents of four Vietnamese daughters, p. 263) and Mij Duong were chiefly responsible for this effort.

From Japan we received the proceeds of an Easter church collection in 1974. Another substantial donation came from Caritas, Italy, via the Apostolic Delegation in Saigon. And, of course, we continued to receive material and financial help from various US-based groups, including the Tom Dooley Foundation, An Lac Inc., and Friends or Families For Children groups scattered about the country. FFAC in Colorado also channelled to us any donations they received.

Chapter 9

HY VONG INTENSIVE
CARE NURSERY
USAID Grant and Funding

IN NOVEMBER 1973 we expanded our work into a fourth and
fifth facility. Ilse Ewald designed and opened Hy Vong (Hope) as an
intensive care nursery, and within a few weeks she and Birgit Blank
were looking after about a hundred babies. Allambie was relocated
near Tan Son Nhut airport with Doreen Beckett, an Australian
Sister of Mercy, in charge. She was assisted by nurse Julie Chinberg
from Texas, and Peggy Hammond. The financial commitment for
these two new nurseries was beyond our means, but we had been
encouraged to proceed by the US branch of FCVN, which before its
break-up had promised us necessary funding. By the time we moved
into the new nurseries our seven-month official relation with the
Denver-based FCVN had been terminated (see ch. 7).

The old Allambie was renamed Rathaven, to be used as staff
living-quarters, meeting place and warehouse. Jo Russell and her
sister Mij Duong (from Adelaide) worked there and were responsible for supplying the four nurseries. The office was still at
Newhaven and run by Luu My Le, our general secretary.

As soon as the Allambie children and staff were settled in the new
premises, a training course was organized for all the child-care
workers by our newly acquired social worker/teacher, the dynamic
and highly articulate Kim Tien. At this time we were employing a
total of about 200 Vietnamese staff in all the houses, some of whom
had been trained as 'mothercare' nursery nurses.

As we struggled to raise funds and to hurry bureaucratic
procedures, Margaret continued to be preoccupied with broader
issues.

7 December 1973, Saigon, MM to WG: First, be assured that the press reports are misleading. The Shell Company here lost only one third of two weeks' supply of oil in the recent fire. There are two other oil companies functioning here. Other news is normal. The country is beginning to feel the effects of war. Previously these effects were cushioned by foreign resources; now the locals will have to pull themselves together.

One of the things that has been churning through my head is an idea as old as time, which hit me between time zones on my return from the States recently . . . It seemed to me then that any country or coalition of nations or governments or welfare departments or religious or political groups of whatever dimension or bias and under whatever pressure of urgency or contingency – any such decision-making groups who, in the making of their decisions or compromises, threatened or were unable to protect the children hovering in the periphery, if not priority, of their scope . . . who were unable to protect life but were responsible for life, and by their inability to give it a priority were responsible for the death of children . . . such groups should set the children free.

Ignore liberty and the pursuit of happiness, focus on life; abdicate responsibility for the children to volunteers who would deputize for, or be deputized by governments, welfare departments, religions, et al. The sole responsibility of the volunteers would be to let the children live, and to send them to where they could. The organization would be partisan and for the profit of children. It would also be official anywhere where children do not profit. It would be supported by individuals interested in the profit of children as a priority. The children would be citizens of the world. The organization would free the children from slavery and death, and would be called in Hebrew EXODUS. It would have no President, since all members would be deputizing. It would operate without humility or apology.

Reading summaries of the series of documents produced in Geneva in 1949 mainly as an aftermath of the Nuremberg trials, known as the Geneva Convention, I found no mention of children. There is no legal framework giving children extra-national status, mainly because the Convention dealt with crimes against people who were assets to and not liabilities of their societies.

The Geneva Convention was drawn up before the Holt programme started. I do not know what has been done since in a
legal sense. I gather that appendages of the United Nations,
which deal with children, have rights which are, however credit-
ably or demonstrably, moral only; no legal rights. International
law respects territorial boundaries and children remain territorial problems even if there are thousands of needy in one
place and thousands of people who could help in another.

At this time we were receiving a regular 8,000 dollars a month and
other occasional large contributions from supporting groups in
Germany, the USA and France. Considerable donated supplies of
medicine, food and clothing also came from these countries, as well
as from Canada, Australia and Belgium. To run the nurseries we
needed 25,000 dollars a month, over and above the donated
supplies. USAID Saigon, aware of the work being done by the
newly-named Friends For all Children, encouraged us to request a
grant for the fiscal year 1974 from the expected Child Welfare
funding:

27 December 1973, Saigon, RT: We have a very good chance of
getting a grant here. The USAID people have encouraged us to
apply, and I have filed an application for 150,000 dollars
according to their instruction. It does seem that we shall get
100,000 dollars, about one third of our budget for the year; this
will be helpful. We have decided to turn Allambie into a pilot
project for mentally retarded and handicapped children, and
now that the pressure is eased with the hope of this grant, I am
forging ahead ... I was very worried about the future of a
growing number of non-adoptable children – it was bothering
me deeply. Then on Christmas Eve I saw the light: I knew that the
only way we could justify the enormous rent we were paying on
Allambie was to turn it into a teaching institution, and train up
not only child-care workers, but psychiatric nurses.

The International Rescue Committee which had previously run a
convalescent home for children undergoing plastic surgery at the
Barsky Unit, now had USAID funding to open a clinic for orphans
in a wing of the Adventist Hospital – formerly 3rd Field Military
Hospital. FFAC together with several other agencies had been

pressing for this for some time. The clinic opened its first beds in December.

On 2 January 1974, Lydia Brackney writing to Wende, confirms that our current situation consisted of 'No Money, more babies, some anxiety, plenty of good will, bunches of optimism, occasional tense moments, lots of fighting spirit, and No Money. The story starts and ends with No Money but in between there is a lot going on.'

Marg's account of her fund-raising progress in Europe returned to her reflections:

January 1974, MM to RT: It is dangerous ground to tread on if you begin to insist that a child who cannot survive in his own country must be given a chance in another *without unreasonable delay.* Equally, I have to say that it seems high time that some official and multilateral sanction be given to the question of adoption. I wish that UNICEF would begin to indicate priorities a little more explicitly . . .

Noting the way in which we seem to have acted in the circumstances of our own small slice of history and geography, viz., according to our lights, and without the slightest discretion, it may well be you who should break this disgusting and murderous silence. I am beginning to see that if you act as if you know everything, and speak discreetly but without fear of consequences, people will start to take initiative and possibly heart. If we don't make a stand, nobody will.

Everywhere I have stated that our work depends on us not seeing the whole problem – we have to see the few children in our care and limit our attention to them. I said that if we started to see what we are not doing, we would be able to do nothing at all. As it is, we are doing something. Which is a hell of a lot better than doing nothing. This has the curious effect of making people think that they can do something, too. Hopefully they will . . .

God help us, it really is a case of David and Goliath. We have only courage and a little time. I wonder how little time and how much courage? God only knows where it will end.

3 January 1974, WG to RT: News here about Vietnam is not good at all. At least the anticipated military offensive is now being predicted for 1 March instead of the middle of February . . .

Hope the North Vietnamese are reading the editorials in the US papers! We need all the time the *Denver Post* can give us.

Staff meeting this morning so I must hurry to clear a path from the door to the table.

Meanwhile, the IVAC team, sponsored by USAID had arrived in Saigon:

21 January 1974, RT to WG: I have just agonized through the last of the IVAC meetings which lasted for fifty minutes – then it was time for their next appointment. I probably blew the whole meeting by interjecting strongly and distracting the Chairman from his planned summarizing statements. I succeeded in arousing him, unintentionally, to table-thumping madness.

Sr Kateri from Catholic Relief also spoke up and said that when it is a question of life or colour, then we must opt for life and disregard colour. She was challenged by one of the IVAC social workers, but defended her point with vehemence. We agreed, of course. IVAC may be politically expedient in the USA, but here in Vietnam, as you well know, it is a glaring example of misplaced priorities and misspent funds.

After that I decided not to go along to the farewell dinner being held for them at the Circle Hippique, an elegant private club left over since French Colonial days. I thought to save a little of the tax-payers' money. Edie [de Chadenedes] went along to represent FFAC and was congratulated most warmly by Dr Oanh and Miss Quoi from the Ministry of Social Welfare on the programme she had drawn up for a new facility for children with 'special problems'. Dr Oanh told Bob King of USAID that this programme should have a number one priority in any funding . . . Edie's proposed programme appears to be the most breathtaking breakthrough in Social Welfare since the establishment of the department six or eight years ago. This is certainly good for our image.

2 February 1974, RT to WG: Laurie Peters [the Vice-Consul] has been giving art classes to Allambie children the past few Sundays, and her husband Lee has been overhauling all our broken-down buggies. The art classes ended up in chaos and poor Laurie described the horror of it . . . kids eating the glue and pasting

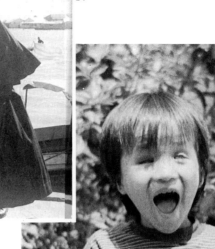

Special Cases.

14 Collecting children by ferry from
Providence Orphanage, Culaogieng (1969). All
three girls (now in Belgium) had eye problems.

15 Jason, a paraplegic boy, from Sacred Heart
Orphanage, Danang. He survived the C-5A crash.
16 Cuong, totally blind, from Providence
Orphanage, Cantho. He died in the crash.
17 Sr Rose and Sr Raymond help a group of
polio children on their way to school at Phu My.

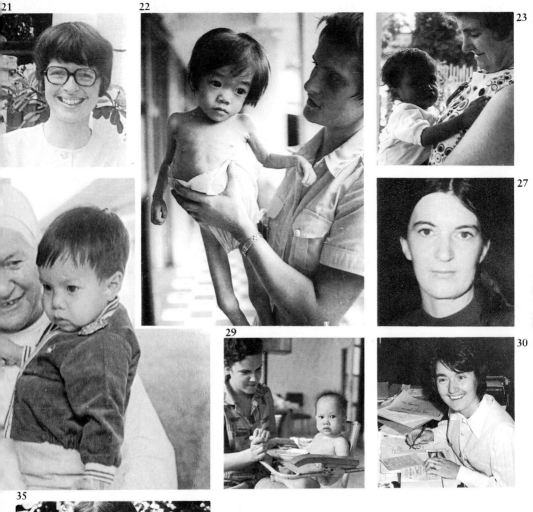

Some Staff and Helpers. 18 Peter Trueman, with Margarita on her baptism day. **19** Christie Leivermann. **20** Mary Cusack. **21** Susan McDonald. **22** Ilse Ewald, with Ut, at Providence Orphanage, Cantho. **23** Anne Barry, with Jacqueline (Jade) at Allambie. **24** Peggy Hammond. **25** Sgt-Major George Miles, at To Am. **26** Sr Rose-Marie, director of Phu My. She is holding two children who are about to depart for Europe. **27** Margaret Moses. She died in the crash. **28** Dolly Bui. She, too, died in the C-5A crash. **29** Yvette Charamont, feeding Lara at Peter Trueman's house. **30** Mary-Nelle Gage, preparing visas and embarkation cards. **31** Lee Makk. She died in the crash. **32** Sr Angela, at Sacred Heart Orphanage, Danang. **33** Rosemary Taylor, with Vanessa, who died a few weeks after this photograph was taken. **34** Doreen Beckett, at Allambie, with Coi (1974). **35** Birgit Blank, with twins, Sun and Flower, now in the USA. Birgit died in the C-5A crash. **36** Sr Ursula, in charge of the Good Shepherd Nursery. She, too, died in the crash.

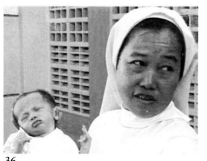

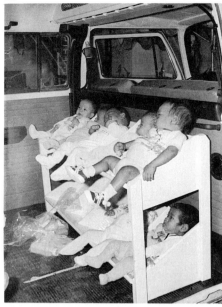

39

40

41

42

On the Move to New Homes. 37 Sr André, French Superior of Vinh Long. The two girls with bags in the cyclo are setting off to families in Switzerland (1967). **38** Travelling to Tan Son Nhut airport, on the way to Europe (September 1973). **39** This young lady is on her way in a cyclo to the airport, en route to Switzerland. **40** 7 October 1968: Australian soldiers help with some babies awaiting departure from Tan Son Nhut airport. **41** Rosemary delivering Anna Renate to Berlin (25 January 1971). **42** Minehaha meets her mother in Montreal.

pictures over all the tables and benches and walls; then after decorating the walls with the crayons, they proceeded to eat the crayons, etc. It must have been a riot. Laurie's mother in Minnesota has been sending us lots of art equipment, and toys, decorations, and furnishings for the nurseries.

February, Staff Memo: Sponsorship: any house with long-term unadoptable children might like to obtain sponsorship for them. This would continue even when we take the child back to the orphanage of origin or elsewhere. The income would be a great help to the institute caring for the child.

Photos: Apart from our immediate staff and our own chosen escorts, no one may photograph in the nurseries unless by permission from the office.

This was followed by an appeal for a member of staff to volunteer as accountant to which there was no landslide response!

At this time two experienced Vietnam veterans, Barbara Baden and Jon Tierney (the ophthalmologist) returned, and were of great immediate service. Barbara nursed at Newhaven while Susan McDonald was abroad escorting children to their new homes; and Jon examined our children with eye problems.

Wende Grant came to Saigon in February to assist with the re-registering of our operation under the new name. We were invited to attend the inauguration ceremony for the new Deputy Director at the Ministry of Social Welfare, Dr Bach. Apart from two other Caucasian women from the UN, we had the honour of being the only foreigners present. On 8 March 1974 we signed our agreement with the Minister, Dr Phan Quang Dan; this recognized the change of name, and (as already mentioned) granted FFAC the added great advantage of full power of custody over the children in the care of the agency. While Wende was still there, we attended a meeting at USAID in Saigon, where we were now told it was doubtful that there would be any funding available for FFAC.

On Monday 21 January that year, a release from Senator Kennedy's office had announced that USAID had allocated 7.2 million dollars to provide emergency child welfare services in South Vietnam, and to facilitate the adoption of Vietnamese war orphans by American citizens. The funds were to be spent through contracts with private voluntary agencies. Senator Kennedy welcomed 'this sign of progress in an area of deep public and congressional concern': 'For too long this administration has found it easier to equip armies than to help the children orphaned by war.' He went on to say that 'the new programme should finally make it possible to sweep away some of the bottlenecks and red tape in the adoption process'. The connection between USAID money and the 'bottlenecks' is obscure. The real bottlenecks remained unaffected. However, the grants did stimulate the interest of hitherto almost dormant agencies who had previously not concerned themselves with adoption work, or simply had not succeeded.

The appointment of several new experts to the USAID staff in Washington and Vietnam was announced by Dr Daniel Parker, the Administrator of USAID, who spoke of his frequent meetings with the US-based experts on Vietnamese problems. He said they had a 'much more precise grasp of the size of the problem' with their new set of statistics on adoptable orphans in orphanages. But USAID statistics would never be able to describe the problem. They spoke with a sense of accomplishment of orphanage surveys, but we knew how certain orphanages resented the interference and arranged their own statistics. Moreover, a large proportion of the orphan population would never be included in the statistics: the newborn babies who were pouring into the orphanages by the thousand each month. Most of them would be dead before they were two-months-old, and so occupied no place in the orphanage registers. These mites came into the world without official registration and left in the same way. Some orphanages (as I've already mentioned) had their own burial grounds. The great USAID survey which came up with the figures of 5,000 orphans available for adoption certainly did not include this large number of short-term survivors.

As soon as it became known that USAID funding was available for child welfare projects in Vietnam, our supporters in America were anxious for FFAC to receive some of the funding. The original Congressional appropriation for child welfare in Vietnam had been for 5 million dollars and then expanded to 7.2 million. Ten per cent of the appropriation was earmarked for assistance with adoptions, but FFAC's chances, we were told, were poor, since 'another politically powerful agency' would be submitting requests for funds. At least 90 per cent of the total 7.2 million dollar allocation was to be disbursed to voluntary agencies for programmes of orphanage improvement, child nutrition, day care, foster care, prevention of infant abandonment (entitled 'family services') and others.

Margaret and Wende argued with USAID Saigon that FFAC had more children under care; provided more medical service for ill, malnourished and handicapped children; and had arranged more adoptions than all other agencies in Vietnam combined; and that surely FFAC should qualify for a grant as a nutrition centre or for medical care as well as for their work as an adoption agency. But we were told that, since FFAC had done 85 per cent of the adoptions during the preceding year, 'we will certainly give you praise. But it is just money we can't give you.'

Wende returned to Colorado from Saigon and left the same day for Washington, where she visited the offices of some US senators who seemed interested in the allocation of the funds, and sought from them an explanation of the distribution policy. She then wrote to each of the senators, summarizing her questions and particularly pointing out that in relation to the number of orphans cared for and being adopted, agencies were clearly being funded in almost inverse proportion:

28 March 1974, WG to RT: Washington was neither very encouraging nor discouraging. At the present moment it seems that Senator Williams' office will help us . . . I alternate between feeling that I wouldn't want their money if offered on a gold platter, and then realizing that it is my money and I resent so much of it going to a fancy agency office in New York. Someone should use some of it for the children!

Some senators, in the course of answering Wende's letter, evidently cabled USAID in Saigon for information:

3 April 1974, MM to WG: The business of USAID money is, I am informed, turning into a bit of a fiasco here, with everybody except, oddly, us going broke.

The senators' enquiries brought the following response to FFAC:

24 April 1974, Matthew J. Harvey, Assistant Administrator for Legislative Affairs, AID, Washington [extracts]: Let me say at the outset that we value highly the contribution to the inter-

country adoption programme that is being made by FFAC and AID hope to make a substantial grant to that Agency in the very near future.

... It is our intention to ensure that the financial resources available to FFAC are sufficient to permit that organization to continue its commendable work in Vietnam.

At last on 10 June we signed our USAID grant offer for 100,000 dollars (the figure mentioned the previous December), which we planned to use for local staff salaries for one year. The nurseries were told to give appropriate increases to the Vietnamese staff, worked out on the basis of each worker's family situation and dependants. The USAID money enabled us to hire more local staff and change to a more efficient three-shift schedule. We were happy to be able to employ the maximum number of women, who had very few and poor job opportunities, and sometimes large families to support:

18 June 1974, Saigon, RT to WG: USAID grant: I have already filled out umpteen forms and gone from office to office trying to sort out how actually to lay hands on the money. We ought to have it within a couple of days. Ironically, all the houses have increased staff, raised salaries – as I told them to, and made other changes ... finally within a few months I can foresee that the USAID money will scarcely be covering half the salaries. Oh well, it was nice while it lasted, I suppose.

I can't concentrate much tonight as I am on guard at Newhaven and they have many very small babies and sick children. I feel too nervous to sit for long without jumping up to inspect the children.

The grant didn't affect the destination of the children for adoption. FFAC in Saigon continued to work closely with adoption agencies in Germany, Sweden, France, Canada, Switzerland, England, Belgium, Australia and Finland, besides the USA.

On 4 March 1974, Anne Barry had arrived from Australia to take over the administration of Allambie, replacing Sr Doreen Beckett, who moved on to fresh pastures at To Am. Anne, like Marg, was a long-time friend of mine since schooldays and I was delighted that another such eminently capable person was joining us. On 10 March, Anne wrote to her family in Adelaide with some vivid first impressions:

It's Sunday and I must have been here almost a week. The happy screams of ninety toddlers are penetrating the closed office door, for they are all out swimming in the pool. Peggy [Hammond], the physical therapist here, has just had it filled in with cement to a suitable depth for the little ones, and chlorinated. I usually go and play with them when they come out.

I am trying to get to know half a dozen at least each day – and the staff, too. I have fun with them exchanging English for Vietnamese. They have a delightful sense of humour.

. . . I think I was completely numb for the first few days, and I rather wish I could have stayed that way; there are aspects to the Vietnamese situation that all but overwhelm me. First of all, it's the extent of Rosemary's operation which involves orphanages all over the country, and then it's her own 'Homes' in particular. I have just finished seeing over the last of them, and I am at once dismayed and amazed at the number of rooms in each house and the number of babies and the size of them and the kind of nursing and medical treatment and sheer care they are receiving. The impression was so strong I was physically affected. I walked around town in a kind of daze that lasted hours after visiting Ilse's Clinic [Hy Vong Nursery]. Those babies were so minute and numerous, I just could not believe what I saw.

The next thing that dismays me, but differently, is the war, or whatever it is here. Soldiers are everywhere. I hate everything about the uniforms all over town, the guards sitting on tops of buildings or in doorways with their guns; the convoys of trucks that blare through town with their sirens blasting several times a day; the amount of air activity above the clouds; the helicopters whining overhead; the barbed wire everywhere; the guardhouses on every little bridge and the sounds of shelling in the distance day and night. Then there are the maimed boys in and around the hospitals. I can't bear the sight of all this and find it most upsetting. Doreen pointed out the Hall of Justice in one of the main streets, with a mammoth-size statue of a crouched soldier, raised gun in hand, facing it. What an ironic sight. I hate it.

. . . I dressed a convoy for France the other day and really it was exciting. Those little kids looked so beautiful. They were excited because they knew they were going somewhere but little did they realize the full import of this 'outing'. Such an event is full of mixed emotions here. The Vietnamese staff, who have grown very fond of the children find it hard to wave them goodbye, but then they know that a family is better for them than a 'Home'. I shall never forget those little kids and the staff and that first convoy.

My correspondence with Wende discusses the children's problems:

24 March 1974, RT to WG: Minh: the second child proposed to this family. She had a seizure the other day. I think the doctor diagnosed it, eventually, as a chronic condition related to the calcium level in her body, and one which would require continued treatment.

Crystal: this child is fortunate to be in a foster home with Mr and Mrs Iken from the Dutch Embassy. If the family would like to have first hand information they could write to the Ikens.

Blancmange: the boy seems to have recovered from the ear infection but he is so unusually gross. We are afraid there may be some problem associated with his size and his pudding-like face. I think it would be best not to place him for the moment – we ought to watch his development a little longer.

Stiff Legs: we think we have finally come up with a logical explanation. The doctor at Grall did a biopsy on the muscle of one of our children and sent it to France for analysis. The verdict was that the contracture could have been congenital. That did not suit me at all; so many children would not be suffering from such a congenital defect – the odds were against it. But they also said contracture could be, and probably is, caused by malabsorbed intramuscular medication gradually causing atrophy of the muscle. This is highly probable. The problem is not with the knee but with the thigh muscles. The doctor at Grall will probably prescribe some form of therapy to loosen up these muscles.

At least twelve of our children exhibited this syndrome.

31 March 1974, RT to WG: Now at 11 p.m., I shall begin to run through your list of families and see if I can keep awake till the end. So far, of course, the night is just beginning.

Linh: I now have a birth judgement for her. I was able to add her name to the last list of judgements requested at court.

César Chávez: We are about to apply for the passport. Hope the Immigration approval comes soon as the boy is in splendid condition.

F. Boy: is coming down from China-Beach Orphanage on Tuesday. We shall repeat the medical as the old one has expired. We shall also extend the exit visa since that, too, has long since expired. The child ought to be leaving soon unless we have problems extending the visa.

John of the Cross: He is a great lump. Sad that he will have to wait around for a non-preference visa which are at the moment current to December 1973. His filing date was March '74.

Troy (family temporarily in Australia): I am trying to get a visa for the child from the Australian Embassy but it is so difficult to find them open. Those Australians are incredibly lazy . . . seem to work about two half days a week!

Ramon: was scheduled to depart, but his medical certificate said possible syphilis, so further tests had to be done. We are awaiting the results; ought to have them tomorrow.

Elizabeth: We have just obtained birth judgement and are about to make application for the passport. A copy of the birth certificate will be sent to you as soon as it comes back from translation. Similarly for Doty, Abraham, Bruno, Brian, Roy, Nuoc-Mam and Thomas More.

Medical visas cannot be used for polio children, neither can parole visas. We are trying to get Coi in on a medical visa which would apply to her case because of her critical condition. I still don't have the passport but hope I can devote some time to it this week.

22 April 1974, RT to WG: Abraham is in a cast. He had a break in his thigh which is very peculiar, like a sliver of bone which has partly broken away from the main bone . . . Otherwise he is doing well and much more handsome than in his previous photo. The cast ought to be off within a few weeks, I expect.

April 1974, RT to WG:
  Andy: died.
  Non-preference visas waiting period has advanced three months recently.
  Sylt: Ilse feels that he is a twin to another little girl we have called List. The two should be placed together as we do not want to risk separating twins.

April 1974, Newsletter: In Hy Vong Nursery there are currently 150 babies, using seventy-five cans of milk formula a day. When the warehouses run out of supplies, and we have to buy at retail price from the local pharmacies, milk for just this one nursery costs us 135 dollars a day or 4,000 a month.

  Before Christmas I spoke of our dream of setting up a facility for our 'special children'. . . Allambie has been called the model nursery for Vietnam. The staff there have been specially trained in 'play therapy', and it is quite hilarious to see the children in different groups, at sandbox, climbing, building, singing and dancing, or swimming in the pool, children and staff together. There is school for the older children.

  The children at Allambie are divided into families of six or eight. Each family has its own room and the same child-care workers assigned. The night-duty 'mother' sleeps in the room with the children. If you drop by at bedtime you will find 'mother' bringing in a tray with cups of milk for her pyjama-clad children who are seated on the floor: colouring, playing with toys, even singing. Then after the milk the older children reach spontaneously for their toothbrushes.

  Each room is named after a country and when a child first comes to the nursery, he is assigned to 'Canada' or 'Africa' or one of about ten countries. This avoids the horror of referring to rooms by numbers. On the bedroom door and walls there are bright posters and photos of each child's adoptive family, with letters from the family posted in English or French and Vietnamese. Each child has a cloth bag over the end of his bed in which he keeps his treasures. The older children take this bag when they leave the nursery to go abroad.

  Kim Tien moved to To Am to give a new course to the child-care workers. The first class from Allambie graduated with a little ceremony in early January. The British Ambassador and his wife, the US Consul as well as many representatives from the Ministry of Welfare and other agencies and institutions were present.

Edie de Chadenedes, our early childhood development specialist, left a week ago. The Allambie children and staff said farewell to her with an 'activities' afternoon, which was a tribute to her work during her six months with us. Because of her training and example, the staff had learned to enjoy their work and to appreciate its dignity and importance . . .

Peggy Hammond, who worked with Julie Chinberg in close association with Edie, describes an outing from Allambie:

. . . because the children were rather confined we tried to take them on outings and errands whenever possible. They always clamoured round the little Renault, hoping that it was their turn to go for a ride. The children also enjoyed 'dressing up' for these outings, and putting on new clothes. One night we took Linh and eight other children to dinner in an outdoor restaurant. Anne and I were anxious about taking so many, but they behaved so well that we soon relaxed. Another day we took them to see the ocean at Vung Tau. We packed lunches of peanut butter on french bread and an orange drink; we stopped along the way to buy bananas and papaya. Vung Tau is about two hours east of Saigon. For most, it was their first trip to the ocean and their excitement grew as we approached the seashore. Some of the children chattered enthusiastically and others were silent with awe. The beach was almost deserted; there were only a few squatting women selling food. We hired an inner-tube for each child and they dashed into the water, the happiest children we had seen in a long time. Coi was due to leave for the US the next day, and this was a farewell treat for her. She had been brought to Allambie ten months previously with a serious kidney dysfunction. Surgery removed a large bladder stone but the doctors could do nothing to improve her kidney function in Saigon. She required further surgery in the US. She had been wearing a catheter ever since her surgery and for fear of an infection was not allowed in the water. This day we disregarded all restrictions and she was the merriest of all the children.

Thanks to the special intervention of Laurie Peters, we finally succeeded in obtaining Coi's visa on medical grounds, and Mary-Nelle escorted her to the USA in April, 1974, intending to spend some weeks fund-raising while she was there. Coi was sad to leave the familiarity of Allambie, but her very life depended on her going. Her surgery was successful and she is now living with her family in Vermont, with an adoptive brother and sister also from Allambie.

1 May 1974, Memo from Julie [Chinberg] at Allambie to RT: An assistant Dean at the University of Saigon Medical Faculty, Dr D. H. Anh, may be willing to do some autopsies for special cases that would be learning experience for his students. Shall I pursue this further?

Enclosed is a receipted Adventist Hospital bill. As a matter of interest the assistant administrator of the IRC [International Rescue Committee] Clinic says we are the only agency paying our Adventist bills. Other agencies have apparently refused to pay until their USAID grants come through.

It is suggested by the hospital that as we have the legal right to vaccinate (in our contract) we ought to have made our own FFAC stamp and use this on the vaccination records of the children.

9 May 1974, MM to WG: I got back about a day ago from Australia. Brian McGowran and Mij have things well under way for the licensing of the Vietnamese Orphan Fund operating officially for the support of the children in care of FFAC.

With a certain snideness I applied for 24,000 dollars (US) from Australian Catholic Relief ... When I left ten days early, this application had been authorized by the relevant bishops in the land but had not yet passed the body of laymen.

On 1 June 1974 I went with Susan McDonald to St Paul's Orphanage, Bien Hoa. Sister pointed out to us one crib where we found a small part-Caucasian boy, about ten months old, with grossly distended abdomen and fleshless limbs, covered with purulent ulcers and swollen lymph nodes, with draining ears and upper respiratory infection. He had an abscess on his protruding spine and was curled into a foetal position. Later it was found that he weighed $8\frac{1}{2}$ lb and was filled with ascaris [round worm]. We were told he had just been found abandoned in a Lambretta, and were asked if we would be able to do something for the child. For a moment my optimism wavered, but Susan picked up the little fellow confidently and we took him back to Newhaven where he was appropriately named De Profundis. After two months of Susan's medicine and tender-loving-care, with a supplementary diet of a special protein formula, the change in De Profundis was dramatic. With abdomen flattened, limbs fleshed out and ulcers healed, he became a bright-eyed little boy with a great sense of fun, and less like an orphan than any other child in the nursery.

4 June 1974, MM to WG: The war goes on. We have forty cases of measles at Hy Vong. Ilse is in Europe and Birgit is carrying on. Julie comes over when she can, whereupon I light off for Rathaven which is still tenantless and almost supplyless. We have closed the thirty-nine rat holes here (there is still one I cannot find) and have cleared the debris from the water tanks. We are now trying to make some sense of the storm drain system. Oddly, while I watch the supply of disposable diapers dwindling, I am rather pleased that at last there is rain. It makes me feel that at least the elements are weeping for this God-forsaken country, when neither you nor I nor any of us have the time to weep.

Chapter 10

THE CONVOYS AND
A VISIT TO CAMBODIA
August – December 1974

IN AUGUST 1974 Wende Grant, Naomi Bronstein of Families For Children [FFC] (Canada) and Dolly Bui and Margaret Moses from Saigon went together to Phnom Penh in response to reports about numerous orphaned and abandoned children needing help. Wende gives an account of the visit, which was in the end cut rather short, so far at least as FFAC was concerned:

We found Phnom Penh a beautiful old city and the Cambodians friendly and startlingly honest. The Hotel Le Phnom offered us a choice of large rooms with old, dilapidated furnishings. There were no light bulbs in the wide hallways; the water was cut off periodically; and the windows rattled with the constant rocketing. Still, the city, and particularly the hotel, had a nostalgic air, hinting of past intrigue and romance.

There was no romance or mystery about what was happening to the Cambodians. Thousands of refugees were living on the streets and the hospitals were overflowing with war-wounded. Two captured young Khmer Rouge soldiers, one a woman, were pointed out to us; the woman was to have her arm amputated the next day. The look of fierce hatred she returned in response to our tentative smiles remains with me still.

We spoke with Welfare authorities concerned about their inability to cope with the growing number of homeless children. Once they overcame their caution of foreigners and realized that our concern was genuine, they were eager for any assistance we could offer. While Margaret and I discussed needs and procedures, Naomi and Dolly arranged the adoption of fourteen orphans by Canadian families. Within two weeks we escorted a convoy of children back to Saigon, en route to Canada.

The plea for assistance from Cambodian Welfare touched us deeply; they actually asked us to take over the National Orphanage. Margaret stayed on in Phnom Penh better to assess the situation. But the project was short-lived. A few days later she was recalled to Saigon to replace Rosemary, who had to go to Australia suddenly because of family illness.

In September, back in the States, it was reluctantly agreed that FFAC did not have the resources to expand into Cambodia, and (even if the money could have been found) it was also quite clear that the Khmer Republic would not last long enough to justify the investment of time and resources to run the National Orphanage.

When Margaret came to Colorado next, we wrote (on 14 October) to an aide of Senator Williams, reporting on our visit and explaining our action and concerns. FFC, Canada, however, found themselves able to respond, and by December they had set up their own nursery, Canada House, in Phnom Penh, and worked out an agreement with the government. Dolly and Anna Charet ran the nursery, for the three months or so left.

Convoys of children flew regularly to Europe and the USA via San Francisco or via Paris and New York. Sometimes the escorts would be members of the Saigon staff, who profited by the trip to snatch a much-needed break, or to contact supporters and discuss problems. Sometimes the escorts were our friends and collaborators, or short-term volunteers from abroad, and the trip provided them with a valuable opportunity to see the situation in Vietnam for themselves. They would take advantage of an excess baggage allowance on the incoming trip to bring supplies that Maria Eitz had assembled in San Francisco, John Wetterer in New York, or Minnie Gallozzi in Paris.

On Pan Am we needed, and were allowed, one adult escort for five children, later reduced to one escort for two or three children depending on their age. On Air France we were at first permitted only one escort for ten children, but later reduced to five children, when Air France experienced numerous times the degree of unwelcome disturbance and mess that could be created by ten restless children with only one exhausted adult to care for them.

One of the earlier 'horror' trips, back in November 1973, is related by Ina Orr, who with Nancy Wheeler was escorting twelve children to the States via Paris with, on the same flight, twenty more of our children escorted by four adults, including Minnie Gallozzi and Dolly Bui who were going as far as Paris:

Because of the fog in Paris we landed in Nice, were delayed there one hour, then returned to Paris. We, thus, missed the connecting flight to New York and had to stay overnight. We were taken to the airport nursery with all our supplies. Four women (including three from Terre des Hommes) were to look after the children that night. We were told to be at the check-in desk at 9 o'clock next morning.

After enquiring at 'Lost and Found' for our suitcases next morning, we presented our tickets at the check-in counter at 9 a.m., and waited. At 9.20, a stewardess and a woman from TdH came from the nursery carrying some of the children and our 'New York arrival' bag, which they left with our luggage at check-in. The stewardess said the plane would leave at 9.30 instead of 10.00.

While Nancy waited for our tickets I returned to the nursery. I saw all our bags were almost empty and the clothes strewn over the floor. The basket that had contained sixteen baby-bottles and two and a half cans of formula was empty except for two dirty bottles. I started to pick up the clothes and sort out which were ours; we needed them for changes on the plane. Then the girls from TdH started shouting in French. I indicated that the clothes were ours – we had brought three large bags of clothing. The stewardess spoke to the girls in French, and nothing was said to us except that we would have to carry our own luggage as they had the children.

The stewardess was carrying a baby and it vomited all over her uniform. Nancy, returning with the tickets at that moment, grabbed the baby just as the stewardess was about to drop him. All the while the three girls continued to shout at us in French whenever we tried to pick up our belongings. Nancy and I were very upset and told them repeatedly that we could not take twelve children all the way from Paris to New York without diapers, clothes and milk. We even asked for the formula in French, one word that we had learnt, but still they refused to give us any.

The stewardess and the TdH girls picked up the remaining children, all except eight-year-old paralysed Bong. He was sitting on the floor crying because he was afraid he would be left behind. The others left without telling us which departure gate we should go to.

I picked up Bong who was dripping wet from not being changed since the night before. Nancy collected ten dirty baby-bottles and put them in the basket. She also picked up one green plastic bag of clothes containing a few pairs of baby shoes, two undershirts and a few diapers. We carried the bags, basket and boy out to the desk and found no one there to help us. We could never get to the plane in time with all this luggage – it would take us several trips.

Eventually three men came over and offered to help. The girls from TdH saw us and started again shouting in French. We stood at the gate but refused to board until the luggage arrived. As Bong was so wet and heavy I boarded him while Nancy waited for the luggage. The steward brought up the bags and the girls started grabbing them: they were angry, explained the steward, because we were taking all their clothes leaving them with none for the next day's convoy, and they had spent the whole morning getting the children ready ... Nancy told him that most of our clothes were still in the nursery and that we had no milk and very few diapers. By this time Nancy was in tears, and leaving two of the bags of clothes with them, she boarded with the little bit she had saved.

Once on the plane, we found several of our children soaked from the waist down, still wet from overnight. As we had only two undershirts and one pair of sleepers, some of the children had on only plastic pants. All the children had diarrhoea and we had no clean clothes. Many of them were cold but all our sweaters had been taken in Paris.

We were forced to feed the babies sugar-water all the way from Paris to New York because we had no milk. No one had told us whether or not the babies had breakfasted. Also missing were Bong's special shoes, Pierre's two elastic hernia bandages and

Hien's red bag containing her Vietnamese dress and letters and photos from her family.

When we began dressing the children for arrival in New York, we found that even the arrival packets had been tampered with and many items were missing. Philip had three shirts but no pants, and Bong's purple pants from yesterday's flight had been stuffed into one of the baby's bags. We knew the packages had been made up with great care in Saigon and contained everything needed.

The whole experience was most upsetting for all of us, especially for the older children and Bong, in particular.

Eventually, Terre des Hommes stopped meeting the convoys unless their own children were involved. Minnie Gallozzi and her group Les Amis des Enfants took over this role and made sure there was always sympathetic help available to exhausted children and escorts.

We tried to prepare convoys as carefully as possible, but there were always factors beyond our control, requiring reserves of initiative and physical stamina from the escorts. Planes were frequently delayed or diverted due to weather or mechanical problems; there were missed connections and unscheduled stopovers without adequate assistance or accommodation. There were health problems provoked by change of climate, change of diet and excitement; there was diarrhoea, vomiting, and restlessness. The health of the children, often precarious on departure, could degenerate rapidly during the long flight, and it was important to have escorts who could cope with such emergencies. In 1973 I had been obliged to hospitalize a severely dehydrated two-year-old in Honolulu, leaving her while I continued on with seven other children. A few days later I was, myself, incapacitated with amoebic dysentery for a second time.

Maria Eitz in San Francisco was an important link in the chain transporting the children from Saigon to their adoptive families in the US. Maria met every incoming convoy, brought provisions to care for the children at the airport, and organized the flight transfers. When there was no immediate connecting flight, she took the escorts and children back to her home for the night. Her own nights would be spent in vigils with sick babies, reducing their fevers, relieving congestion with her vaporizer, or painstakingly hydrating them drop by drop. If a child's condition seemed to warrant it, she would call her doctor or hospitalize the child. Then she would return the escorts and children to the airport for the last lap of their journey.

Co-ordinating schedules of escorts with such variables as their own availability, the available plane space, date of expiry of visas, the number of children ready, and the children's travel fitness, required no mean genius. As soon as I realized Mary-Nelle Gage's talent in this field I hastily abdicated the honour of organizing convoys, whenever possible.

August 1974 was surely a high-point in her brilliant career. Mary-Nelle recollects this time:

That summer brought us several specialized volunteers, in addition to the normal flow of representatives from our support groups throughout the world. Already in the first half of August, fifty-four children had left with eighteen escorts, and there were nine more escorts ready to travel before the end of the month. Dolly and Le were working to capacity to process the children's papers.

Prospects were further complicated by the arrival of a much-needed and long-expected nurse, 'Patsie Dolores', whose qualifications had been widely sung. Patsie's first announcement on disembarking (in a luminous yellow vinyl rainsuit) was that there had been a mistake, and that she had realized upon take-off in San Francisco that her rightful place was in the States. We quickly came round to that same opinion after she announced a prescription of antibiotics for *every* child at Allambie, sight unseen. The next discovery was that she had no qualifications whatsoever, except for time spent as a patient in hospital, and her obvious interest in illnesses and things medical. She was even at that moment anxious about her breathing, suspected TB, and incipient measles.

It was obvious that Patsie had to be added to the list of escorts for immediate departure, a list which already included Wende, Naomi Bronstein (with nine of the FFC Cambodian orphans) and three short-term volunteers.

Arrangements were made for Naomi and the Cambodian

orphans to travel by Pan Am, with Wende and two more escorts. Suddenly, Naomi announced that she preferred to travel Air France, via Paris to Montreal since the connections were easier. We revised our plans, and started processing the children on Air France. After submitting lists of names, birth-dates, and adopting families to Air France, we were told that there were no confirmed seats beyond Rome, whereupon Naomi wisely conceded that the Pan Am flight after all might be more appropriate, and it also would permit an additional two escorts, Linda and Patsie, for the same number of children.

Once more we changed course in mid-stream. Mai-Huong, a long-suffering Pan Am agent sat late one evening preparing the tickets and cabling the families of the arrival time of their children. We were almost finished, long after closing time, when Mai-Huong answered the phone. As she listened, her expression began to droop, then drag. And then: 'Now Mrs Bronstein, what is it you plan to do?' I grabbed the receiver from a startled Mai-Huong, shouted at Naomi, and stormed out, after cancelling the Pan Am flight.

Meanwhile, Maria Eitz learning of the Rome reservation dilemma with Air France had contacted the American Ambassador in Rome to request special help, and arrangements were made for Embassy families to accommodate children and escorts during their lay-over. With that obstacle surmounted, Naomi thought she might as well go back to Air France.

I could not give up, but pleaded a case for the two extra escorts and the escort engagement we had with Pan Am for both Wende and Naomi's ticket to Saigon. Naomi agreed. Since it was now too late for the Thursday Pan Am flight, we began negotiations for the Saturday Pan Am flight from Hong Kong. The free escort tickets to Hong Kong on Air Vietnam needed special negotiating since we had no regular arrangement with Air Vietnam.

Patsie had been with us for almost two weeks and her reputation had become increasingly colourful. Naomi and Wende were paralysed with fear at the prospect of her being responsible for children on the flight. Wende set about convincing her that her suspected measles and tuberculosis contact might be serious. She urged Patsie to remain calm and quiet in flight and to busy herself only with the luggage rather than risk further contamination through close contact with the babies. Patsie agreed to this prudent plan.

But even the luggage was fraught with peril. After processing through Immigration, the children and escorts went upstairs to the departure lounge. I followed the escorts' luggage through Customs. Patsie had brought with her a medium-size medical library and her bag was further strained with newly-acquired souvenirs. Upon checking her case, after one latch was undone the entire piece of baggage exploded, spewing thick volumes and large clothing items all over the area. I had not the vestiges of energy remaining to engineer the feat of repacking. I fetched Patsie and she managed to repack and close her case before departure.

16 September 1974, M-N. Gage to WG: Six-week delay in visas: just before Rosemary left [for Australia] we were warned that there would be a new system for all passports, involving a journey through the Ministry of Social Welfare and the Ministry of Interior for each application. A dragon in Social Welfare is opposed to adoption and wanted a full-scale investigation to locate the mother, whenever there is a named mother on a birth certificate [hardly ever the actual name, which is not known, but one supplied by the orphanage when the birth was registered] in order to help her find other means for the care of the child rather than giving it up for adoption . . .

Wish you could have seen Rathaven. The surplus shipment from USAID has just been delivered: AFRO hair dressing, Endust furniture polish, horseradish sauce, and Schweppes Bitter Lemon . . .

23 September 1974, M-N. Gage to WG: Ruth Routten [an American Airways stewardess who often flew as an escort for adopted orphans] was here for a day and showed me the pictures she took of the Cambodian convoy. She also told me that Maria Eitz got a message that the nine children were routed through ROME with no way out of Rome, and that going to Rome would cost her 2,000 dollars! So I guess my worries were nothing in comparison with Maria's, who twice telephoned the American Ambassador in Rome to solicit his help.

Margaret, recalled from Cambodia, addressed herself to the problems of the crowded nurseries where children were waiting at least eight or nine months before joining their adoptive parents in France. In a letter of 18 September 1974 to Dr Dan, she proposed that the licensed French agencies be permitted to register with Social Welfare in Saigon and that the children processed under their aegis be allowed to leave Vietnam before the completion of adoption procedures, as was the case for children going to the States and Australia, for whom proxy adoptions could be completed in the Vietnamese courts.

When I got back at the end of September, Margaret was freed to escort a group of children to the States and consult with Wende. At that time Marg had one principal idea in mind: to draft a new adoption law for the use of the Ministry in Vietnam. While the licensed agencies were required to follow complicated procedures and report all phases of their programmes to the Ministry, the private adoptions by orphanages and lawyers continued without surveillance. More generally, there was a frustrating wait suffered by the children destined for Europe. Wende and Marg spent many days designing a law and procedure that protected biological parents, adoptive parents, and children. Their concept included safeguards but eliminated useless steps in the adoption process. It put more responsibility on the licensed agencies and precluded private or independent adoptions. The rights and needs of the children were given priority.

Marg returned with the outline to Saigon and we had high hopes that our basic ideas would be approved and translated into legal procedure. In January 1975, an International Conference on Children and National Development was due to take place in Saigon, and I had already been asked by Dr Phieu, who was to chair the adoption committee, to read a paper on adoption. We thought that the Ministry would have time to look at our proposals afterwards.

In Saigon, we were experiencing a serious shortage of supplies. We knew that large quantities were sitting in Arizona awaiting shipment. We had approached USAID/ADRR for assistance in airlifting the supplies, but to no avail:

24 October 1974, MM to WG: Jay [Ruoff] was his usual compromising self about airlifts. He said they are recommended for

emergencies and publicity only. Jay says everyone is hungry and he is thinking of funding the Red Cross to set up soup kitchens in Saigon.

Do something, Wende, anything. This is war and famine and nobody is budging an inch. I feel calm and smiling and bloody. Rosie is gay and dangerous and looking for a diversion.

25 October 1974, MM to WG: We are using Pelargon milk now, not SMA or Guigoz. God knows how long Pelargon will last out. I just wrote to Brian McGowran in Adelaide and told him to start shipping Lactogen, if Australia has any to spare ...

Spirits are taut and bright here. How are they your end?

While Marg was dealing with these problems of supply shortage and nursery overcrowding, with plant management and principles, I continued to concentrate on the children's dossiers, sending abroad information on available children, and processing the documentation. Lists of documents for already placed children alternated with searches for suitable families:

25 October 1974, RT to WG: Megan: this is a part-black child, who looks rather more native Australian than American – just a guess. She is quite verbal, and her language suggests she is at least five-years-old. She came to us from Qui Nhon Orphanage and Sister said she had not been there for long.

When questioned Megan said that before coming to Saigon, she was out in the street. She says she has an older brother and sister and a younger (either) brother or sister. She said that her mother was at home (in the house). When asked why she left her mother, she said because her mother did not love her. 'Why doesn't your mother love you?' 'Because I don't love my mother.' 'Why don't you love your mother?' 'Because my mother does not love me.'

These answers were given without any prompting, though Megan spoke very quietly and hesitantly, probably due to shyness of the company. She seemed to be happy to be at Allambie.

Megan shows she is intelligent and aware. She has obviously suffered from family rejection. Must be careful that she is put into an environment where she will not suffer further rejection.

Mary-Nelle's October newsletter gives an account of the current staff responsibilities, and the special help we were receiving:

Between June and August there were several short-term volunteers who gave valuable service. Visiting escorts brought in needed supplies, unpacked boxes, sorted clothes, typed, took children on outings, gave extra attention to some of the babies, and gathered information to continue their support work back home.

Ilse Ewald has shifted her responsibilities from Hy Vong to the provincial orphanages. She makes frequent trips to the Delta, taking supplies and food, bringing back abandoned children and those in need of intensive medical care.

Julie Chinberg moved to Hy Vong to share the nursing with Birgit Blank. We are continuing to make improvements at Hy Vong so that we may establish it more as an intensive care clinic, complete with laboratory, as the orphan clinic is always so crowded ... We need more laboratory equipment and more isolettes.

Paulette Peterson (Petey), a novice with the Sisters of Loretto, but very experienced in day care and pre-schools, has established a spectacular programme of learning games and activities and crafts at Allambie. A pre-school teacher has been hired to assist her and continue her programme after she leaves in early January. Positive reinforcement with treats and affection are her technique for teaching altered behaviour, talking and walking.

Jo Russell is continuing her programme with the handicapped and retarded small children at To Am. She has made many contacts with various medical facilities in Saigon, including the neuro-surgical unit at Cho Ray Hospital. She makes periodic trips to orphanages in Danang, Nha Trang, Qui Nhon, also taking supplies and bringing to Saigon children in need of surgery and intensive medical care. Since Doreen Beckett is moving to Hy Vong as administrator, Mary Cusack (who arrived earlier in the year and has spent several months organizing supplies at Rathaven) has taken over administration of To Am.

Christie Leivermann has returned and is now organizing the pharmacy and warehouse at Rathaven. She is also serving as a relief nurse for Susan McDonald at Newhaven. Newhaven is enjoying a classical period with the arrival of new children from the Greek and Roman periods: Aristotle, Aeschylus, Plato, Socrates, Athena, Aristophanes, Jocasta, Agamemnon, Tiresias, Sophocles, Euripides, Marc Antony, Julius Caesar, Cleopatra, Electra and Orestes.

The Rathaven warehouse has been in use during the past month as a clearing house for donated surplus food and supplies from USAID. CARE and USAID contributed quantities of baby food, juices, frozen meat and rice which relieved our food budget. We have been disbursing the supplies to orphanages and voluntary agencies. Dolly Bui and Lydia Brackney (our past master in the art of bureaucratic form-filling) arranged for the customs clearance for the Canadian airlift, and organized the unloading and transporting of the supplies to Rathaven.

John Carr, a Jesuit brother, has recently joined us. He will remain at Rathaven and assist with all our electrical, engineering and other maintenance problems.

Five blind children left Saigon for treatment in Australia, thanks to Elaine Moir and her Orphan Medical Fund. Elaine spent one month in Vietnam, travelling to many orphanages, locating and arranging documentation for children who could benefit from eye-surgery in Australia.

Anne Barry (administrator at Allambie) has arranged for several of the handicapped children to attend a special school here in Saigon, run by a psychologist.

Sunday mornings are a special time in Allambie when a local Cub Scout Troop and Scout Leaders arrive to set up their tents and flags on the lawn. Most of the Allambie children participate in the activities with the Scouts. Several of the older boys learned the traditional Dragon Dance for the mid-autumn festival, a children's holiday which we have just celebrated. Allambie was decorated with large red plastic ships, fish, stars, birds and multi-coloured lanterns. Each child was given a small lantern on a stick and came out on the lawn in the evening to watch the Dragon Dance. After the songs and dances, refreshments of mooncakes, nuts, rock candy and tea were served. It was a night of magic, all aglow with the lanterns and the enchanted faces of the children.

I had asked Doreen Beckett to take over the administration of Hy

Vong, so that the nurses would be freed to concentrate on their increasing medical responsibilities:

2 *November 1974, Anne Barry writes home*: Doreen's job is to bring together three of the strongest personalities and get them to work together as a team in Hy Vong nursery. That is just one aspect of the job. She has obvious organizational skills.

. . . I enclose photos of some brand new arrivals at Newhaven Nursery, Antony and Cleopatra . . .

Life here is interesting. Eleven government Ministers are supposed to have resigned, and the Commanders of the Armed Forces have changed. Demonstrations occurring daily – sometimes on a widespread scale, sometimes more local. Thieu constantly issuing statements like 'anti-government attitudes are of communistic origin', and so on.

I have stocked the larder as we are prepared for a *coup*. It could happen tomorrow or in a few weeks or months. It looks inevitable. Rosemary and Margaret are distressed that after so much negotiating with the Minister Dr Dan, it seems he, too, has resigned . . . American aid is being cut, cut, cut. It's hard for someone like me to know what that is going to mean here . . . Buddhists and Catholics are demonstrating everywhere and that pretty well means everybody is unhappy with the regressing state of the economy and the widespread and public corruption of officials.

Rosemary is up to her eyes in work. She returned from Australia a bundle of energy and I would guess that her optimism dwindled in the first sixty minutes. Her task is ENORMOUS, OVERWHELMINGLY COMPLEX, COMPLETELY IMPOSSIBLE, AND NEVER-ENDING. HER SPIRIT IS REMARKABLE, HER METHODS COURAGEOUS, BREATHTAKING, HAZARDOUS & DICTATORIAL. Without her the whole team would fold up. *Because* its structures comprise a complex maze of ingenious channels of operation totally dependent on her leadership: simple, forthright, autocratic and TOTALLY ALTRUISTIC. How does that sound as a pertinent observation, from one who has participated and observed for eight whole months now? The amazing aspect of all those capitals is that I don't feel they are in the slightest way exaggerations.

Fortunately Marg was able to reassure Wende (in a November letter) that Dr Dan had read about his resignation, but not resigned. Our official status required us to attend numerous meetings. Marg and I usually shared the burden, or delegated other staff members to represent FFAC, so that no one person had the frustration of losing too many working hours. But in preparation for the International Conference the meetings became more frequent, and both of us felt obliged to attend together:

> *23 November 1974, RT to WG:* We lunched with Dr Dan and made a bargain that if I went ahead and gave the talk on adoptions at the Conference, he would expedite visas for fifty non-America-bound children, so that we could get them out of the overcrowded nurseries. However, Dr Dan hasn't yet had time to give the matter further thought or sign the necessary approval. Even if he does, we simply don't have the manpower to process all those extra visas . . .
>
> Dr Dan had more or less said that we were supposed to write the 'Definitive Work' on International Adoption, and give him the book by the end of November so they could print it and send it to all the international delegates. This was clearly impossible in the time and at the next meeting I explained to Dr Phieu, the Chairman (former Minister of Welfare), that we were regretfully unable to participate in the Conference because of more immediate commitments. But Dr Phieu turned to Catholic Relief Services and the International Social Services and Holt and told them they were to gather up any statistics we needed, even if necessary to write the paper, but I MUST deliver the paper. Thereupon, they all expressed their willingness to support me because no one else wanted the job. Phieu said it need be a paper of ten to twenty-five minutes only, dealing with our experience of adoption in Vietnam. I had to concede we could manage that much.
>
> When you come in January, please bring one or two of your daughters. They will be living proof of what we are trying to say. Dr Dan really does seem anxious to promote inter-country adoption and to convince people here that it is a good thing – that the children are happy, etc.

Marg was trying at this time to set up an isolation ward at Newhaven, and to start the children at Newhaven on a dose of

Fansidar as a prophylaxis against pneumocystis carinii. A pilot group started on 21 November had all shown weight increase and the babies' sunken/worried-eye syndrome was disappearing within a few days, though coughs and so on persisted. They were keeping strict records of the group receiving prophylaxis, which could be phased in only very gradually to avoid too many children at once reacting with vomiting and diarrhoea. Susan McDonald went to the States during the autumn and consulted with Dr Werner Dutz, a specialist in pneumocystis control. He kindly gave her a crash course on the disease, and promised to provide autopsy reports if the lung biopsies could be sent to him. Susan wrote a comprehensive report on all she had learned from Dr Dutz, and shared it with her nursing colleagues back in Saigon.

Dr Jack Redman from New Mexico had recently been successful in treating a case in the States. Once he had been alerted to the possibility of the disease, he recognized this form of pneumonia in baby Jahnna, whose illness was not responding to the usual medication. This was the first time one of our babies had recovered from a confirmed case of pneumocystis carinii, and it brought us new hope. Dr Redman wrote up his experience in the *Journal* of the *American Medical Association* of 16 December 1974.

From the time the prophylactic dose of Fansidar recommended by Dr Dutz and Dr Redman was started at Newhaven in January 1975, there were no more deaths attributable to pneumocystis carinii.

26 November 1974, RT to Magdalena Weinmann (Freunde de durch RJT . . . Waisenkinder) in Berlin: Thanks for the ampicillin donated by Schering. We have plenty of oral but not much IV. We also need colimycine, bactisubtil (or biolactyl, etc.), B-complex syrup, antibiotic eye ointments, and 25 gauge butterfly needles . . .

We are gradually acquiring a few items for our laboratory, but can't advance very far without a lab technician to operate it.

At Newhaven we are setting up an isolation room. Would you be able to send us oxygen tents . . .?

2 December 1974, MM to WG: The year has been a slow tug-of-war with disease, with perhaps the most noticeable achievement being official recognition of the fact that children are dying here.

It is a point that has been difficult for us to establish, oddly. In September, the total number of children who left Vietnam from all agency centres was thirty-nine. The total number of deaths was thirty-nine. The Vietnamese and American officials sat up when they read that. Statistically, it is dramatic. But they never saw the children alive nor did they watch them die . . .

I am feeling a bit glum: three deaths in three days.

3 December 1974, WG to MM: One of your admirers sent a cheque, a letter and an article he wrote about you. Thought it would cheer you up – tide you over till I get there to dispel gloom, spread gaiety and laughter . . .

We had 247 pieces of mail over Friday and Saturday! Everyone gets so damn sentimental with Christmas and starts thinking of babies and orphans and mangers or cradles – things like that.

9 December 1974, RT to WG: From 3 p.m. until almost 6, I was talking with Miss Quoi at Social Welfare. I walked in, meaning to stay for a few minutes to discuss a special case with her. It concerned a Black-American wanting to take custody of his seven-year-old daughter Giang Thi Ngoc Diep, now in Good Shepherd Orphanage, but the mother refuses to let the father acknowledge the child and have his name put on the birth certificate. The father visits the child constantly and there is no question of his paternity. I hoped Miss Quoi would appreciate the complexity of the problems we are facing and would lose some of her nit-picking mentality. Since there were several ways of approaching this problem, I thought we would have more chance of succeeding if we followed Miss Quoi's advice from the outset. In fact, she could advise nothing that would be remotely helpful in this case (see p. 245).

Here are a few lines to add to your Christmas newsletter: For the last months we have been existing on assorted scraps of whatever milk we can find at retail sources and the odd cans we have in our own stores until more milk becomes available in wholesale quantities. You can imagine how much this has demoralized the nurses. An epidemic of pneumocystis has further demoralized us and sent our hospital bills soaring.

I'm afraid the acute anxiety for the health of the children, our grave lack of sufficient nursing staff, together with statistical harassment by USAID and Social Welfare, and the slow-down on all bureaucratic operations (aggravated by the forthcoming Conference) – all this does not constitute any sense of happy anticipation for the coming Christmas.

12 December 1974, WG to RT: Do we have your permission to shorten the questionnaire-report you filled in for CRS [Catholic Relief Services], copy it and send it to all US senators? You may call it tongue-in-cheek, but I would say yours are clear answers, stripped of bureaucratic nonsense. The vote for foreign aid will be coming up soon and some senators are trying to stop all funding to Vietnam because of the huge allocation for military support. It might be a good way to remind them that the child welfare allocation should be continued or expanded. I think your report is a masterpiece, and would like to see it publicized as it is and not cut back to some bare statistics.

In the middle of your frustration and worry, please take a minute to think of the hundreds of children who did *not* die, but lived to go home. They are cutting teeth, crawling, learning to talk and walk, looking wide-eyed at Christmas displays in the stores and buying fifty cent gifts to exchange at the school Christmas party.

My only memory of Christmas Day that year was of Margaret hauling a load of odd furniture to Newhaven, and of Mary-Nelle surveying the chaos in her front yard on Christmas afternoon, finding it the last straw, and promptly bursting into tears. I was dumbfounded; Mary-Nelle was departing from her script. She was not supposed to cry and I told her so. The rest of the staff were permitted to have moments of weakness and discouragement, but we depended on Mary-Nelle's unruffled equanimity.

30 December 1974, RT to WG: Medical students (as proposed for us by Dr N.): No, no, no. We don't want students. We want specialist doctors with experience – not a bunch of know-it-all medical students. We have enough to put up with at the moment. We want either someone who can TEACH us something or someone who can WORK.

By the end of the year, Naomi Bronstein of the Canadian FFC was setting up the nursery in the wake of the visit to Phnom Penh with which this autumn had begun. The young Canadians, Dolly and Anna Charet, stopped by Saigon on their way to Cambodia:

31 December 1974, MM to WG: The arrival of the Canadian contingent and its departure was breathless and a bit earlier than expected. I spent a lot of time speaking privately with the two girls and telling them something about the running of the houses. I felt obliged to give them all the help I could as they had not received much information.

Morale has been low and I feel 'my great optimism and cheery spirits' are needed to keep the show on the road.

Chapter 11

INTERNATIONAL CONFERENCE ON CHILDREN AND NATIONAL DEVELOPMENT

Papers on Adoption and on Pneumocystis Carinii
14–23 January 1975

THE LAST MONTHS of 1974 and the early months of 1975 saw the arrival of at least eighteen foreign volunteers, nurses, specialists, and general helpers, mainly for short-term service, to replace outgoing and temporarily absent staff. Even then the nurses were spread too thinly over the four houses, where medical responsibilities were increasing day by day. The convoys, too, were another drain on the permanent staff and left gaps to be filled in every nursery. Pat Zirk, a computer programmer from New York, arrived at this time to take over the administration of Allambie; Marg's mother, Margaret Moses Sen., had come up from Australia in December to render what assistance she could, and her presence was another godsend. When Naomi Bronstein brought her first fourteen orphans from Cambodia to Saigon in January, two of our nurses accompanied her for the onward trip to Montreal, though we could ill-afford to be without them.

Early in January, Wende Grant and her two daughters, Thi and Tia, were on their way to Saigon, where they arrived a few days before the International Conference was due to begin on 14 January, at the Thu Duc Conference Centre. I had given an advance copy of my talk on adoption to the Ministry of Social Welfare, who were supposed to translate it into Vietnamese and print multiple copies in both languages. In fact, they copied only the English text. Either they baulked at the considerable work involved in translation, or diplomatically wished to prevent the dispersal of copies in the vernacular. At the Conference itself, I delivered a somewhat abbreviated version of my talk and handed out copies of the complete text. I ended with a special plea to the Ministry:

Since the Vietnamese Government in approving Adoption Agencies has obviously reinforced its approval of inter-country adoption, let us hope for a few logical consequences yet to be realized:

1. That the licensed Agencies will be allowed to function as Agencies and not be harassed by suspicion and non-co-operation on the part of the Ministries.
2. That Agency adoptions, with the greater security they offer the child, will be expedited over non-agency adoptions.
3. That lawyers will be discouraged by legal measures from involvement in adoptions which do not offer the protection of an agency in the country of adoption.
4. That the Ministry of Social Welfare will bear always in mind their reason for being . . . in this case, the WELFARE of the child. This means a speedy solution to the problem of homelessness. The Ministry must not degenerate into *one more obstacle course* for those bodies struggling to promote child-welfare.
5. That the adoption procedure will be made more relevant to the welfare of the child and will become a genuine safeguard and protection, rather than the hollow and legalistic formula it is in its present form.
6. That no POLITICAL, MILITARY or FINANCIAL consideration will be permitted to separate a homeless child from a loving family.

A member of the audience promptly rose up and addressed the assembly, introducing himself as the President of the Junior Chamber of Commerce in Saigon. He voiced protest at proposal 3, which would take adoptions out of the control of lawyers. I pointed out that the president of the JCC was better known as Lawyer Phu, who might be considered to have a strong vested interest in maintaining the autonomy of lawyers in the adoption process. Apart from this, my talk passed fairly uneventfully within the conference chamber. Outside the chamber, however, the speech caused a stir beyond my expectations. André Vung, Director of Sancta Maria Orphanage,

ORPHANS OF WAR · PART I

used my speech to provoke the directors of other orphanages, who had themselves understood probably not one word of what I had said and certainly had given no serious thought to the total context. André called an unscheduled meeting to condemn me and request my expulsion from Vietnam. The Sisters of Providence and the Sisters of St Paul de Chartres, who had known me well for years and who had given us most of the children for adoption, did not follow the sheepish throng that trailed after André, but a few of them attended his meeting to observe the proceedings.

The newspapers for the following days revelled in melodrama. I emerged as a diabolical villain and André the white knight, flashing his shining sword. I was embarrassed by the unwelcome notoriety and depressed, even angered, by the credulity of some of the orphanage directors who had reacted with such shallowness, wasting their emotions on hostility towards me instead of directing them more fruitfully towards finding solutions to the problems of the orphan children.

When tempers were still high, Marg commented to Dr Dan that the speech would probably lead to my assassination. Dr Dan responded without hesitation, 'Well, in your contract it says you are responsible for burials!' And there were other reassuring reactions: at the Justice of Peace Court, the judge was a scholarly man whose understanding and compassion I respected. He had known me for seven years as I presented myself each week to sign adoption contracts. At the court session following the Conference, I walked into the judge's chamber hoping irrationally that if I kept my eyes lowered he wouldn't notice me. I was relieved to find from his friendly smile and comments that he hadn't fallen a credulous victim to the newspaper reports. A few days later, I was called downstairs from my office at Phu My. A young Vietnamese man, unknown to me, explained that he came from the School of Social Work and his professor there had spoken so glowingly of my speech that he just wanted the honour of shaking my hand. Both extremities of reaction I found quite astonishing.

Wende Grant went to the Conference carrying posters that exhibited happy Vietnamese children who had been adopted by American families. For ten days there were group discussions on child health-care, delinquency, nutrition, education, and day-care. There were also heated discussions on the adoption of Vietnamese orphans abroad, but no one paid any attention to her two girls, although they had been introduced to the adoption section of the Conference.

FFAC's other important contribution to the Conference was to bring over Dr Jack Redman to address professional colleagues on the subject of pneumocystis carinii. We were eager to promote an awareness of this fatal disease amongst the medical profession in Vietnam and to develop ways of preventing, diagnosing and treating it. Dr Redman both presented his paper, and also met with the FFAC nurses to help them set up the preventative programme. At the same time he initiated a successful course of treatment for three-year-old Aeneas, who was judged to have a fulminating case of pneumocystis carinii.

The Conference took place against a background of shelling and increased military activity. We became more intensely aware of the fragile military/political situation in Saigon. And if Saigon seemed less secure, what about Cambodia, where the news was increasingly bad. Wende Grant, once back in the States, worried about the two Charet sisters now with the forty children in Phnom Penh, and kept in touch with Naomi Bronstein.

Both Marg and I wrote frequently to Wende:

4 February 1974, MM to WG: I have just a few minutes to write . . . and all I can think of saying is that it was lovely to have that 'family' reunion in January. I think that other things might have happened in January, too, but I was probably only dreaming.

At the moment I am in the middle of preparing Rathaven to accommodate the overflow of Hy Vong nurses, as I have two clear days before the next French-speaking people arrive. Rose and Ilse are going to Europe on Thursday, and Mary-Nelle is going East side to the States on the 13th. Jo and Ruth Egar are leaving 8 February.

We are about to apply for an amendment to the USAID grant as it seems we have only about 6,000 dollars left in it. At this particular moment, that should be fun. I'll let you know.

11 February 1975, WG to MM: If I could be of any possible help – doing papers, discussing cases with Miss Quoi, holding babies, filling out embarkation cards, preparing convoys, sorting clothes in the warehouse – let me know. Somehow I feel uneasy.

It seems as if President Ford will not get his supplementary appropriation for Vietnam and Cambodia. Perhaps Congress will approve a token amount. If Thieu was truthful about the 330 million being imperative to continuing his government, we'd better start planning to withdraw along with the others.

Wende had taken particular interest in a little girl called Diep-Marie, while she was with us in January. On 4 February, I sent her a report by Anne Barry:

Diep is a dear little eight-year-old, Afro-Amerasian girl: tall, slender, healthy and with a good physique. Her peculiar charm is her shyness, which often shelters the most winning of smiles. When Diep first arrived in the nursery with her friend, Elizabeth Dung, in early October 1974, she was extremely timid and fearful. She hid behind Elizabeth's vivacious personality and was a long time learning trust. When questioned about what she remembers, Diep spoke of a family of ten but it is difficult to tell whether she is speaking of her orphanage experience or earlier. She is extremely shy and cautious about speaking of herself.

Apart from this shyness, she is normal in every respect. At school she is a conscientious pupil, though it is too early to assess her ability. She especially likes art and spatial aptitude studies. She is most athletic, and loves best of all to climb and swim, and to play with her doll.

Wende, too, remembers her encounter with Diep-Marie:

In the classroom at the bottom of Allambie garden, Diep-Marie was sitting at a blackboard, writing 'I am a girl. I am a girl', in remarkably neat letters. With her close-cropped fuzzy hair, it may have been difficult to distinguish her sex until one saw her face. She had perfectly formed features; her skin was very dark. Had an artist struggled to design a face to typify the beauty, dignity and pride of an ancient race, he couldn't have matched the breath-taking Diep-Marie. While all of the children were beautiful, there was an ethereal quality to the symmetry of features, grace and colour of Diep-Marie ... Her written assertion of self – 'I am a girl' – completed the visual poem.

Diep-Marie was one of the children who died on the C-5A three months later.

On 6 February, Ilse and I escorted a group of children to Europe. We wanted to enlist more assistance, bring back penicillin, and discuss freight transportation with Air France in Paris. I also made profitable contact with the support groups, Song in Belgium, and Freunde de durch RJT . . . Waisenkinder, in Berlin. We were both back in Saigon by 15 February. Meanwhile, Mary-Nelle had left with a small group of children for the States. She intended to do some fund-raising while she was there. As things turned out, she did not get back to Saigon before the evacuation.

Since we had many children with special needs and handicaps in the nurseries, our success in finding homes for all of them with the least possible delay was naturally dependent on the agency having a long waiting list of prospective adoptive parents, ready to accept children with all variations of age, sex, racial background, physical health, and psychological development. But even though the primary goal of FFAC Colorado was to have numbers of selected, suitable families available, nonetheless the agency felt a degree of moral responsibility not to give parents unrealistic expectations and to keep to a minimum the number of families that might be finally disappointed:

26 February 1975, WG to RT: The news about Vietnam doesn't improve. If your crystal ball is any clearer than ours, do let us know your thoughts. We have 367 families with applications but no children assigned. We have eighty-four families with children assigned. Even if we lose 10 per cent of the active families, we will still have 330 with applications to whom we will be assigning children throughout the next twelve months. Then there are 400 waiting for applications, with a normal 30 per cent drop-out rate.

The question is: should we stop accepting pre-applications and just tell families we can't see any chance of their getting a child? Can you see two years ahead? one year? two months? two weeks?

You have mentioned March 1976 as the time our contract is up . . . If Saigon holds out beyond that, are you going to want to renew the contract . . .?

Every day there are more indications in the news that there will be no more US money for the Thieu government, and that without it Thieu will fall from power in six to eight months. It all comes back to the question as to whether we should continue as usual or whether we should just try to deal with the families already on our files.

Big Cuong from Tan Mai Orphanage had been at Allambie for some months, but we had not yet chosen an adoptive family for him because we had certain questions about his development. Marg and Lucienne LeGall (one of our close associates) were conducting interviews with all the older children; it was important to hear what they had to say about themselves, as well as what the orphanages told us. It had been obvious many times how the children's desire to suppress painful memories would cause them unconsciously to distort the facts and interpret time-sequences very freely. One day, seeing Marg and Lucienne speaking with other children, Cuong had come to the door, pointed to himself, and said 'Maman'. They took the hint and realized it was time to interview Cuong:

28 February 1975, Interview with Cuong, MM and LLeG:
Cuong is a slightly cross-eyed Vietnamese boy of about five years with his front teeth missing.
  His manner was plaintive. He was on the verge of tears initially and the interpreter spoke with her arms around him. He had a complex, almost an obsession about the fact that he had (still) no family. As far as his teeth would permit, his speech was normal and his comprehension good. His concentration span was normal. He cannot yet distinguish colours, write nor recognize numbers, etc. His IQ-range would seem to be 92–98 (normally educable if motivated) and his present problems in school, etc. are directly related to the fact of not belonging, which in turn induces reactionary behaviour. Once in a family, he should make normal progress.
  The following are answers to direct questions: He said he came from 'upstairs' and had lived there for a long time. He liked swimming but they wouldn't let him swim with the others because he ducked them under. He said he liked school but he was only going to the pre-school classes. They wouldn't let him

go to the afternoon classes with the other big children because he messed around. He said he often fought with the little kids, but added defensively that it wasn't just his fault. His friends had gone. He wanted to go to France, not America. He didn't care about brothers or sisters, he just wanted a mother and father. A big brother would be all right. He didn't want any sisters or any little ones around.

He remembered living in Gia Kiem (near Tan Mai on the road to Dalat) with his father, a cook, and his mother, a washing woman, who worked for 'Tonkinese'. His parents were Vietnamese. He had . . . been abandoned because 'they didn't want me'. He said he made trouble in the family. He still thought about his mother, nobody else.

He said that his favourite colour was black. We showed him a heap of crayons and asked him which colour was black. He took the red one. While he was fiddling with the crayons, the Vietnamese-Caucasian child laid up next door with chickenpox came in to see what was going on. The interpreter asked him if he played with Cuong and he said no, because Cuong was crazy.

Cuong said he liked to eat, was eating at the time a potato, and that the food here was good. He said that he would rather have a mother than be here and that he would like to go soon by plane to France. Then he made off with some matchboxes.

Cuong's French family was chosen shortly afterwards. He received photographs and information about his new parents and was an excited and proud little boy when he boarded the C-5A that crashed on 4 April. He died within the hour. His new name was to have been Aubin (Dawn) as he was coming from the East.

4 March 1975, Interview with Lien, MM to FFAC Colorado: Lien is a Cambodian-Vietnamese girl of ten years with a warm smile and beautiful features. She wore earrings and a silver cross both of which she said had been given her by the Sisters at Soctrang. She had a direct gaze, good carriage and an eloquent face. During the interview she showed almost every emotion except anger and bitterness.

The following are replies to direct questions: Lien lived the first six years of her life in a military camp somewhere in Military Region IV. She was the only child of a Cambodian soldier in the

Vietnamese Army and of a Vietnamese woman who used to sell candy to the children at the camp, with Lien at her heels. When Lien was five her mother died after a long illness which Lien said was 'grippe' (flu). They had been living in a tin shack on the camp with two military wives/widows whose husbands were not there. After she saw her mother die and be buried, she remained in the camp until a little after the death of her father about a year later. He was brought in from fighting and died from bullet wounds without regaining consciousness. She was there when he died.

The two women then took her to 'the market place at Khanh Hung' for 'a few days', returned her to the camp 'to collect a few things', and then 'threw her' into the Providence Orphanage at Khanh Hung. Neither the two women nor her mother's mother, who had visited the camp a few times previously, ever came to visit her at the Orphanage.

She said the Sisters were good to her, and that she spent most of the time with the Sisters, helping with the little ones. She said that her father had been a Buddhist, her mother a Catholic. She said that she wanted to be, but was not, a Catholic.

She had been taught at the Providence school by a Vietnamese lady (not a Sister) for a short time 'not long before she came here'. She 'left school' because the 'teacher hit her'. At this Lien shed two tears, so the line of questioning was not pursued.

Her best friend here was Ngoc-Diep, a little girl whom she knew must soon return to Vinh Long. She likes the little ones here, but did not know/like the other [four] children of her own age. She did not like swimming. She could do the 'easy things' at school. Her favourite colour was yellow, although she thought that was a bizarre question to ask a girl of her age.

The Sisters had sent her here 'to be happy'. She liked it here, mostly 'the Americans' here, but did not hesitate longer than politeness required before accepting the offer to stay with Mme LeGall until her new family was found.

Lien is a happy-natured, gentle little girl and seems of normal intelligence. She is sensitive, quiet and very lonely. She is not at all aggressive and one feels that her only outlet will be the security of an understanding family [MM].

But Lien also would die on the C-5A, together with her friend Ngoc-Diep.

7 March 1975, RT to WG: New passports: already one group of dossiers has passed Welfare under the new system [submitting separate dossiers concurrently to the Ministries of Social Welfare and of the Interior]. We are seeing some light at last. There will be many passports issued in the next weeks.

Pan Am announces the establishment of a flight from San Francisco to New York soon; we shall use that as a lever with Air France to persuade them to restore our excess baggage privilege.

In February and March sixty-six new dossiers were lodged with the Ministries, and more than forty exit visas and passports collected before the service closed down.

7 March 1975, RT to M-N Gage: Come back – we miss your sparkle. Remember we are trying to tie-up all loose ends by March 1976 [sic] – solve all Vietnam's problems that are within our scope to solve, and then get out . . .

I've just been to Court and to the bank. I'm writing this downtown at my little coffee-stall near Air France.

5 March 1975, inter-nursery memo from RT: According to the packing lists, the next shipment of supplies will include: 44 choirboy robes, 15 black priest robes (?), 1 washer; 1 portable sewing machine; 1 dryer. Please get your orders in early . . .

Ears: a formidable number of children sent abroad need surgery on their ears. The treatment for ear infections, even over a long period, seems to be ineffectual. Could you discuss this at the weekly nurses' conference? When writing child-reports please indicate holes in ear-drums. We ought to warn parents of the possibility of surgery, or hearing loss.

The nurses continued to hold their usual meetings, and discussed the treatment for chronic ear infections at their next meeting on 8 March. The same day I sent out another inter-nursery memo:

Yoghurt sugared costs 600 piastres a bowl, and unsugared costs 400. Therefore, we are ordering unsugared and each house can add some sucrative agents, e.g. – raspberry cobbler, fruit, lactose (of which we still have a large supply) or simply sugar. The yoghurt is made by the baker from our own powdered milk supply and the cost is written off against extra milk we have given to the bakery responsible. The brilliant idea behind this reintroduction of yoghurt into the diet is to replace the intestinal flora destroyed by antibiotics and thereby eliminating the necessity for bactisubtil, biolactyl, and other more expensive flora replacement pharmaceuticals.

That morning Wende had phoned from Colorado to say that she had determined on evacuating the Canadian Orphanage from Phnom Penh. The US affiliation of FFAC was essential to accomplish this, and as all commercial flights in and out of Phnom Penh had been cancelled for several weeks, they would have to evacuate via Saigon. I told the nurseries to prepare all nooks and crannies for the fifty Cambodian children.

Chapter 12

EVACUATION OF CANADA HOUSE
AT PHNOM PENH

12 March 1975 during the Communist Takeover
by Wende Grant

BY NOW the British Embassy, which handled Canadian affairs in Phnom Penh, had been evacuated and it was becoming increasingly dangerous for the orphans at Canada House. On 8 March, I called Naomi Bronstein and told her I was determined to see what I could do as the Director of an American agency registered in Vietnam to arrange their evacuation from Cambodia to Saigon. Naomi agreed that I should try, and that she would join me as soon as she could. A call to Rosemary in Saigon on Friday evening produced an escort ticket, which was cabled to San Francisco's Pan Am office by Saturday. I spent that day preparing a dossier, so that we could if necessary adopt some – or all – of the children should that prove the only way to get them out.

On the plane Ruth Routten introduced herself to me. Ruth was the airline stewardess who had been using her available free plane passes to fly to Saigon with supplies to help the orphanages, and had often acted as an escort taking groups of children to the US. Now she cheerfully offered to go along with me to Cambodia, an idea that had been seeming more dangerous and impossible as time went by. Ruth's instant acceptance of the scheme restored my confidence in the credibility of the attempt.

Margaret Moses was there to meet us at Tan Son Nhut, at 8.30 a.m. on 11 March. She had the day's meetings mapped out and we started off immediately. We went first to someone in USAID, who contacted an official in the American Embassy. A friend in California had already approached Senator Tunney for assistance in evacuating the Canadian nursery; the Embassy was already in receipt of the Senator's cable requesting that every assistance be made available for the rescue project. We were already guaranteed a flight into Cambodia and a plane to take the children out.

An aide of Dr Dan's explained the procedure for securing the permission of the Vietnamese government to bring the children into Saigon for some months. The plan was meeting with surprising acceptance and as the day progressed our optimism grew. A phone call to Air America, mentioning several names, secured a seat on an early morning flight to Phnom Penh. Very early on Wednesday morning I boarded a plane with five men. There had been only one available seat. Ruth cheerfully loaned me her flight bag and said she'd hitch a ride into Phnom Penh in a day or two. The plane wasn't pressurized or heated; I clutched Ruth's flight bag that held every item I had with me and hoped not to freeze to death. I carried some 3,000 dollars, fully intending to buy or bribe exit authority for the children as a last resort.

It was well-known that Air America was run by the CIA, and also known that Air America flew regular flights within Vietnam and to adjoining countries. Entering through the rear of the small plane, the cargo had been clearly visible. It consisted of furniture. There was a couch, chairs and tables. There were no closed cartons or crates that one could have imagined as holding guns, ammunition, or even secret documents. The front compartment consisted of two single seats and two facing benches with a table between, where I sat with three other passengers.

One of them advised me to watch carefully as we landed in Phnom Penh and I might see some rockets hit the airport. There was nothing I wanted to see less than a rocket hit, but I looked as directed and did see two puffs of smoke on the runway. Some of the men put on flak vests and helmets before getting out. For the hundredth time that morning I wondered what I was doing and how to get myself out of it. One of the others agreed to give me a ride to Canada House. Entering the gates gave the impression of stepping into another world. It was an old wooden house with the main living quarters on the upper floor. The large yard had flower beds, trees and grass with children's play equipment. Around the play equipment were laughing children; Dolly and Anna Charet were out, but Anha, the Cambodian cook, manager and house-mother, gave me iced tea. She talked to me in French which I didn't understand: I answered in English which she didn't understand. It was, however, very friendly and peaceful but I was overwhelmed with a sense of my mission being ridiculous. The plane trip, the rockets at the airport, the burned-out sections of Phnom Penh that we had driven through on the way from the airport – I must have imagined or at least exaggerated them in my mind.

The Cambodian secretary for Canada House arrived to talk to me. He spoke Cambodian, French and English, and what he said jolted me back to reality. He wanted to know if I had come to take the children out. I said I was going to try. He agreed that it was a good idea and started to describe his own children; how they were good and obedient, studied hard and were intelligent. He would like them to live, he said with great dignity, and asked if I could take his children out and place them for adoption, too. He had been working on adoption papers for several months and knew the meaning of placing a child for adoption. As kindly as I could, I refused, explaining that if we succeeded in taking any children out, it would only be orphans.

The Charet sisters were relieved that I had come. Explanations tumbled out: they were determined not to abandon the children, but so far neither the British nor US Embassies would consider evacuating the orphans along with their personnel. It was impossible to complete adoptions because officials were unavailable to sign papers. Foreign embassy staff had advised the girls to flee without the children; and to commit suicide should the Khmer Rouge take Phnom Penh before they could evacuate.

For several days we made the rounds of Cambodian officials – who stayed at home most of the time – and the US Embassy. Mr Dy Bellong was one of the officials who listened to our request. In August of 1974 he had discussed child welfare needs with us and given every assistance. A friendly and energetic man, he had invited us to his lovely home, introduced to us his adopted four-year-old daughter, discussed his older children, and served us tea. In March of 1975 we were again at his home, seated in the garden drinking the inevitable tea. Gunfire and the roar of planes filled in frequent pauses in the conversation. Dy Bellong seemingly had difficulty following the discussion. He gazed at the chickens and the more exotic birds marching through the garden. Several times he interrupted his own sentences to name a particular bird. His eyes shifted to the house, the trees, the sky. Slowly, without expression, he listed the steps we should take and the people we should see. With automatic courtesy he bade us goodbye and good luck. Even as he foresaw his death and the deaths of his family – the end of his own world – he carried out his duty as Member of the Executive Cabinet of the Republic in charge of the Intergovernmental Relations Office for Foreign Aid.

We were trying to get people to put forth extra effort to save forty-three orphans, knowing there were tens of thousands, including their own children, who would not be saved. After several days of repeated visits, the permission was given. An official letter had arrived from the Vietnamese government to say the children would be accepted in Vietnam and that Friends For All Children would be responsible.

Naomi Bronstein and Ruth Routten arrived Friday afternoon on another Air America flight. Faced with no space at Canada House or at the Hotel Phnom, we went to the home of Mr Middleton, the British Chargé d'Affaires and the only British official left in Phnom Penh, and asked if we could stay with him. With utmost courtesy he invited us in, found sheets and towels and opened lovely bedrooms that had been closed up, awaiting the inevitable takeover.

A young Cambodian physician in the Ministry of Interior was responsible for signing the children's joint passport and exit authorization. We saw him late Thursday afternoon. As he spoke with Dolly Charet in French, I saw that his body was twitching uncontrollably; Dolly explained later that the man knew he would be killed. He was worried about being able to fulfil his duties until the end and he wanted to be sure someone would care for his infant son. He had asked Dolly if she would adopt the child if he could get him out of the country.

On Saturday morning, Anna Charet and I set out to get my adoption papers signed for the six-week-old twin girls I was adopting from Canada House. Naomi Bronstein, Ruth Routten and Dolly Charet finished final preparations for departure. In the afternoon a woman came to Canada House to relinquish her two-year-old daughter. The woman was a refugee and had been seriously wounded; she could walk only with great pain. All alternatives were explored; she was offered food, clothing and money to care for the child but the woman was adamant: when the food and money were gone, she would still be unable to support herself or her little girl. Her pain and the child's anguish underscored again the agony of Cambodia. In the end we decided to take her, but when the *laissez-passer* came, the child's name was not on the list and we had to leave her behind, with one other little boy.

On that Saturday, 15 March, the shelling was markedly intensified. Anna and I were a block from the American Embassy when three shells came in so close that all the bystanders flattened themselves against the curb.

At Canada House that afternoon the children were taken into a sandbagged bunker beneath the house and heavy firing continued until the following morning. During the night there was no way for us to know where the fighting was, but we feared that the airport might be taken.

The rice flights resumed on Sunday, proving that the airport still held. At times that afternoon we could see half-a-dozen supply-planes stacked up, circling and waiting their turn for a steep descent and landing. The plane came for us on Monday morning. All children were dressed in three complete layers of clothing, both to ward off the cold temperatures of the plane and to ensure some supply of clothes in Saigon. Tiny babies were packed four and five to a bassinet. Strong nylon netting was laced over the top so that the whole basket could be strapped in a double plane seat, and the infants couldn't bounce out in the turbulence. Supplies of infant formula were packed, along with essential papers and medicines.

The Cambodian staff prepared the large truck that had been loaned by a friend in Phnom Penh. It had heavy wooden sides perhaps two feet high and then a canvas cover over a higher metal frame. The children were loaded along the sides in the hope that the wood would deflect flying debris if a rocket hit close by during the drive to the airport. The Cambodian child-care workers, the young guards, the secretary and Anha, the cook, packed and loaded while their tears fell. Anha picked flowers and put them in our hair. She told me that when we returned she would make good meals for us.

As we drove slowly out of the gate, the entire staff walked behind the truck, saying goodbye, wishing us luck and crying. We could only cry. The US Embassy sent a radio-equipped car to synchronize our arrival with the landing of the plane. The truck backed up to the plane as it taxied to a stop. Children and supplies were rapidly transferred. In seven minutes we were taking off for Saigon. Christie, Ilse, Birgit and Dr Merritt Stark were in the plane to help with the children. [WG]

Chapter 13

EVACUATION PLANS
Easter Week, March–April 1975

THE EVACUATION of the Cambodian children to Saigon was an operation of almost unbelievable virtuosity and conducted with total discretion, unmarred by media leakages. In Saigon, Margaret had obtained the entry authorization. Immigration had been alerted and Welfare officials were at Tan Son Nhut airport to facilitate entry. The children, by-passing formalities, were taken immediately to the nearby IRC [International Rescue Committee] Clinic for a preliminary check-up, and then on to a special facility in Thu Duc that Lucienne LeGall had rented and equipped in two days.

Friends For All Children had guaranteed responsibility for the children and they were listed as being under our 'guardianship', but their care and all expenses were assumed by the Canadian agency. FFC assigned them to families, and the children left by commercial planes as their entry visas were granted by Canada or the USA. Within a week, Thu Duc became an unsafe area and the remaining Cambodian children were brought to Saigon where they camped on the floor of Rathaven pharmacy. Their scheduled Air France flight was first delayed, then cancelled.

Dr Phyllis Kaplan, a psychologist, returned to Saigon in mid-March for the two weeks of her Easter vacation and made up-dated reports on all the 'special need' children she had come over to work with the previous December. Right up until the last days we were to continue with plans for developing our laboratory, improving child care, and the functioning of the nurseries. At the end of February 1975, FFAC nurseries were caring for 533 children, officially registered with the Ministry. There were also more than fifty children still resident at Phu My, whose departures were being processed by FFAC; this number increased daily as more of the orphans still in the northern provinces (Quang Nam, Binh Dinh, Phu Yen) were able to be brought to Saigon to await departure. The adoption formalities for most of these children were completed or nearing completion. Following normal procedures, we had sent altogether 179 children on regular commercial flights in the first months of 1975.

The central provinces fell one by one to the North Vietnamese with tens of thousands of refugees converging on Danang, Qui Nhon, and Nha Trang. On 26 March we met with the Minister of Welfare and members of other voluntary agencies to discuss ways of assisting the refugees. Dr Dan spoke bravely of relocating them within a month in areas outside the cities. It was an incredibly unrealistic proposition given the magnitude of the task, and probably he knew it in his heart. In Military Regions I and II there were an estimated 800,000 refugees according to the information sheets we received.

27 March 1975, memo from MM to RT: In the event of a communist takeover, it is assumed that all children in the FFAC facilities would be evacuated by the US government, whether they were placed by FFAC in Colorado or by agencies legally affiliated in other countries.

The time frame involved seems to depend on whether or not Danang falls. If it does, it is assumed that it will fall within two weeks. After that, Nha Trang. If the troops stranded in these positions cannot get out, then it is assumed that Saigon will fall within or after three months. The unpredictable factor is the rain.

At the moment, a takeover is more likely than a coalition. It is unlikely that the present government will be allowed to last until the normal election time, which is October. It is also unlikely that the Communists, Viet Cong, National Liberation Front or whatever they are called, will sit down to discuss a coalition.

I think I am saying that we should proceed as usual, which seems on the face of it a pretty damn stupid thing to say. If Danang does not fall, most of the above cancels out for quite a while. Apparently, there is so much panic there with the one million refugees; plus the normal population; plus the fact that the army is trying to board its wives and families; plus the fact that the people are choking the streets so that the buses cannot get to the planes to board them; that the planes are (a) leaving every forty-five minutes instead of every twelve, and (b) are coming out one-third full in order to clear the tarmac for the next three planes which are hovering around trying to land and using up all their fuel. There seems to be no one up there who can enforce martial law.

The same day the Ministry sent out an official document to all the welfare agencies estimating the numbers of refugees converging on the provinces of Khanh Hoa, Ninh Thuan, Binh Thuan, and Tuyen Duc.

Sacred Heart Orphanage in Danang had telephoned us to come up and take out the children, and St Paul's Orphanage in Qui Nhon also sent down urgent messages for us to evacuate the entire orphanage to Saigon. It was impossible to find air transport – even Air America refused to take us. Mr Jacobsen at the US Embassy heard our story, promised to phone back and never did. A few days later Danang fell and communication was cut off completely. Then Qui Nhon fell and we heard no more from the Sisters at St Paul's. Some of the orphanages in the middle coastal provinces did manage to evacuate to Saigon or Vung Tau. Phu My Orphanage in Saigon prepared to receive large numbers of refugee orphans and I was able to give Sr Rose some money to buy more beds.

No one knew how much time we had before Saigon would fall. Some thought it might be six months, others not as long.

Wende Grant had stayed on in Saigon after the Cambodian evacuation and Elaine Moir had come to assist with the departure of children for Australia. On Easter Sunday, 30 March, Wende and Elaine worked on the children's dossiers in the Rathaven office, categorizing them according to the progress of their documentation. For five minutes each hour they listened to the radio news bulletins: Danang had fallen. They realized then that there would probably be no time to arrange normal departures for our children, even with expedited visas; Margaret agreed.

An evacuation plan for US personnel in Saigon was already under discussion. The following bulletin had been issued:

Should it be felt necessary for US personnel to report to their designated assembly areas, a coded message will be broadcast over American Radio Service. This message will consist of a temperature report for Saigon of '105 degrees and rising' followed by approximately the first thirty seconds of 'I'm dreaming of a white Christmas'. This message will be broadcast every fifteen minutes for approximately two hours.

If you hear the above message, report, with travel documentation, to your nearest assembly point. Stay tuned to American Radio Station FM 99.9 (primary) or FM 90.1 (secondary) for further announcements.

Attached to this was a map of Saigon and a list of the twelve emergency assembly locations.

There were now about 600 children under FFAC care in the four nurseries, including the remaining Cambodian refugees. The children were cared for in shifts by the 400 local staff and fifteen foreign staff nurses and administrators. Should the situation in Saigon deteriorate, the Vietnamese staff would be unable to report for work, and without them there would be no way in which the rest of us could cope. It would be physically impossible to transport so many children to the airport or to the helicopter pick-up points in the event of an emergency evacuation. The radio newscasts on Easter Sunday were reporting on the panic in Danang and the clogging of all circulation; it could be much worse in Saigon.

No one considered leaving the children behind. It was accepted that if the children did not depart prior to a change of regime, they would never leave Vietnam for the families that awaited them in other countries. The only logical solution in Wende's mind was to evacuate our children before there was an acute shortage of food and medical supplies, before Saigon could be flooded with refugees, before the fighting was too close to the city, and before the airport could be closed by shelling or a panic-stricken populace. Once this was clear, there was no time to be lost and everyone started working on this plan immediately. In the late afternoon I went to Rathaven, and accepted the necessity of an evacuation without further discussion. It was still Easter Sunday.

There were three basic requirements for evacuating the children in FFAC care: government permission for the children to leave prior to completion of the usual formalities; entry authorization into some other country; and means of transportation. That evening we composed a letter to Dr Dan, requesting authorization to remove the children. We prepared memos to the nurseries warning them of the departure and of the need to pack supplies for three days. Each nursery was to submit to the office the names of all resident children in permanent custody with notations concerning their travel fitness. Children in temporary care only should be returned to the family or orphanage of origin; and children in foster care with private families should be brought back to the nurseries.

Long past curfew we learnt in another broadcast that Mr Ed Daly, the President of World Airways, had flown into Danang that day in an attempt to evacuate some of the refugees crowding the city; the attempt had failed and Mr Daly was back in Saigon at the Caravelle Hotel. Wende and Elaine Moir made an appointment to see him in the hope that his airline could help us.

The interview with an overwrought Mr Daly consisted mostly of listening to three or four recountings of his day's adventures in Danang. Wende was finally able to outline FFAC's need and received an immediate promise of a 747 plane to evacuate the children to the US. They weren't entirely reassured by a somewhat precipitate promise, but it seemed at least hopeful. They returned to Rathaven at about 2.30 a.m.

Early on Easter morning, 31 March, the letter to Dr Dan was delivered, since only the Vietnamese government could approve the children's departure. The letter is reproduced in full:

FRIENDS FOR ALL CHILDREN

445 South 68th Street
Boulder, Colorado 80303
Telephone (303) 494–7305

31 Phan-Dinh-Phung
Saigon
Telephone: 24101

30 March 1975

Dr Phan Quang Dan
Deputy Prime Minister
Concurrently Minister of Social Welfare in charge of LDHB
Ministry of Social Welfare
138 Hai Ba Trung   SAIGON

Dear Dr Dan
The events of the past two weeks lead us to believe that it is imperative that we evacuate the children under our care for the sake

of their safety. We would request that a *Laissez-Passer* be given to the children whose names will be submitted and for whom we are, and will remain, legally responsible.

We will arrange transportation for these children, entry visas and completion of formalities of adoption. There are currently approved families available for all children.

As stated in our Agreement (BXH 1928, 8 March 1974) our facilities, in the event of our departure, are to be designated to any charitable organization approved by the Ministry of Social Welfare. We would suggest that the best use of these facilities would be made by the Sisters of Providence and the Sisters of St. Paul de Chartres, whom we would continue to support.

This request for a *Laissez-Passer* does not constitute a request for termination of Agreement. We would greatly appreciate it if our Agreement were to remain valid until 8 March 1976 as stated at the time of signature.

Yours sincerely [signed]
WENDE S. GRANT
Director

The memos to the nurseries were delivered that same morning, and as the information on the children came back to the office, it was collated into lists, by country of destination, with names and birth dates of the children together with names and addresses of adoptive parents. The total information on each child was put on an index card and to this was stapled a photograph and birth certificate.

The idea of the evacuation of the children certainly did not originate with the US government. FFAC did, however, use our contact with USAID to assist in obtaining the authorization. But since the Vietnamese government's approval had to be predicated on the willingness of a host country to receive the children, the US Ambassador hoped we, in turn, would mediate with the US government through our American home office.

At 4.30 p.m., Wende received a phone call from Ray Fontaine, our contact, who said that Dr Dan would be unable to grant our request for a *laissez-passer*. The Holt agency had also requested permission to remove their children, he said, and had been refused. The government was afraid of granting permission in case it created panic in Saigon. Wende professed to understand, but she asked Ray to tell Dr Dan that she was leaving Saigon next day and would give a press conference in San Francisco as the best way of informing adoptive parents they would probably not now have their children.

At 7.00 p.m. Ray phoned back to Wende with a message from Ambassador Martin saying that he was meeting with Dr Dan and the President at that time, and he expected Dr Dan to raise the question of the children and obtain a favourable response:

7.25 p.m., from Dr Dan, through Ray Fontaine, message received by MM: Dan has approved and will take all papers of the children to the Prime Minister tomorrow morning. These papers are to be left with Ray at 123 Doan thi Diem, appt. 31, at 7.30 a.m. on 1 April.

Additional message: Happy April Fool's Day, optional. See you later: Marg.

We spent all that night, 31 March, in the office preparing the lists to be submitted next morning to the Prime Minister. The list-making continued for the next four days and nights, working round the clock and snatching an occasional hour's nap when it became impossible to continue functioning.

Mr Daly's offer of the 747 plane didn't survive twenty-four hours. On Monday it was changed to two smaller planes: one was to go to Australia and the other to the United States. Travel lists were prepared accordingly; children destined for Europe and Australia would go on the Australian plane; those for the US and Canada would take the other flight. But before another day had elapsed, the offer of transportation had changed again to one plane for 300 children to go to Australia. Then it was 'no plane at all'.

Wende, scheduled to leave with her Cambodian twins on Tuesday, 1 April, cancelled her own departure in order to continue assisting with the evacuation of the rest of the FFAC children. By early Wednesday morning, World Airways made a new offer of a DC-8 cargo plane that would hold 600 children – not one less – who were to be boarded in half-an-hour for the most dramatic, action-packed television coverage. The conditions were physically impossible. We could never board so many children in such a short time, and we could not provide adequate escorts for 600 children under those conditions. We had to refuse the offer on Wednesday afternoon. That night the World Airways flight left Tan Son Nhut with an unspectacular load of 60 children from another agency.

The Prime Minister finally authorized the departure of our children. On Thursday, 3 April, USAID called a meeting and promised us a 'medivac' – military hospital-plane – fully equipped for transporting babies. This was the first indication of official US help in the matter of transportation. No other country had yet cared to become involved, although we had asked France and Germany at least to transport their own children. We continued, nevertheless, with our efforts to obtain private chartered planes.

EMBASSY OF THE
UNITED STATES OF AMERICA

US Aid Mission to Vietnam   3 April 1975

Ms Rosemary Taylor
Friends For All Children
207 Hien Vuong St
Saigon

Dear Ms Taylor,
This will confirm the message communicated to you by telephone Thursday morning, April 3.

The Office of Deputy Prime Minister and Minister of Social Welfare, Dr Phan Quang Dan, advises the GVN-authorized inter-country adoption agencies that the Ministry of Interior requires, of each of these agencies taking advantage of the authorization to evacuate overseas children in their care, a list (four copies) of all children expected to be evacuated. The name and age of each child is required. One copy of the list should also be sent to the Ministry of Social Welfare.

Telephone contacts: Ministry of Interior: PTT-24058
Ministry of Social Welfare: Dr Cao Xuan An, PTT-99271

> Sincerely [signed]
> Robert L. King, Chief
> Social Welfare Division
> Relief and Rehabilitation

Late Thursday afternoon there was another message from Ambassador Martin informing us that John Wetterer was arriving on an Air France flight the next day with 2,000 lb of medication. The Embassy had been asked to assist him with transporting the supplies from the airport.

On 4 April, I was surprised to receive a circular letter from the Australian Embassy advising me to leave 'while commercial travel facilities are still available', and warning me that the Embassy 'may not be able to guarantee my safety or arrange for my departure later'. In my eight years in Vietnam I had requested very little from the Australian Embassy. It never occurred to me to regard them as guarantors of my safety or as responsible in any way for arranging my departure. But I was grateful for the kind personal offer of the last Consul, Mr R. Devereux, who invited us to send our luggage to the Consulate for inclusion with his own personal effects for transportation to Australia. In this way, I managed to save several boxes of books and photograph albums that would have been impossible to take out in any other way, given the circumstances of our eventual departure.

Chapter 14

THE CRASH OF THE C-5A

A Collation of Accounts
4 and 5 April 1975

Rosemary Taylor: About 2 a.m. on Friday I returned to Phu My in a Mission Warden car. Kneeling by the bedside for the next five hours, I continued sorting documents and dossiers which were spread all over the bed and the floor. By 8.00 I was back at Rathaven Office.

Wende Grant: Before dawn on Friday Duane, my husband, telephoned from Colorado. A Pan Am pilot had called the Boulder office about a plane in Hong Kong scheduled to return empty to the US. He volunteered to fly the plane for us if Pan Am agreed to the charter. The Colorado Staff were working on it but we should also approach the airline at this end.

Margaret and I were at the Pan Am office as soon as it opened. Al Topping, the Manager, was in conference with the Regional Director from Hong Kong. We waited in an adjoining room and were able to overhear enough of the conversation to make it clear that FFAC would *not* be getting the 747 plane in Hong Kong. Another agency had chartered it.

Before we could talk with Pan Am, a call came in from Bob King of USAID. The US had authorized transportation for the Vietnamese orphans scheduled to leave Saigon, and there was a US military C-5A departing that afternoon. Mr King was offering space for 230 children. If FFAC chose not to take the flight, USAID would approach other agencies. He assured us that the C-5A had seats, seat belts, oxygen and emergency evacuation equipment. Margaret and I discussed the plan for a few minutes and agreed to accept the offer.

We were back in the office by 9.30 a.m. and announced the departure of 230 children for that same afternoon.

RT: A Pan Am plane was still a possibility, but we had spent a nerve-racking week with each promise and possibility evaporating. The children in each nursery had been prepared for instant evacuation and the nurseries had continued in this state of alert and uncertainty day after day – clothes and food piled up in the entrances. We had been up night after night working on the medical records and identification data. The nights were under strict curfew and so in order to circulate we had to call a US Mission Warden car to make the necessary excursions between the office, Phu My and the nurseries at 2 or 3 a.m. We were intensely calm and systematic. Twice the word had been given to the nurseries and to Phu My to dress the children for immediate pick-up. Both times the emergency procedures had to be interrupted and the staff expected to proceed with normal routine.

Although the C-5A was not the medivac plane we had been promised, we accepted it since nothing better had materialized. Time was running out.

We rapidly studied the nursery lists. For this flight we checked off the older children and healthier babies: all of the Allambie children; fifty-two from Phu My; sixty of the healthier babies from To Am; and twenty-two from Newhaven. None of the babies from Hy Vong were considered well-enough to go on this flight.

WG: The buses were to pick up the children from the nurseries at about 2 p.m., for the 4 p.m. flight from Tan Son Nhut. Shortly before noon, I left the office and went into the house to pack my bags. My return ticket to the US had been for Tuesday, 1 April: on that Friday, 4 April, it seemed more like three weeks than the three days since I had sent my two-month-old Cambodian twin girls off. It was with relief and excitement that I now packed and carefully labelled the bags.

When I said goodbye to Rosemary, still intensely absorbed in checking lists in the office, I felt suddenly guilty for wanting so much to leave. Over half the children – all small babies – would still remain. I asked if she would like me to stay until the rest could leave. (As the American Director of FFAC, I could probably be useful.) 'That would be great if you could. Maybe someone could go in your place today?' She returned to her lists and I went to find Margaret to ask her to go to the US rather than to Australia.

In a few pointed words, Marg let me know that going to the US with the first 230 children hardly headed her lists of desirable projects but, nevertheless, she accepted the inevitability of such a plan and agreed to go. While her mother packed a small bag for her, Marg and I found a battered old suitcase to hold the children's documents; there wasn't time to sort out the cards for the children scheduled for that day's departure, so we jammed all the cards into the case. With a 'See you', Margaret left for Allambie to board the bus with the older children.

Birgit Blank left with her adopted baby, Sven. I sat alone in the office watching the others leave. Several reporters called: I told them the Director wasn't there and I didn't know anything. I wondered how my family was coping with the twins, and how long it would be before I could go home to join them.

RT: Phones were out of order in two of the nurseries. We sent a messenger to To Am and I myself raced to Newhaven to tell them to prepare twenty-two of their strongest children for departure in one hour. En route to Newhaven I had met Sr Ursula from the Good Shepherd Sisters at Vinh Long, and invited her to go with the children leaving that afternoon for the USA as we needed nurses to care for them. Although about to depart for Malaysia, she revised her plans immediately, happy to be able to help. After dropping me at Phu My she continued to her convent at Binh Trieu to alert them to this new arrangement. At Phu My, I supervised the dressing and name-tagging of the fifty-two children (a number of whom were in transit from Sacred Heart Orphanage, Danang, and other orphanages in the northern provinces), loaded them in the bus sent by USAID, and accompanied them to the airport, confident in the knowledge that the other nurseries could be relied on to organize their own departures independently.

Susan McDonald: The plane was first due to leave at 11 a.m.; then 2 p.m.; finally 4 p.m. Must have the healthiest children from Newhaven ready at 2.30 p.m. Would there be a bus? The phone service was getting steadily worse as the day went by and there was no contact with the office at Rathaven. Muoi, our cyclo driver, was working full-time in the garden (his favourite work) since all cyclos were banned from the roads by the government.

By 2.30 we had all the departing children and their in-flight luggage (bottles, diapers, pyjamas, blankets) in the yard. There were no pick-up buses so the America-bound children were transported to Allambie in four available cars that were standing by.

As the bus for the Australian children was due to arrive at 3 p.m., we began immediately to prepare them for departure.

Marg phoned from Allambie: 'I'm going on the American plane instead of the Australian, Susan. Wende will be able to stay and help, and go on a later plane. Tell Rosemary I've got *ALL* the documents. Tell her I'm taking all the children's cards with me. Susan, I just called to say goodbye . . . and I do hope I'll see you again, Susan.' She spoke the last sentence in a wistful voice and I responded with 'Oh, Marg' in a voice that said, 'cut the drama'. 'Be sure to tell Rose I've got *all* the cards,' she reiterated.

Babies going to Australia were then assembled in the yard, two to a basket. By the time Elaine's bus arrived at 3 p.m., I discovered I had sent Dean, Don's twin, to Allambie with the other children, and the twins were destined for Australia. The phone was then working so I called Marg and alerted her that there was a well-marked, little, four-month-old named Dean in the crowd of 120 children at Allambie, who should be sent back to Newhaven. Marg seemed amused and said she would take care of it.

By the time Dean arrived back in Newhaven, the Australian bus had come and gone, so I jumped into a taxi and took the baby to the Australian Embassy just two blocks away. Elaine Moir was there looking very fatigued and holding Otto in her arms.

Mary Cusack: We selected sixty of the stronger To Am babies for the C-5A flight, still hoping that the weaker babies would be transported in something better than a cargo plane. There was a plane scheduled for Australia that same day, with fifty of our children, mostly the tiny sick babies from Hy Vong, but also some handicapped children from To Am and Allambie.

I had already told Rosemary that I would stay in Saigon for as long as needed. I was not scheduled to go on any plane on 4 April, but about noon, Elaine Moir, organizing the Australian side of the evacuation, phoned me and asked if I would go in place of Marg who was now going on the American plane. I was to travel only as far as Bangkok on the Hercules transport. There the children would be transferred to a fully equipped 747 and I would continue on the Hercules to Butterworth, the Australian Air Force base in Malaysia, returning the following day on an air force plane to Saigon. I agreed to go.

The bus for the American C-5A flight arrived at To Am. No sooner had this bus pulled out of the lane with sixty of our babies, than the Australian bus pulled in.

RT: At Tan Son Nhut, as we waited on the tarmac, I saw Marg accompanying the Allambie children; she was wearing a dress I recognized as Lydia's. I said nothing to her; I merely grimaced. The situation was beyond words and too unreal for pleasantries. I didn't even realize that Marg intended going with the plane; I had trusted the common sense of the staff to sort themselves out appropriately, with some of them accompanying this flight and some staying over to accompany the smaller babies on the next flight. There was no point in imagining the confusion of this trip with far too few escorts: Christie Leivermann, Birgit Blank, Lee Makk, Dolly Bui, Tina Bui, Sr Ursula, and three other American women who had volunteered to help. But I knew the strength of each one of our nurses, most of whom were experienced escorts, and I knew they would work with a super-human courage.

Phu My children boarded first. As I walked up the steps carrying a baby, I was momentarily stunned at the dimensions of the plane. The first children were taken to the upper level which had a passenger configuration. The babies, sweltering and screaming, were strapped tightly, two to a seat, by the well-meaning air force personnel, who were helping us board the children. The babies were not supported adequately as there were not enough cushions available. I followed after, trying to prevent them from strangling themselves by slipping under the seat belts or smothering as they slid over on top of each other. My mind was numb with horror at the distress of the children, and as the air force worked at top speed to strap them in, I hunted up a canteen of water, found a paper cup, and went around giving each child a drop of water with my fingers since the bottles had not yet been loaded. At that moment Christie

Leivermann was the only escort attending the babies on the upper level. Impossible to say exactly how many children were with her, but we presume all the Phu My children and all the Newhaven children. To Am and Allambie must have had children on both levels.

When the upper level was crammed beyond capacity, I said goodbye to Christie in a state bordering on stupor, and climbed down the perpendicular ladder to the lower deck. I was vaguely aware of the children and adults crowded over the floor of the front end of the plane but I couldn't take in any more details after the shock of the scene above. Pat Zirk, in charge of Allambie, stumbled over to me and her shock reflected my own. We speechlessly supported each other off the plane. Just at that moment, Birgit came over, holding out little Sven to kiss us goodbye, and Dolly, with baby David gave us an excited farewell embrace.

Back on the tarmac we stood by to help load the supplies of milk, clothing, blankets, food and the bags with medical records on all the children. Ilse was already down below in the ambulance after saying goodbye to her adopted daughter Monique. Now I realized that Marg was going on the flight I was immensely relieved, knowing that she would organize the arrival with her usual competence: she knew the children and would ensure that they reached their proper destinations. Marg would assume all responsibility for the departing children and we could freely turn our minds to the children who remained.

Reporters and cameramen began to annoy and crowd us so instead of waiting for take-off, we drove away quickly, scuttling the newsmen as we went.

Back at Rathaven, Wende told us that USAID had phoned: there had been problems because none of the escorts, except for Margaret, had an exit visa and were thus not authorized to depart. At such short notice it had been totally impossible to obtain exit visas and now the escorts might have to leave the plane . . . We sat and waited to see what would happen. When nothing happened we presumed the plane had taken off with all escorts aboard. I went over to Newhaven to report to Susan.

WG: Thirty minutes passed. I was worried about Dolly who, holding a German passport, was married to Bui van To, a

Vietnamese; To had no exit authorization, but had been promised a place on the German evacuation plane scheduled to leave that same day. Dolly and her three dependent children could have gone on the German plane, but she opted to help with the FFAC children on the C-5A. She realized, too, that this would leave more room on the German plane and a better chance of a place for her husband. If, however, FFAC escorts were unable to leave because of lack of exit authorization, Dolly and her children could be left in Vietnam while To was in Germany or France . . .

Sometime after 4 p.m. the phone rang; it was Jay Ruoff of USAID. I braced myself to hear that the FFAC staff and children had been refused permission to depart. I remember the conversation as if it were an often-played recording:

'Wende, this is Jay Ruoff.'

'Yes, Jay.'

'How are you feeling?'

'Jay, I'm feeling sorry for myself that I'm still here. I want to go home.'

'You have to hold on, Wende. I have to tell you something.'

'What is it?'

'The plane has crashed. It went down just outside Tan Son Nhut.'

I could say nothing.

'Wende, there are some survivors. You must get your best medical personnel and emergency supplies and get out to Tan Son Nhut immediately.'

'All right, Jay. We will do that.'

'Wende, are you all right?'

'I'm all right, Jay. We will go out right away. Thank you for calling.'

Running for the house it was already clear to me that I couldn't think about it. I could only try to do what was necessary. First, I had to find out that it was a minor accident; that there were some injuries but no deaths. Ilse Ewald and Naomi Bronstein were the first two people I saw in the house. Within two minutes we were heading for the airport, but decided on the way to go to the Adventist Hospital instead.

Arriving at the emergency ward we saw an ambulance pull up and Christie stepped unaided from the back. 'Thank God,' I thought. Surely if Christie was uninjured the others couldn't be dead. I began to rehearse in my mind something clever to say to Marg, who would surely be terribly annoyed with me for making her take my place on that flight.

On the ambulance with Christie were some children who were carried into the emergency room, three or four to a stretcher. They were muddy and silent but appeared to be without injury. We asked Christie what had happened. 'The whole God-damned back end of the plane blew out; that's what happened,' she replied with sheer anger. We asked for Dolly, Marg, Birgit. She said they had been on the lower deck; she had been on the upper; she didn't know.

More ambulances pulled in, tyres screeching and sirens wailing. Ilse, Naomi and I reviewed our memories of what each escort had worn. As the stretchers were whisked from ambulance to emergency room door, we scanned the occupant for the yellow slacks of Birgit, Dolly's white slacks, Margaret's navy-blue dress. We checked the injured who were laid out in rows on the floor of the emergency room; none of them were FFAC staff. I spoke to one of the C-5A crew members who was sitting in the emergency room, asking about those on the lower deck of the plane, trying to make him understand how many children and staff had been on the lower level. He told me how God knows every sparrow that falls. I stared at him, stupefied. Finally, I comprehended what he was saying and stumbled outside.

Rosemary and Susan ran in from the street gate. Their faces were white and contorted with pain.

SMcD: At 3.45, I was in Newhaven where the women were rearranging the house after the departure. There were several ill babies needing attention. Penumbra had watery stools, but the IV was running well. Charles had a terrible cough. The children with measles seemed to be improving except for Perth who needed to be sent to the IRC Clinic; Mai would take him. Hong, Lieu, Suu and Lien arrived back at the house after boarding the children on the C-5A: 'Too many children,' Hong said, 'and the plane was *big* – but the Newhaven children ... they were the best ... didn't cry.' Hong's eyes were all excited and happy as her eyes mostly always were. I was feeling decidedly anxious and was wishing it was over.

Rosemary walked into the house shortly after 4.00, terribly

uneasy. I poured her a cup of coffee. 'The plane isn't safe – nothing like we had been told. Nothing on the floor – no mattresses – just the bare floor. And I don't know how they are going to be able to watch all those babies. Only Dr Stark and Christie were with the babies upstairs.' 'Really it is awful.'

The phone rang. It was Rayneld: 'Do you have any extra girls to send to IRC? Something went wrong with the plane and the Adventist Hospital called us to send women to take care of the children.' I asked her to repeat the message; she had no further information.

I dialled IRC and they confirmed Rayneld's report: 'They are bringing in your babies wounded.'   .

Rosemary and I ran out to the road, got in a taxi, and rode in silence to the hospital. Down Phan Dinh Phung, then Pasteur, then Cong Ly – the taxi ride seemed to last forever. Army ambulances, ambulances from other hospitals, trucks, jeeps were all screaming into the hospital driveway as our taxi pulled up. We ran over to the crowd and were met by a tear-faced Wende. 'Over half are dead. *All* in the lower section of the plane were killed.' Ilse was with her – an agonized unbelieving Ilse. 'Dolly, Marg, Monique . . . they're dead.' Christie was also there, with Wende and Ilse. She was stunned and her pants were muddy. I mumbled, 'I'm glad you're alive,' and she said she was, too.

Rosemary and I ran up to the paediatric ward – Ward 6 – it was packed with children and nurses and doctors. Some of the children were crying . . . others silent and confused. Some of the children were wet and muddy – most of them were naked. 'These are OK,' the nurse called.

I took two and ran downstairs with them to see about transportation. Some friends were already standing by with cars, anxious to help. Then we began running, trip after trip, carrying two children each time from the paediatric ward on the second floor down the steps, through the corridors to the parking lot and the waiting cars. Then back to the paediatric ward. Ambulances continued screaming through the gates. The whole place was wailing. 'There's something wrong with this child's eyes,' a doctor said. 'That's Tiresias,' I said, 'he has always been blind.' 'And these children here can't move their legs,' another doctor said. 'They've had polio.' Olaf sat on the bed wearing his usual smile. Anne Frank was lying

The Canadian Nursery in Cambodia.

43 Wende Grant at the British Residence,
Phnom Penh, March 1975.
44 Canada House Nursery.
45 Children in a sandbagged shelter
at Canada House, 15 March 1975.
The Grants' twins are the 2nd and
4th from the front, in the row
on the left, then aged 7 weeks.

43

44

45

46

47

48

52

53

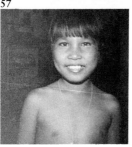
57

54

4 April 1975: the Crash of the C-5A, and Some of the Children who Died.

46 Vincent, from Tan Mai.
47 Diep-Marie, holding Basham.
48 Tran Dinh, from Qui Nhon.
49 Desmond.
50 Minh and Thanh, from Baclieu.
51 Elizabeth Dung.
52 Ngoc-Thanh, from Phu My.
53 Dennis, from Danang.
54 The scene of the crashed plane.
55 Xuan-My, from Sacred Heart, Danang.
56 Helen Rosalie, from Qui Nhon.
57 Lien, left in the market place.
58 Big Cuong, from Tan Mai.
59 Thy (Roi) blind in both eyes, was
   abandoned in a Pleiku dispensary.
60 Andrew, from St Enfance, Vinh Binh.
61 C. S. Lewis, at Allambie.
62 Tien and Be, from Sacred Heart, Danang.

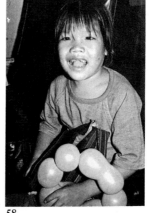
58

59

50

51

55

56

62

61

Evacuation of Saigon.

63 26 April, at Tan Son Nhut airport. Babies in boxes waiting to be boarded on the last evacuation flight.

64 The refugee ship, the *Green Port*.
65 Rosemary, Doreen Beckett, and Ulla, on the *Green Port*.

on another bed, looking around for some attention. Passeron was contented and smiling at all the activity. Down the stairs and to the cars with two more children. Grateful that there were some children to be carried.

A truck was coming and being directed to the morgue. Rosemary and I ran over – two stretchers were pulled off the truck. 'Nine here,' the driver said. 'All babies, all children.' Some had heads bashed in – all were wet – all were naked. Their skin matched the brown of the stretcher. Blood-matted hair. Some limbs missing.

I ran back to the emergency room and went from cot to cot – two older children, and the rest were adults I didn't recognize – then out to the operating room area; no one in surgery yet. Some adults were lying on stretchers. Over in the X-ray department, there was a pale, comatose woman with an obvious fractured skull and IV fluid running rapidly into a vein in her left arm. 'Know her?' the technician asked. I wanted her to be Margaret. I went over and looked closely – she was bruised and drained of blood, about Margaret's size and age – but she was not Marg. 'Is anyone in surgery now?' I asked. 'This one will be first,' the technician said. No more places to check. None yet in intensive care. Margaret, Birgit, Dolly, Tina, Michou, Lee, Sr Ursula were not there. I went back to the parking lot. Naomi and Wende were sitting in a van, weeping in disbelief – shocked at what was going on around them. Pat was in anguish; most of the children she had bid goodbye to an hour before were dead. Dick Lucas was there supporting her, and full of grief himself since the boys he had fostered were also dead.

Rosemary walked across the lot to where I was standing.

'Marg is dead – and Dolly and Lee. I can't find them anywhere. They're not in surgery or X-ray or the Intensive Care Unit or in the emergency room.' We didn't say anything else. Rose went into the emergency room and got us each a cup of water. The saliva in my mouth was now very thick mucus and the back of my throat was dry and hurt. The water tasted good.

Girls arrived from Newhaven – Lieu and Hong. Hong – who knew Dolly and her children so well – came and looked at me with the same look Ilse had, a look that said 'make this all different – make this not true.' All she said was 'Dolly' weakly, then sobbed. A TV camera was instantly there to catch her tears. She turned away from the camera and I held her for a while.

All the trucks and ambulances and jeeps were now being directed to the make-shift morgue – stretchers and bodies inside and stretchers and bodies outside. A fence separated the morgue area from the crowd of people. Ilse was standing by the fence, looking through. At first the guard at the gate refused to let me enter, then Rosemary and I managed to get through. Three stretchers lay on the ground before the doorway, all with large green rubber bags containing bodies in them. I unzipped one – the body of a naked woman with long hair – her skull crushed and her body very white. Was this Marg? I zipped the bag back up and we left the area.

FROM STATEMENT OF CHRISTINE D. LEIVERMANN TO THE AMERICAN AIR FORCE
4 April 1975 [dated 7 April 1975]

Loading of Passengers and Baggage on the C-5A
By the time I arrived on board the airplane, most of the passengers and baggage were already boarded. Most of the older children and many of the adults were downstairs. A few small children were with different members of our organization who were also scheduled to take the flight that day. I asked a crewman where the majority of the little ones were concentrated, and he directed me to the upper deck of the airplane. I went upstairs and helped strap children into their seats. Many of the smaller children were strapped two to a seat, so I went around trying to straighten them out a bit and make them more comfortable . . . I said goodbye to friends that had helped load the children and were now disembarking. Then I went downstairs to check on supplies. People were going about their business, and I took some spare baby bottles upstairs and instructed some crew members on what to give the children to drink. Then I returned to the section of babies near the stairwell.

Upstairs, many of the adults had no place to sit for take-off. As we prepared to take off, I mentally reshuffled children in an arrangement that I thought would offer maximum care for the children and seats for the adults. I planned on asking one of our (FFAC) nurses to come up and help once we were airborne.

Recollection of Events from Take-off through Rapid Decompression and Subsequent Crash Landing
. . . A crewman asked me if I knew how to brace for take-off – I said

'Yes', and he went back to his station a few rows ahead of mine. My position consisted of the first two rows directly in front of the stairwell, the short row next to the stairwell, and assisting with the row next to the emergency exit doors. My position for take-off was between the first and second rows in front of the stairwell. After the plane had levelled off, I began to give out more baby bottles and collect the empties in my station. I took the empty bottles back to the galley and waited in line to fill them with sugar water. Someone handed me a carton of milk, and I had just finished it when there was a tremendous explosion. Someone said 'Oh my God, my Jesus God, no!' I believe that a black crewman injured his leg at this time. After a few seconds, I stepped over and around the debris that had accumulated in the galley after the explosion and went back to my station. I looked down the stairwell and saw a large body of water. I assumed the plane was going to drop into the ocean and started thinking about the fact that neither the children nor myself could swim. A crewman came up to me and put his arms around [me] and asked if I was all right, and if I was scared, and if I would be all right. I answered 'Yes' to all three questions. He explained that the cargo door had blown off and that we would probably land all right because it's [sic] happened before and the planes usually landed okay. Some crewmen ... appeared to be handling a radio or something similar. Someone said the wiring was gone. Then the oxygen masks fell from the ceiling. I only found two that worked in the first row. When I pulled on the tubing to start the flow of oxygen, the unit came out of the ceiling. When I straightened the tube and gave only a gentle tug, no oxygen came through the mask. The tubes were not long enough to reach the babies in their seats. I put on one mask and had to unstrap the babies and lift them up to the oxygen. This proved extremely awkward, so I finally decided to just give it to the babies that looked like they were in greatest need. Many babies seemed to be bordering on the unconscious, but one was turning cyanotic,[1] so I picked him up and held him to the oxygen until the crewman signalled that oxygen was no longer needed. The time involved seemed to be about two minutes, but I am in no way positive about this. I remember looking to the forward section of the plane and seeing everyone giving oxygen to

[1] Cyanosis: a bluish-purple discoloration of the skin and mucous membranes usually resulting from a deficiency of oxygen in the blood.

the children. I don't know if they had the same problems with their oxygen masks.

After the oxygen was no longer needed, we began strapping and padding the children more securely in their seats. I occasionally turned to look down the stairwell. The air was much warmer, and the wind was causing scraps of paper to float around the stairs. The land was rising up quickly and I could see rivers, rice paddies, houses, etc.; the crewman came up to me again and asked if I was okay. I answered 'Yes'. The rush of air seemed to be getting louder now as we neared the land. My babies were all very still and quiet. Most of the adults were hovering over their charges and preparing for landing. We started to brace for landing. I was still securing my children, and I could see people crouching between seats, some of them trying to shield children with their arms. I crouched between rows one and two in front of the stairwell and braced myself. The plane touched down and seemed to bounce back up in the air and come down again. Some part of the plane broke off, and started on fire – (I don't know whether the break or the fire was first) possibly the wing. Some flames came up the stairwell and were followed by intense heat. I started to feel very panicky as I couldn't reach all the children at once. But the plane kept sliding forward and left the burning wreckage and the intense heat behind us. During this time, I was bounced around a bit; the life raft inflated; some seats near the life raft were pulled off the ground and overturned with the children still strapped in them; ceiling panels fell down on top of us; and tremendous blasts of mud, water, and weeds were shooting up the stairwell. There were many grinding, grating, and shearing noises. I glanced to the left and noticed a hole worn in the side of the plane and I saw some of the rice paddy through that hole.

Rescue Efforts and Subsequent Evacuation of Survivors to include Extent of any Injuries I have Sustained

After the plane stopped, I stood up and started to wonder how we would get out. The children in my immediate rows seemed relatively okay, and I hadn't registered yet that the overturned seats had children in them. I climbed over the rows and saw that the exit doors about mid-plane were open, so I proceeded to the centre of the plane. Some children were already out of the plane on the right side, and one of the injured crewmen was there as well. Two of the children had rolled nearly face down in the mud, so I jumped to the ground (about 6 to 7 feet from the emergency door) to turn them face-up. After I turned them over, I noticed that the crewman was bleeding severely through a makeshift bandage on his head. I noticed the sound of helicopters landing very close by. Someone had thrown a knotted rope out of the door, so with the rope and a boost from one of the crew, I went back into the plane. We found some bandages, and I handed them out to Dr Stark who was with the crewman previously mentioned. I went back to my section and started handing children out the central door. (The exit nearest to my station was jammed.) We formed a chain to hand the children out an exit on the right side of the plane. We righted the overturned seats, and found the children in apparently good health despite their ruffled appearance. The last part of my section to be evacuated was the area next to the stairwell. I could only see an arm because a number of panels from the ceiling and wherever had fallen on top of the seats. I panicked and called over to a crewman that some kids were buried under the debris and I didn't know if they were alive. He was busy sending another section of children out the left exit doors, so he asked if I could check them. I crawled over the seats and proceeded to pull the debris off the children. I found them alive and in apparently good condition. I handed them to a crew-woman, and she handed them out to one of the helicopter crew. Only after I had handed her the last child from those seats did I notice that she had injured at least one arm. I helped her out of the plane, and we proceeded to a waiting helicopter. I asked one crewman about the bottom half of the plane – he shook his head 'No'. All of the other children had already been evacuated, so I joined her in that helicopter ... I looked down and saw some crewmen still at the crash site, and the piece of smouldering aircraft-remains some distance behind the plane. We proceeded to the Air America landing strip, where an ambulance was waiting for us. We went directly to the Adventist Hospital. While boarding the ambulance, I asked where the other children were. Someone told me they were fine.

Once at the hospital, we proceeded to the emergency room. Just before I entered it, I was stopped by one of the Vietnamese hospital co-ordinators for our organization. I explained what had happened, and she ran off to telephone one of our nursery supervisors. I went into the emergency room. An American doctor questioned me briefly and called the American Embassy. Until this time, none of the other passengers or crew had arrived at the hospital. An American lady at the hospital gave me a glass of water, and we went to sit on the bench outside to wait for the others to come. Some ambulances from other hospitals arrived at the hospital, then the ambulances started to come in with the victims. The hospital grounds started to crowd with reporters, concerned friends and staff, and onlookers. The emergency room was filled to overflowing, so all children were routed upstairs to the paediatric ward. The flow of ambulances slowed down, and I was directed to a table where a nurse checked my blood pressure and pulse. I got up to wash my face and a doctor asked me how I was. I told him I was okay and he went back to the injured people. The ambulances started coming in again with the dead. They were directed immediately to the morgue. I waited in the emergency waiting room and went out to check whenever an ambulance came in. Some of the crewmen were also in the waiting room – one of them had his camera and asked me to take a picture of him in his 'crash clothes'. He then decided the light wasn't good enough and returned to his seat. I saw the black crewman wheeled through the emergency room on a stretcher... Sometime during the time I spent in the waiting room and outside with the ambulances, I think I heard mention of previous trouble with the cargo door on the C-5A. I don't know who said this, as I was interested only in the ambulances. I left the hospital later that evening and went home.

SMcD: The last of the ambulances arrived. The children had been returned to the nurseries and it was getting dark. Someone drove me back to Newhaven. The entrance lights were on. Sang, Lieu, Hong and Nga stood in the doorway. 'Passeron ...' Lieu said, and her voice and look indicated that Passeron hadn't come back. 'Passeron is OK. He is in the hospital.' 'Eric and Aeneas aren't here,' Sang said, and she showed me the list of those who had returned. Maybe they were at To Am. A friend drove me over to To Am and I walked from room to room, down the rows of cribs, trying to find Eric and Aeneas. To Am girls would hold up babies they did not know (Phu My babies) but none of these babies were ours. To Allambie next. Empty Allambie. A house that had been full of older children – now the upstairs rooms were dark and only a few children played on the main floor. Staff workers sat in the doorways weeping. Pat stood among the children quiet and desolate. Baby Anh was there and we took her back home with us. No Eric or Aeneas. Maybe in the morning we would find them at the hospital or at To Am.

Michelle on night duty had just woken up and had to be told what had happened.

WG: Many months later I learnt that it was Dick Lucas who had taken Rosemary, Susan, Christie and me back to Rathaven.

Marina Bui, Dolly's surviving daughter, aged fifteen, was sitting on the front steps of Rathaven, crying. She asked for her mother, sister and brothers. We told her they were all gone in the crash. Christie found a sedative in the pharmacy for her. As Marina's sobs quietened, we looked to the gate and saw her father Bui van To walking across the courtyard. Seeing him approach was a continuation and intensification of the nightmare that had started shortly after 4 p.m. that afternoon. He had heard of the crash and asked for Dolly, Tina, Michou and David one at a time. 'Gone, To,' was answered to each name. He accepted the news with incredible courage. After listening to the information we had, he took Marina home for the night.

Mary Cusack (accompanying the children bound for Australia): We had a long wait at the Embassy and another long wait at the airport entrance. Our supply of boiled water for the babies was almost depleted and we were anxious lest the babies become dehydrated in the oppressive heat of the bus. One of the Embassy officials told us the delay was due to security checks. (The airport was heavily guarded at all times and even more so now. It was impossible, practically speaking, for any unauthorized person to set foot inside the airport precincts.) I heard a fire engine and ambulances scream out of the gate. I could see a fire in the distance: someone said it was a plane. I imagined it must be the sabotage of some army plane.

Finally, we were allowed to drive on to the tarmac. We unloaded all the babies from the bus and loaded them into the Hercules, together with the green plastic garbage bags full of diapers, clothes, formula and bread. We had no more water save for what the plane could supply. Diane pulled up in the old Dodge van in which she had brought all the other luggage. For the next two hours the adults crouched on the floor, or crawled between the babies, trying to get fluids into them. I had to fight off an overwhelming desire to sleep.

At Bangkok airport some Australian officials started organizing us, moving the children into the airport lounge. Throughout the evacuation, government, military and Red Cross officials took control, and with few exceptions ignored the personnel who had lived and worked with the children. It had become a power game for 'officials only' and any intrusion by the Vietnam staff, who were so well-acquainted with the needs of each child, was highly resented, or at least ignored. The experts and officials were so caught up in the excitement and the publicity of this happening, as they bustled about cheerfully, little wonder they ignored our shabby presence and used their own smartly dressed volunteers. We were so tired, frustrated with politics, nationalism, officialdom, chattering middle-aged ladies, domineering nurses and know-all doctors who couldn't even recognize scabies, that we would only protest when there seemed a real threat to the well-being of a child. We became bystanders in a bizarre pantomime.

At Bangkok airport I first learnt of the crash of the C-5A plane. I tried to get some information but no one seemed to know anything more. One pompous Foreign Affairs official (Australian) gave us to understand that even if he did have any news, he certainly wouldn't communicate it to us.

As arrangements were made for my continuing flight to Butterworth, and then back to Saigon, for the first time I felt really afraid. I was suddenly homesick. Friends tempted me to continue on the 747 with the children to Australia. But something deep inside told me that now more than ever before, I was needed in Vietnam. The staff would be very low in numbers and in spirits and there would be so many new problems to deal with. So I said goodbye to the children and continued on to Butterworth.

RT: All the medical records, ID cards, clothes and supplies had been destroyed. Some of the identification tags had been lost. The remaining nursery staff set about identifying their own surviving children and checking on those still hospitalized. The sorting-out process lasted for several days.

Elaine Moir, who was responsible for organizing the Australian-bound convoy, was assisted by Julie Chinberg, Mrs Moses and May

Cope. Mary would accompany the children only as far as Bangkok and was due to return to Saigon next day. Many of the babies sent to Australia were the smallest and handicapped children from Hy Vong. Julie had made the choice, based on her assessment of the child's ability to withstand a longer or shorter plane trip. For some of the older handicapped children we had been undecided in choosing who would go to Australia and who to the USA. We were happy with either country as long as a home was assured. In a rare moment of levity long before dawn that morning, we had drawn lots, Wende for the USA and Elaine for Australia: I held out the cards, face down, while Wende and Elaine took turns to draw one. We were dropping with fatigue but laughed till the tears streamed down as the cards were chosen and each of these little ones we knew so intimately had his or her destination thus decided. We laughed with and at each other as Otto, Danielle-Mai, Phi-Truong and darling little Venus were chosen for Australia, while Marcia, Andrew, Vincent and Genevieve were chosen for the USA. Four went on to a new life in Australia, and four that same day were faced with the mystery of eternity.

In To Am nursery, Elaine Norris and Sr Rayneld were left to sort out the confusion. In Hy Vong, Kathy Garland was alone since Doreen Beckett was still en route back to Saigon after delivering a group of children to Europe. Susan McDonald still had Michelle Boutagh to help at Newhaven. Diane Bennett from To Am went across to Allambie to help Pat Zirk who was alone and suffering indescribably from the death of more than half her children.

The living still had to be cared for; there was no time to dwell upon the tragedy. I myself was numbed beyond the possibility of emotion. All the remaining staff knew what had to be done and did it with a minimum of wasted words. In the back of my mind I knew that I could 'think about it later', to use one of Marg's favourite phrases. Seventy-eight children had died. Of the survivors, ten were in hospital and only three of these appeared seriously injured, Hung, Elaine and Ly, all of whom were eventually 'medivaced' out of the country. It took us many days to identify Hung, the most critical case. Hung and his sister, who was uninjured, were the only two surviving children whom we knew for sure to have been on the lower deck of the plane. We had seen in the newspapers a photo of them sitting together before take-off.

175

I went to Phu My, sobbing for the first time as I broke the news of Margaret's death to Sr Rose. I asked her to come to the nurseries next day to help identify the Phu My children. I must have then returned to Newhaven.

SMcD: A few minutes later, Rosemary walked in. We had to get word to Australia that Marg and Lee were dead. We phoned for a Mission Warden car from the US Embassy and went to the house of one of the Embassy secretaries. There was no possibility of a direct phone line to Australia, but the Australian Embassy promised to cable Canberra immediately. We returned to the nursery.

I felt incredibly dusty and sweaty and thought Rose must feel the same – so I drew her bath and made up the bed with clean sheets and put out Mary-Nelle's bright pyjamas for her to wear. After her bath, Rose said 'We'd better go to bed – tomorrow we'll have much to do – and it won't help us if we haven't tried to rest.' So Rosemary went into my room and I slept on the couch in the adjoining room. I left the lamp on and the radio on low – hearing the message every hour – that there had been a plane crash – that fewer than half survived. From time to time I'd check on Rose who seemed to be sleeping, with an exhausted expression on her face. Michelle was up for the night to nurse, and came into the room occasionally for a sip of coke from the icebox in the corner. It was April and quite warm in Saigon.

WG: Failing repeatedly to get a line for a call to Colorado, I asked the US Embassy for assistance and they sent a Mission Warden police car to collect me at Rathaven; it was after curfew, about 8.30 p.m.

At the Embassy I was ushered into the office of Mr Lehman, the Minister Plenipotentiary, and sitting alone at the great desk, I waited for my call. Within minutes I was talking with Deanna Carnie at the FFAC office in my home in Boulder. Reluctant to waste time, I cut short her expressions of joy to hear me alive, gave her the list of known dead and told her over half of the children had been killed [it was fewer]; I didn't yet know which children had survived. 'We will wait now for a chartered Pan Am 747, Deanna. Rather than take another military plane we will wait for the Vietcong. They couldn't do worse.' Then I realized that Deanna's eighteen-month-old twins, Hansel and Gretel, had been aboard the C-5A with the other Allambie children.

Christie and Ilse were talking quietly in the office at Rathaven when I returned. Christie was calmly describing what she remembered of the crash while Ilse was absorbing the certainty of Monique's death. We talked for an hour then went to bed. A little sleep was essential if we were to cope with tomorrow.

Before dawn on Saturday, the night guard woke me to take a phone call from Colorado. Pan American Airways had agreed to divert to Saigon a 747 plane, scheduled to fly from Japan to California; it would pick up the remaining FFAC staff and children that afternoon.

Everyone was at work early Saturday morning. In subdued voices, nursery Directors read off the names of the children they had sent on the C-5A, qualifying each name with a 'returned' or 'did not return'. Rosemary checked the names against the master list, writing 'dead' after more and more names. Miraculously, almost two-thirds of the children had survived. And when Le and Chinh returned from a round of the hospitals to seek possible survivors we knew that Hansel and Gretel were alive and without serious injuries.

To and Marina came early to Rathaven. To had been prevented by the airport police from boarding the German evacuation plane the day before. The German Embassy had another plane leaving that day and they had promised To they would intervene with the airport authorities to permit him to board, since he had the necessary German authority. (In fact, the German Ambassador personally interceded and he was able to leave.) To carried a box of photographs, all he had left of his life with Dolly, Tina, Michou and David. Marina was to travel as previously decided, on the Canadian evacuation plane with the remainder of the Cambodian children and the FFAC children scheduled for adoption in Canada.

Bud Turner of USAID also came by Rathaven early Saturday morning. He collected the passports of the departing FFAC staff so that he could get exit visas for us and avoid a repetition of yesterday's problems with the airport police.

The counting and checking continued throughout the morning and early afternoon. I took the phone calls, mostly from reporters after a story; I either hung up or explained that we were expecting a call from the US and could not tie up the line. One official caller requested FFAC's permission to cremate the bodies of the dead children. I gave permission.

John Wetterer arrived mid-morning; his Air France flight had been delayed eighteen hours. He walked across the Rathaven courtyard as To had the night before, but John's face wore a happy smile. Obviously, he knew nothing. I had to tell him what had happened. Unbelieving, stunned, John immediately agreed to depart that same afternoon as an escort on the Pan Am plane.

MC: Next morning I was the only civilian on board the Hercules returning to Saigon. I felt sorry for the crew who were obviously afraid of everything about Vietnam, as well as of the possibility of sabotage at Tan Son Nhut. When we landed, I waited for the crew to descend so that we could all go together to the airport lounge, but they were not permitted to leave the tarmac. I was therefore alone and very tense as I faced the immigration authorities with no visas to authorize my departure or my return. The officers were astonished, and referred the matter to their superior, who at last seemed to believe my story. He let me through.

It was siesta time and the streets were quiet. I went directly to To Am. The staff there were grief stricken but were continuing to care for the remaining children. To Am had lost eighteen children; forty-two of their children had survived the plane crash. Br Andrew and Br John came to offer some comfort. Upstairs, Elaine and Rayneld, looking very worn, were flat out preparing new lists for the chartered Pan Am 747, which would take the rest of our children that same afternoon. Rayneld, Elaine and Diane were going with them. I was staying at To Am with a number of the children who were not going to adoptive families abroad.

RT: 324 children had to be prepared again for departure, new supplies packed and identities confirmed. Several of the Phu My Sisters went around to the nurseries to re-identify their children and then came to see me at Rathaven. I had boarded the C-5A first with the Phu My children and they were all seated on the upper deck: they had all survived.

All the remaining staff except Doreen, who had just returned from her European convoy that morning, Mary, Susan and myself, would go on the 747 to care for the children. The LeGall family from Thu Duc would take over responsibility for Allambie.

WG: The grey USAID buses, windows screened with heavy wire mesh, arrived at the nurseries at 3 p.m. The house administrator checked the children one by one against her list as they were carried from the house to the bus by the Vietnamese staff. Once loaded the bus doors were closed and did not open again until arrival at the airport. That afternoon I went on the bus with the To Am children, carrying the escorts' passports with their newly stamped exit visas. Some of the Vietnamese staff holding the children were crying; the foreign staff were silent.

The bus was waved through the gates at Tan Son Nhut and pulled up at the terminal whereupon a policeman boarded and scrutinized the passengers. I was told to take all the adult passports through the usual departure procedure. The USAID man volunteered to help me and as we entered the terminal building, the bus doors firmly closed, rolled on through the barrier and across the airfield to the plane.

After filling out the embarkation data on three or four passports I noticed my USAID friend had disappeared. No doubt he had realized before I did that we were already beyond the immigration barrier. Jamming the incomplete cards and passports into my purse, I submitted the completed ones, had them duly stamped then walked out the door unimpeded, and across the field towards the Pan Am 747 I saw in the distance. A car was approaching; Rosemary beckoned me to join her in a search for a missing bus. We located it alongside the wrong plane and led it back to our 747.

RT: The Pan Am 747 was configured throughout for transporting children. There were special supplies aboard; cardboard cartons to box the babies safely, milk, diapers, plastic bags and blankets. There would have been adequate space for all of our children had we not attempted to use the C-5A the previous day, but it took the tragedy of the day before to convince Pan Am that we needed them, and only after an American friend had stepped in with a down-payment of 150,000 dollars against the total cost of 230,000.

This time, as we loaded the babies on the 747, none of the Vietnamese staff were allowed to board. There had been talk of sabotage of the C-5A and some of the escorts were nervous on this account. As far as we could see, there was no one else on the plane, except for our children, eleven FFAC escorts and the Pan Am crew.

I could not imagine how Christie would ever have the courage to board another plane, but without any fuss she had merely changed her muddy clothes of the previous day and shouldered her share of the nursing responsibility as if yesterday had never been.

While we were boarding the children in the Pan Am 747, a Canadian plane was taking off with Naomi Bronstein, Marina Bui, the remaining Cambodian children and about twenty of our own children destined for Canadian families.

WG: Ilse, Christie, several stewardesses and I were in the tail section of the 747. Ilse and I sat together for take-off, each gripping tightly the seat arms in fear. We discussed nothing during the long trip except the needs of the babies in our section of the plane. Caring for the children was a marathon of feeding and changing diapers. Low-sided cardboard boxes were under each seat, stowed like carry-on luggage. A tiny baby was in each box. Some larger boxes, too high to slide under a seat, were wedged between seats. These held larger babies. After take-off we pulled boxes from beneath seats as if opening dresser drawers. Crawling on the seats, we examined the contents of each drawer, holding, feeding and changing the little inhabitant before returning him or her to the folds of the red Pan Am blanket that lined each box. Soon we were confused as to which child had been fed, which had been sleeping when checked and so passed over. An empty box could mean that a stewardess was carrying that baby up and down the aisles to still his crying. Had she fed him at the same time?

By the time we were approaching Japan, we were looking for signs of dehydration and respiratory distress among the smaller and weaker babies. Christie had infusion sets ready for several tiny babies. Necessary preparations for landing to refuel forced her to wait. Babies were returned to their boxes and carefully covered. The cardboard 'drawers' were closed by pushing them under the seats again. At the last minute we slid into our seats, pulled fast the belts and waited for disaster. It was a smooth landing.

We had landed at a military airport. The US Military made its presence known with a detail of medical officers who boarded the plane and started examining the children. I stared at them in a stupor and could only wonder what in the world they were doing to our children. They brushed me aside with a muttered, 'orders ... children ill'. I persisted, saying these were our children and if we needed medical help we would request it.

A sergeant, I think it was, stepped in to reason with me so that the doctor – a paediatrician, no less – could continue his inspection tour of our children. The sergeant was more polite but just as sure of his, and his officers', US-army-given right to examine our children on our privately chartered plane and cart them off to hospitalization in Japan. I argued bitterly that FFAC held custody of these children, that the nurses who had kept the children alive for months were on board, and that we would make the medical decisions regarding our children.

In the middle of this increasingly heated discussion, the Pan Am captain emerged from the front of the plane to introduce himself and to announce that reporters were waiting to come on board to photograph the children. 'Absolutely not,' I snapped. Patiently, he explained that he had received a cable requesting the news coverage from 'the highest US authority'. 'From the *very* highest authority,' he added. Trying to match his patience I told him I didn't care *how* high the authority; our children were not going to be used for any purpose. 'I certainly respect your authority and your wishes,' he said, and left to tell the reporters they would not be allowed on board. Wonderful man, I should have expressed my gratitude. He was to be the last person for weeks who recognized my responsibility and authority as Director of the agency holding custody of those 324 children.

The press disposed of, I returned to my argument with the military paediatrician. He and his colleagues had selected about twenty of our children to be hospitalized in Japan. Hurried conferences with the nurses confirmed that they had chosen children with superficial problems; problems well known to the nurses. They had missed completely the tiny infants, badly dehydrated and in respiratory distress, who waited in the back section for the departure of our military medical specialists so that Christie could put them on IVs.

After my threats to stop the flight and demand hospitalization for all 324 children, the doctor agreed to remove only the two worst cases. He showed them to me. Samantha, somewhat under a year old, had a boil on her head. I stared in disbelief. 'That is a boil,' I said. 'It could break inwardly and cause brain damage,' he said. The other child, a girl of about four or five, had eyelids crusted closed from conjunctivitis. Again I said, stupidly, 'That is conjunctivitis.' 'And could cause blindness,' he said.

The friendly sergeant again interposed. He would get his wife and her friends from the US base to stay with the children in hospital, he promised. He would see that they got the best care and that they were sent on to the US the moment they were better. I made him sign a letter guaranteeing that the children's complete medical records would be sent on to me.

Volunteer Red Cross nurses, mostly military wives, we assumed, replaced the Pan Am stewardesses. They took over the perpetual feeding, changing and holding of babies that made it possible for us to provide necessary, minimal care for the children for the following ten hours to San Francisco. By then FFAC people had been awake at least 24 hours, and that after some fitful few hours of sleep after the crash of the C-5A. I found myself slow in response and awkward of movement. I marvelled at Christie deftly adjusting IV equipment as she monitored the progress of the sick babies. The other nurses seemed equally oblivious to the exhaustion they must have been feeling.

A volunteer nurse who had joined us in Japan seated herself beside me as I tried to concentrate on getting milk from a glass bottle into a cleft-palate infant, and asked me if Christie was a doctor, qualified to insert an IV ... was she at least a registered nurse? I looked over at Christie in her clean yellow shirt and wondered what she had done with the mud-spattered clothes she'd worn through the C-5A crash. I replied that Christie was an extraordinary nurse; that where we came from nurses certainly were allowed to insert IV needles; that she shouldn't worry. It was funny for a moment. Then visions came unbidden. The nurses fighting for the lives of children discarded at birth. Hy Vong full of babies who couldn't survive, with Birgit standing over them, using talent and abilities born of desperation and determination and keeping so many alive. Now Birgit was dead. And Margaret who managed so many impossible situations – gone. Dolly, with her gallant spirit, killed – and so many children with them ...

I wanted to get to San Francisco. Friends would be there who would feed the babies, hospitalize the very ill, organize and plan and, most of all, give us time to think about what had happened and to cry about it. 'Don't worry,' I repeated to the volunteer nurse. 'That nurse knows what she is doing'.

During the latter part of the flight from Japan to San Francisco, one of the Red Cross nurses came crawling down the aisle checking the children and filling out a US Immigration and Naturalisation I-94 form for each child. Since these children lacked passports and regular entry visas for the US, their entry would be authorized by a special parole visa for which they were eligible in the circumstances.

We explained the identification bracelets to the nurse, helping her locate and decipher a few, then went back to feeding the babies while she crawled over and around the boxes, transcribing the information on to the I-94 forms. Had she been able to mark, indelibly, the forehead of each child thus processed, the plan may have had a modicum of success. As it was, babies were removed from the boxes to be fed just before the nurse reached them, and returned when she had already passed their row. Babies already registered were moved a row further back where they would be duly registered again as the nurse worked her way systematically towards the tail section of the plane. Allambie and Phu My children, who had survived the crash of the day before, had already been recorded in the first-class section; as they wandered the length of the plane, bored, restless and curious, they were stopped again for the issuance of still another I-94 form.

Further complicating the task of completing a single I-94 for each child were the multiple bracelets on most of the children. One ID bracelet gave the child's nursery name; another the name of his nursery of origin; some listed the adoptive family's name; still others identified the brand of formula the child drank or country to which he or she was destined. Most children wore an FFAC identification. On one encounter with a child the nurse may have recorded one bit of information as the child's name and, on a second check, discovered an entirely different name.

These I-94 forms were duly turned over to Immigration at the Presidio. On processing the children out of the reception centre, we were supposed to find the I-94 form for each child. This was to add immeasurably to the confusion over the identities of the children.

Chapter 15

AT SAN FRANCISCO
PRESIDIO

Accounts by Mary-Nelle Gage and Wende Grant

M-NG: I had flown to the States in February and since then spent some time on a fund-raising stint in St Louis, Boston, New York and Washington. For Easter I stayed in Kentucky at the Mother house of the Loretto Order, trying to snatch a respite before resuming duties in Saigon. But as the political situation in Vietnam deteriorated with merciless rapidity, I kept a constant vigil with radio, TV, and newspaper accounts, and phone calls to and from Connie Boll in Connecticut, former Vice-Consul Laurie Peters at the State Department in Washington, and Susan McDonald in Saigon. I anguished over my friends and our more-than-500 children, caught in a desperate situation. Then, on 1 April, Pat Adams called from St Louis to say that Maria Eitz was trying to get in touch with me; that there seemed to be an imminent evacuation afoot. I called Maria immediately, and she instructed me to come to San Francisco right away: the evacuation was indeed in progress, and my help was needed to help receive the children.

Several volunteers were already at Maria Eitz's when I arrived, looking after the children who had come in on a Pan Am flight earlier that day. Ruth Routten was there and she escorted some of the children on to their new families early the next morning. She greeted me with tales of the Cambodian evacuation of Families For Children's Canada House. I remained at Maria's side, talking, making and taking phone calls. We loaded a truck with baby supplies from Maria's garage and headed out to the Presidio, a military base made available for this occasion. Army officers were on hand to question us and direct the work of preparing Harmon

Hall gym to receive the children. Mattresses, sheets, blankets, cases of premixed baby formula, crates of disposable diapers were being carried in. Red Cross personnel set up a canteen. An operations office with a blackboard for posting flight information, desks, chairs, and phones was set up.

By mid-afternoon on the 2nd, we had word that our children would arrive that night. But in the evening, the notice changed to read that Ed Daly's World Airways flight was bringing only a small number of children of another agency. A large room had been set up at the air terminal as a press room and was full of reporters and cameramen. The unloading area was floodlit and swarming with porters and the press. Army buses filled with Red Cross medical volunteers rolled into place, ready to provide 'laps' for the children, as they were carried one by one from plane to bus and so on to the Presidio.

I had returned to a local Loretto convent. On Friday, 4 April, I woke to learn that there had been a plane crash and that our children had been on board. I was stunned. Gradually, through news broadcasts and a phone call from Denver some facts began to emerge, and then the names of our dead friends. I do not know any words to describe the wrenching, the tearing, the crushing that attacked and mangled my spirit. But as always, there was no time. As soon as we could, Connie Boll and I began negotiating for a commercial plane to bring our children and friends to San Francisco. Connie called Bob McAulay in Connecticut, and George Carnie in Colorado, and together they managed to charter a Pan Am 747. Bob McAulay agreed to provide the funds to secure the plane. On our way back to the Presidio, we picked up several newspapers; Naomi Bronstein's photograph was on the front page, crying and clinging to a sobbing Vietnamese woman carrying two babies.

The Presidio housed three worlds now: that of the Red Cross and medical team of volunteers; Maria Eitz's staff that had become 'Operation Orphan Airlift', tracking evacuation flight schedules and arrangements; and friends of Rosemary – Anne McCrudden, Lola D'Orazio, Evelyn, Petey, Connie, myself. We neither knew how to comfort each other, nor how to give way to our grief. We were caught between despair over who was lost, and relief over who was spared.

Press calls for interviews were unrelenting. Maria and I telephoned some family of surviving staff to give them any information we could. Susan's parents, Bill and Marguerite McDonald, flew to join us immediately. In the middle of the afternoon a regular Pan Am flight arrived in San Francisco airport with three of our children. Dreading the press coverage, we arranged to collect the children discreetly before they entered the terminal. George Carnie, President of the FFAC Board, meanwhile had arrived and dealt with the press. I then met the McDonalds off their local flight from Denver; and a friend, Barbara Hunt, who drove us in her van back to the Presidio. There we hoped to board one of the fleet of buses that was drawn up to meet the chartered Pan Am 747. However, rigid security measures had in the meantime been invoked since President Ford was to meet the flight, and to our horror we were not allowed to join Petey, Connie, Lola and Anne, who had kept us places on the buses. The 'laps' to receive the children had been checked and secured for several hours!

Determined to be at the plane door to help as the children disembarked, I led the McDonalds back to Barbara's van and told her we must drive ourselves there. While we speculated how on earth to get out to the plane, we realized that we were by now driving alongside the official army bus convoy. Somehow, Barbara managed to slide her van into the line of buses; Bill donned his Washington County sheriff badge; the police checked our van with a flashlight, caught the reflection of Bill's badge – and waved us through. Barbara parked the van, and found a clipboard and pen for me. The tarmac was well-lit; guards with shotguns perched on adjacent roofs; areas were roped off for the press and contained by police. There was a group of VIPs out on the open tarmac, so I hustled over to be near them, determined to board the plane. But my requests were either totally ignored or brushed aside. Barbara, Bill and Marguerite and I then joined the press section, so that, if nothing else, we could at least witness the arrival.

Eventually, the plane taxied on to the floodlit tarmac. A long period of time elapsed before the stairs were wheeled into place, and the door opened and a medical team boarded. Some time later, stairs were wheeled to the rear door, where Christie and Michelle emerged carrying ill infants on IVs to ambulances waiting at the foot of the stairs; they made three or four such trips. Then President Ford, surrounded by his entourage, boarded and, all smiles, emerged carrying a child. Meanwhile, we inched our way closer to the plane until we were right next to the Red Cross helpers waiting to mount the stairs. We merged with the group. I thrust the clipboard and pen at Barbara, who made a quick inventory of the staff on the flight: Susan was still in Vietnam; Barbara had to break that disappointing news to the McDonalds. I managed to put a foot in the plane and catch a glimpse of a smiling John Wetterer, badly in need of a shave. A baby was handed to me, and I was ushered down the steps and into a waiting bus. But I was an extra uncounted lap, which threw the bus into total confusion. I had to be formally identified. At the Presidio I handed over my baby to the waiting arms of a Red Cross volunteer and ran out to meet the rest of our staff: Kathy, Michelle, Christie, Ilse, Rayneld, Elaine, Pat and Diane.

WG: The plane landed shortly before 10 p.m. in San Francisco, some twenty hours after departure from Saigon. It was still 5 April in San Francisco. We had been awake for over thirty hours. The supplies of infant clothing and baby formula were exhausted. The very sick babies had been moved to the tail section of the plane to facilitate their being taken quickly to hospital. They were promptly removed by a group of doctors. But the rest of the children and escorts had to wait until President Ford came on board to meet us, or to greet the children, or to be thanked – I wasn't sure which. Except for George Carnie, our friends and relatives were not allowed aboard the plane to greet and help us. The daughter of the Director of World Airways came on board and I could not fathom what she was doing on our privately chartered plane.

After an interminable wait, the President left carrying one of the cleaner and more completely dressed babies. Then long lines of complete strangers boarded, picked up a child each, and departed. I asked what was happening to the children and was told to sit down. Our children were no longer our business and we were not with them. The nightmare of the past forty-eight hours closed in and I wept. Crying seemed to be effective, and someone found cars to take us to the Presidio.

In Harmon Hall the stunned and exhausted children were laid three or four to a mattress with a volunteer 'baby holder' by each child. The helpers ranged from teenagers to grandparents, who held, patted, juggled, or talked to his or her assigned child. Nurses and doctors made health examinations, and supplies of diapers, bottles, clothes, and baby formula were piled in strategic locations about the room. Army personnel kept a buffet table supplied with coffee, sandwiches and doughnuts. To anyone from Saigon, the room was too cool and damp, and totally confusing.

In one of the adjoining rooms, tables had been set up and phones installed to make office space for the agencies. There a group of FFAC staff and friends tried to organize the tasks that lay ahead. Six or eight phones rang constantly. Which children had died on the crash? How many children were left in Saigon? Who was going to check on children taken from the plane to hospitals? What documents did we have on the children? How many children destined for Germany did we bring? Germany was on the phone . . . France was on the phone. Were we sure it was chickenpox rather than smallpox that marked some of the children? Washington was on the phone . . . New York, Pennsylvania, Quebec, London . . . Did we want to move the children into foster homes in California? Agencies all over the country were on the phone with offers of approved adoptive homes.

Those of us who had arrived with the children drifted off, three or four at a time. We took taxis to a hotel and went to sleep.

M-NG: Connie Boll had obtained some complimentary rooms at the Jack Tar Hotel for our Saigon staff; Barbara took them there in states of shock and exhaustion to try to rest. Lola, Petey and I listened to Christie as she related the crash experience over and over. She couldn't stop talking about it; we were desperately hungry for every detail. Finally, we all slept for a while, before returning to the Presidio to work.

The system for identifying the children had been well-organized, at least in principle; as each bus travelled from the plane back to the Presidio, a medic in charge had given each child a letter and a number according to the bus and seat it was in. But unfortunately, significant information was lacking – such as the fact that 'Pelargon' on an infant's identification band was not the child's name, but its milk formula; and 'Hy Vong' was the nursery he had just left, not his own name. When the bus lists were duplicated and distributed, we were confronted with pages of 'Pelargons' and 'Hy Vongs', that made the business of identification much harder. Where were the children taken to hospital and who were they?

Locating children even in that one building was a challenge, as volunteers took them away into examining rooms, playrooms, and so on. To further complicate matters, the army or 'Operation Orphan Airlift' set up a system requiring a portfolio on each child with immigration forms, footprints, medical releases, etc., *ad infinitum*. With each change of shift, the composition of the required portfolio changed. By the time one learned a process, a new directive was issued. We could not send a single child to its new home for at least twenty-four hours simply because the maze was too complicated for a staff of 'normal' adults. To have to face the Presidio in the wake of the C-5A crash was the final injustice.

WG: Sunday, 6 April 1975: In the morning we were back, rested and more rational. It was now more apparent that an enormous effort had gone into organizing the arrival of the children, with hundreds of volunteers – doctors, nurses, and baby-sitters. But the FFAC nurses, who knew the children, were wandering around on the side lines, not integrated into the child-care programme. They could only observe and offer advice on a particular child. While baby-sitters wore heavy sweaters in the cool room, many babies accustomed to 90 °F temperatures lay in only a diaper and under-shirt on the mattress on the floor. Despite screens set in front of the outer doors, a cold draught constantly swept in under the screens and across the floor. For the most part, our suggestions were neither sought nor appreciated when offered.

Identification of the children – when we saw a copy of the lists – was a challenge. On the 'B' bus, for instance, there had been twenty-one children: B-1 was listed as 'Tin Guirasco Fac', and B-2 was 'Alice Spring FFAC'. Each person carrying a baby had found his or her child's bracelets and written down the information by the seat numbers. Besides the 'Pelargons' and 'Hy Vongs', the destination 'France' also seemed a sensible name to many baby holders. If a bracelet had been lost, some baby holders resorted to descriptions: Ariella became 'Tiny' and Dorothea 'Pretty'; Princess was 'Prinless'; Minh, 'Miner'; a child destined for Luxemburg was named 'Lux Enbollrg'; Tiresius was 'Tierequill'; Olympia was 'Olympia Fraclinkc'; and a child listed as Ne Tuan was also noted as having 'Loose stool' (I know what happened to that baby holder). To add to the fiasco, some numbers were left blank; some had the designation 'No Name'; and one had 'No Child'. Did the baby holder scoop up an empty blanket from the plane and only discover the error when on the bus?

Chaotic as it was, at least we had a place to keep the children until we could arrange for their onward travel. We met that Sunday morning in the hotel to organize and delegate tasks before returning to the Presidio shortly before noon. A doctor who had been on the plane the night before stopped me before I reached the office. 'This is a medical disaster,' he told me. 'You have twelve hours to get these children out of the Presidio.' Doctors, he told me, had been working several days without sleep. We had brought in children with measles and chickenpox; no one could handle so many children in such poor health: some of the babies had pneumonia and others looked on the verge of it. More flights of orphans were due and the facilities couldn't hold them all.

But what did they think the operation in Vietnam had been for the past eight years, if not a 'medical disaster'? And what did they think had been happening in the Vietnamese orphanages functioning with staff, equipment, medical care, and supplies inferior to that which we had in our Saigon nurseries. Where did they think we could take the children, and who would be better equipped to handle this medical disaster? I sought out Maria Eitz who had played a major role in organizing this reception centre. Surely she could straighten out this newest twist in the continuing nightmare. She told me not to worry. A group in Wisconsin (I believe it was) had set up complete facilities to receive and care for the FFAC children; airlines had donated space on flights, and all the children could be moved to Wisconsin. I told her that we would take the children home to Colorado rather than move them to yet another half-way place. It was decided, meanwhile, that the FFAC children would be moved temporarily to another building on the Presidio, to make room for new arrivals in Harmon Hall. FFAC was to process children out of the base with all possible speed. We phoned the FFAC Board members in Colorado and asked them to set up facilities, supplies, volunteers and medical care for several hundred children.

John Wetterer offered to take France-bound children to Long Island for temporary foster care. In the face of a twelve-hour 'eviction notice', I approved his plan. Connie Boll offered the same service for the children destined for Germany. With John and Connie willing to accept the responsibility and enormous effort in taking over the care of so many children, it began to look more possible that we could get the rest to Denver.

During that day I finally saw my daughter Lisa, who had flown to San Francisco to help care for our Cambodian twins. Lisa was pale with dark circles under her tear-reddened eyes. 'I named one of the babies after Margaret,' was the first thing she told me. I began to realize what my own family had endured and the pain that would continue. We went together to see our babies, still at Maria's house, where they had been taken when they arrived on Tuesday night, by now five days before. Lisa and the babies were packed to take an afternoon flight home.

Some parents arrived to pick up their children from the Presidio. Late Sunday evening, still on 6 April, the first fifty children left for the Denver Life Center in Colorado.

M-NG: Meanwhile, Connie and John were setting up temporary nurseries on Long Island and in Connecticut to care for children destined for Europe, while their immigration and travel formalities were being arranged. Christie was despatched to Darien, Connecticut with several babies. John Califf of the Lutheran Service Society in Denver established a temporary nursery in the Denver Life Center.

Connie secured the use of Hugh Hefner's (founder of *Playboy* magazine) bunny plane to transport some children to New York, and some off-duty 'bunnies' helped to care for them on the trip. With the luxury of hindsight there are a few humorous moments which at the time were rarely appreciated. But, certainly, the bunny plane episode elicited a chuckle on the spot.

Even in the shadow of the Golden Gate Bridge we were not spared the tragedy of our nurseries, when tiny Dorothea died in hospital, and was buried, not only with the dignity she deserved but amid the curiosity of the press and entangled in military regulations.

Elaine, Rayneld, Lani, Diane, Jerry Peters and I were chauffered by mortuary limousine to the cemetery where a simple and reverent graveside service was held.

After a vain attempt to get a second plane to travel to Vietnam to fetch the rest of the children and bring our staff home, we decided the best we could do now was to head back to Denver to sort out the paperwork in close contact with the FFAC staff in Boulder and the children at the Life Center.

Chapter 16

CONTINUING EVACUATION
AND ARRIVALS IN USA
5–26 April 1975

THE REMAINING FOREIGN STAFF in Saigon – Doreen Beckett, Mary Cusack, Susan McDonald, rejoined about ten days later by Ruth Routten and later still, Ilse – returned with me to the nurseries to continue with what was left to be done. We met daily for lunch, which was prepared by the To Am cook and brought by Mary in the Volkswagen to Rathaven. It was a welcome break for us all and helped us co-ordinate our efforts. First of all Doreen closed Hy Vong and sent her few sick babies to Newhaven, as Susan was the only nurse. Some of the children left in Allambie and To Am were brought to Phu My, and a few were taken back by Sr Sylvie to the Delta. Most of the nursery equipment, furniture and food supplies were given to Phu My. But then more children poured in from provincial orphanages, as the Sisters commuted back and forth from the Delta, bringing children who had been promised mostly to families in France and Italy. Over the next three weeks, the population of To Am, Newhaven and Allambie built up again to maximum capacity, and this after most of the local staff had been dismissed and extra supplies dispersed.

A visit to the Italian Embassy by Mary was unproductive. Nothing more was heard from Italian officialdom until the children destined for Italian families were safely evacuated to the USA, thanks to American diplomacy and at American expense. Marguerrite de Gunzbourg from France, helped by Marie-Rose Hung, laboured over the confusion of the French adoptions, which were being handled by several different agencies in France. They tried to obtain authorization for the children to go directly to France and succeeded in the cases of two or three small groups, but it became apparent they would never succeed in processing all the children in this way, since the Ministry services were breaking down. On 11 April, five children were sent on the Air France flight to France and Scandinavia. To evacuate a large group directly to France, despite the legal *laissez-passer*, would, it seems, have been a diplomatic *faux pas* the French were not prepared to commit. As in the case of Italy, it seemed that only when the children had reached America would the French Embassy facilitate their onward journey. And this is what happened: the French Consul in San Francisco was most helpful and issued the necessary documentation with merciful efficiency.

Susan and Mary had a tremendous task trying to run the nurseries at full capacity, cope with the daily new arrivals, and at the same time prepare for complete evacuation as soon as a plane became available. Doreen had found some refugee sisters from Tuy Hoa who were happy to move into a fully equipped Hy Vong. The FFAC staff were grateful that the nursery would continue to be used for the welfare of children, since it had been set up so beautifully for this purpose. Lucienne and Jo LeGall, our long-time collaborators, moved with their family into Allambie to care for newly arriving older children. Doreen then moved over to Rathaven office and took charge of all financial matters, housing contracts, vehicle disposal, and made up powers of attorney for legal transfer of property.

As our hopes rose and fell with the reports of possible planes, the city resounded with the noise of military activity. Mary made us laugh with a story of what luckily turned into an emergency practice, when one night after a particularly loud explosion she arranged for all the children to shelter under beds on the ground floor. Flashlights, radios, food and water, and diapers were mustered, and she switched off the power and lights. (It was the sound of the ammunition dump blowing up at Bien Hoa Airbase, just fifteen miles away.)

We read in the *Saigon Post* of the Australian government's decision to take an 'unlimited' number of orphans, providing that they were going to Australian parents. Our Australian friends had set up facilities to care for children temporarily, but the government refused categorically to accept children in transit to other countries.

I checked several times with the Embassy in Saigon to see if there had been any change of policy; Australian planes were available, but the government would not budge. Only the United States took children irrespective of their ultimate destination.

Ruth Routten arrived from San Francisco on the 15th. She rang me at Rathaven to announce her unexpected arrival and told us of FFAC's plan to send a plane in two days' time. Since we still had no *laissez-passer*, Doreen phoned the States to see if the plane could be postponed – only to learn that, anyway, it had come to nothing.

> *Ruth Routten*: I accompanied Doreen to USAID as she submitted a list of orphans requiring exit visas and transportation. Although Mr Ruoff had a meeting with the Ministry of Social Welfare that very afternoon, he would not present FFAC's list, since he was planning to use another agency's list as a 'test case'. Doreen persuaded him at least to accept her list. He assured us that there would be no problem in securing an aircraft once the Vietnamese had approved the departure of this new group of children. A US Air Force C-141, equipped with medical personnel, could at once evacuate the children.
>
> Back at Rathaven we reported our limited success to Rosemary, Susan and Mary. After a quick dinner at USAID I spent the night with Susan at Newhaven. Susan was quite aware that Saigon was in imminent danger of falling to the North Vietnamese troops. She had attended several briefings by the US Government Mission Warden's Office, concerning plans for an emergency evacuation, which would probably occur at night. I slept on the couch, fully clothed. My first night was relatively quiet. The shelling was very light and appeared to be outgoing.
>
> *Wednesday 16 April*: Rosemary was continuing in a systematic and calm manner to process normal travel documentation on as many individual children as possible, sending them out on either Pan Am or Air France flights which were still operating. I called Bobbie Nofflet to enlist her assistance in obtaining the new *laissez-passer* from the Vietnamese government.

A representative from an Australian group arrived in Saigon about this time and used Newhaven as a depot for the babies which he collected from various orphanages. They left on an army plane and took with them two of our children, Hymn and Minh Hoa, assigned to Australian families. The Australian Embassy had invited us to send more children on this last flight, but still refused to accept children in transit. Three sick babies could have gone to Australia as a last resort, but by the time we presented the necessary data we were too late: the lists had been submitted and approved by the Minister before he had reportedly resigned. These children had lost their last chance. Little Amos with biliari atresia[1] would probably have died, but the two others, Aurelia and Budapest, might have been saved permanent brain damage and death by timely surgical intervention.

On 17 April, another warning circular arrived from the Australian Embassy, 'strongly suggesting that [I] should now plan to leave the country while commercial aircraft are still operating'. On Friday, the 18th, five more children left with complete documentation for France and Germany on the regular Air France flight.

Ruth, like Doreen, compensated for my own inefficiency in these days. She carried the mountain of files that lined two of the four walls of my room at Phu My into Margaret's empty room, and sat for long hours in the heat, going through the thousands of dossiers. She extracted birth certificates and adoption decrees before destroying the rest. The choice of what to keep and what to jettison had to be made rapidly using what foresight we could command. Finally, we packed up four trunks of documents and our entire master filing-card system. We envisaged no problem in regularizing the status of the children, thanks to the crucial fact that we now held their legal custody under Vietnamese law, and so would be permitted in the adoptive country to transfer custody to the adoptive parents in the name of our agency, without having to have recourse to the orphanage of origin.

Ruth Routten: I kept in touch with Bobbie Nofflet to see if she had progressed in her efforts to obtain departure authorization for the children. On Saturday, 19 April, we considered ways of transporting the boxes of files out of Vietnam. 'Flying Tigers' at

---

[1] Biliari atresia: obliteration of one or more components of the bile ducts due to arrested foetal development, resulting in persistent jaundice and liver damage.

Tan Son Nhut said that they had already ceased their carrier operations, but the deputy manager kindly agreed as a personal favour to put the entire 300 lb of files on a plane with his own belongings.

. . . I next spoke to Major B. about the possibility of evacuating one hundred orphans. He was co-ordinating the refugee evacuation from Tan Son Nhut, and said he had helped a group of orphans leave Saigon the previous night. We presumed this was Fr Crawford and his children. That afternoon, when we delivered the files to Flying Tigers, Major B. said a plane would leave in a couple of days; we would travel with a montagnard group bound for Denmark and could take only a minimum number of escorts, among whom he stipulated Susan and I, as Americans, must be included. More details would be forthcoming on Sunday.

Meanwhile, Bobbie Nofflet had herself been ordered, in the category of non-essential personnel, to leave Saigon that very afternoon, but she refused to go while our situation was so uncertain. At Rathaven she secured an up-to-date list of the children in Rosemary's care for one last attempt. Her own final departure date was set for Tuesday.

Doreen continued organizing the finances, paying debts and the remaining staff's wages, with final bonuses, and distributing extra piastres where they would be most needed. Several million piastres were given to the Sisters who had moved into Hy Vong. Rosemary thought it would pay the rent for the next two years (a useless prevision as it turned out, as the nursery was requisitioned immediately after the takeover, the Sisters and children evicted, and the money in the bank confiscated).

The *Saigon Post* was still in print but large areas were censored and blacked out. News concerning the fall of Cambodia was printed. The quiet days and air of normality produced a false sense of security in us. However, the Vietnamese people were for the most part fear-struck. Radio Hanoi had, according to Le and Chinh, reported that all people who had worked for the adoption of orphans would be considered war criminals.

Fr Joe Turner, a military chaplain remarkable for his dedication to the orphans, who had first helped Rosemary on his Vietnam tour in 1971, now returned unexpectedly on his own initiative to help evacuate orphans; and John Carr had also come back. After dinner at USAID together, Susan and I returned to Newhaven; Mary and Doreen to To Am; Rosemary to Phu My; and Fr Joe and John to Rathaven. Back at Newhaven, we found a military jeep with armed soldiers parked outside our gate; a special news bulletin announced an immediate curfew. We were concerned that we couldn't communicate with Rosemary, but could only wait. The next news bulletin announced the resignation of President Thieu.

We spent an edgy night, as usual fully dressed, bags packed and ready for a possible evacuation by helicopter. I phoned Major B. at midnight (as requested) and learnt that his proposed plane, a 727 belonging to World Airways, had been refused entry by Ambassador Martin. The Major told us that World Airways had requested 450 dollars for each child's transportation as far as Tokyo, with no assurance of onward travel. Nevertheless, I assured him, cost would be no deterrent if, after all, the 727 could come.

Monday 21 April: Rosemary came to Newhaven as usual about 8 a.m. She and Susan updated the arrivals of the previous day: two of the babies needing nursery names were called Hesitation and Resignation. Soon after, Le reported that she could not get into the US Consulate to process the entry visas for the children due to depart on the Thursday's Pan Am flight. The compound was surrounded by a large crowd of Vietnamese, and police and TV cameras were everywhere. As an American, I was able to force my way in and process the visas for myself. Many Vietnamese women were there trying to obtain visas for their American-fathered children.

That afternoon we were told that the World Airways flight was withdrawn.

Tuesday 22 April: Susan and I drove to Tan Son Nhut at 7 a.m. Susan was attempting to get clearance for a Vietnamese friend and her two children. For a short period it seemed that any US citizen could sign sponsorship papers for Vietnamese nationals and they would be evacuated. But when we returned with Rosemary that afternoon, in an attempt to sponsor at least some of the older US-bound orphans via the refugee airlift, the regulations had already been changed, as we learnt after a two-hour wait in the long queue.

Doreen spent the morning trying to contact USAID and at 5 p.m. drove me back to Tan Son Nhut for the third time that day, and a further meeting with Major B. He told me that we would have to evacuate very soon, if necessary without our, by now, 200 children. He seemed surprised, but realized I was serious when I said that we would not leave without the children. He had re-established contact with World Airways; they were again willing to send a plane once we had paid the 450 dollars for each child.

Wednesday 23 April: Br Andrew came to Newhaven, and we broke bread together: Rosemary, Susan, Doreen, Mary, John Carr, Br Andrew and myself. Afterwards, we shared a delicious meal that Mary had arranged. The evening was especially meaningful since Andrew had decided not to leave Saigon. We dispersed early because of the 8 p.m. curfew, and went to bed with the usual expectation of a nocturnal helicopter evacuation.

Thursday 24 April: John Carr departed as escort for four children on the last Pan Am flight from Saigon. The scene at the terminal was chaotic. John had forgotten to pick up his own escort ticket, so I offered him mine, which I wouldn't be needing now. Artillery and mortar fire was quite audible at the airport, and fighter jets were swooping low strafing the perimeter of the field. When the Pan Am plane taxied out with over 450 persons aboard, including all the Saigon Pan Am staff, we were struck by a sense of finality.

Doreen attended another USAID meeting with the other adoption agencies, and reported back that the US Embassy had finally decided to airlift the remaining orphans out of Saigon, beginning that afternoon. The *laissez-passer* had been granted.

Susan and Mary prepared their nurseries for an evacuation, as did Mme LeGall at Allambie, only to hear that the flight was cancelled. New flight departure times were established for Friday. Doreen and Rosemary were maintaining order under the great stress imposed by the ever-changing list of children, escorts and flight schedules. This time Vietnamese staff were authorized to act as escorts. Le and Chinh became very quiet. They had been so anxious to go and only now that their travel status was cleared were they able to appreciate the full impact of what it meant to leave family and homeland for ever.

Each evening the USAID restaurant became more deserted; the menu more limited. By Thursday there remained only the 'absolutely essential people', plus Sr Kateri of Catholic Relief and ourselves.

Friday 25 April: A plane was scheduled for this afternoon. With relief and elation we all prepared the children for departure. The Allambie children were brought over to To Am; the children from Caritas also came to To Am. The yard was very crowded and the children restless in the afternoon heat. After an age of waiting around, the phone rang to say this plane, too, had been cancelled. The Caritas children were sent home after Mary managed to find them something to eat. As the ambulance that had brought the children from Allambie refused to budge, Mary, Le and Chinh ferried them back in small groups.

Again the comforting ritual of supper together at USAID, with only two or three others, amongst them Ray Fontaine. By now it was a foregone conclusion that Saigon had only days left before being taken over by the Communist troops. Ray estimated less than a week, and he was right. That night sleep was difficult; aircraft circled continuously overhead. I thought at first they were C-141s continuing the refugee evacuation, but when Susan and I went up on the roof to investigate we discovered two American-built C-130s flying figures-of-eight over the city, perhaps checking on the movement of heavy artillery around the perimeter of Saigon.

At midnight on Friday the head child-care worker brought in a four-month-old boy, whose breath was laboured. Susan recognized immediately a case of the fatal pneumonia, pneumocystis carinii. She called the Mission Warden for transportation to hospital and meanwhile administered some medication; but the Adventist Hospital had closed down, and all the foreign staff had been evacuated to the States earlier that day. Susan then continued to Grall Hospital, which took the child in. She returned to Newhaven very shaken, giving him little hope of surviving. A phone call in the early hours confirmed his death.

We had only three of our foreign staff – Susan, Ruth, Mary – to escort the, by now, 270 children. USAID suggested we send one escort for every five children and this could include our Vietnamese staff and their dependants. Four of the Vietnamese staff elected to go: Le, the secretary; Chinh, recently administrative assistant at Allambie; Kim Tien, our social worker and child-care instructor; and Thi Ba, a faithful worker who had been with us for four years and for whom we felt responsible since she had no family at all. We needed still more escorts and asked the Sisters of Providence if they wished to send some of their number. They listed eight names, including two priests. We were very doubtful about their efficacy as escorts but at the time we decided that we simply needed more hands, and reluctantly consented to include them. The final list (including by now two LeGall daughters, Brigitte and Regine, and their cousin Sylvie) had already been submitted to USAID when the Sisters asked if they could send two other priests, since the original ones did not wish to leave. We refused. We were afraid to do anything that could jeopardize the departure of the children, who were our only concern.

On Saturday, 26 April, the time for the pick-up of the children was communicated to each nursery; there would be two buses at Newhaven, two at To Am, and one at Allambie. Ruth went to Newhaven and Doreen to To Am with the approved list of escorts to make sure that no unauthorized person boarded the bus; Ilse (just back) and I rode in the ambulance with all the baggage. We checked at To Am on the progress of the bus-boarding and found the unlisted priests trying to board. I was angry and adamant in my refusal. We had no idea what formalities awaited us at the airport, and we would not take the risk of including any unauthorized person on that bus with the children.

Each child was also checked off on the master list before being allowed to board the bus to make sure that unauthorized children would not be shuffled aboard. In that particular convoy we had children who were not well-known to us, since they had been living in the orphanages until now and were mostly destined for European families. This evacuation plane was their last possibility of joining their adoptive families.

Ilse and I continued to the airport so we could direct the buses as they arrived. The airport entrance was heavily guarded and vehicles were carefully scrutinized before entry was permitted. Many vehicles containing Vietnamese were not allowed through. We spoke to the police and told them about our five buses. The Newhaven and To Am buses passed through with no problem, but the Allambie bus failed to appear. Marguerite de Gunzbourg, who had personally assumed responsibility for collecting together and organizing the children bound for France, and who had been instrumental in facilitating our entry into the airport, appeared once again at the gate and waited with me while Ilse drove back the half mile to Allambie to investigate the delay. The bus had not shown up! Ilse crammed thirty children into the ambulance, already loaded with baggage, and in two smaller private cars she jammed in the rest. The police at the airport gate accepted our explanation of why the children were not in the regulation bus, and let the vehicles pass.

Inside, however, as we were trying to follow the buses on to the tarmac, the police objected. They had no authorization to let pass any vehicle other than USAID buses. One of the by now empty buses returned, so that we could load the children into it, and thus satisfy the regulations, but the police would not accept this solution. Nor would they let the children get out and walk. When we unloaded the sweltering children and attempted to walk the 100 yards a police officer drew his gun and levelled it at a four-year-old who was wandering away from the group. It was an incredible impasse. There was no one from USAID there to help us, as most of their personnel had already been evacuated. I glared with all the contempt I could muster at the police officer who had dared to draw his gun on a four-year-old. He scowled as though I would be next. I remembered an emergency number I had been told to phone in case any problem should arise, and I walked on past the police to the Flying Tigers office a few yards away. I phoned the mystery number and help was promised within ten minutes. The affair took considerably longer to arrange. We hassled it out until eventually the children were permitted to board one of the empty buses to take them the last fifty yards.

We were still too far from the plane to walk with all these babies, many of whom were in cardboard boxes supplied by USAID. Once again we had to load up the buses. It was a physically exhausting task, as half the inexperienced non-FFAC escorts were standing by, totally useless and disorientated, clutching their own baggage. Again my patience snapped, and I grabbed the bags out of the hands of some of the escorts and pushed babies into their arms. Mary and Doreen did likewise.

Ruth Routten: The plane was a small C-141 cargo plane with no amenities whatsoever. The older children were strapped in can-vas seats along the side of the fuselage with one common seat belt to secure them. Approximately seventy-five children travelled in this fashion. The remaining children were placed on blankets spread over the metal floor. The tiny babies in boxes and baskets were placed in the rear of the plane with Susan and the other escorts were scattered throughout. I sat in the forward section amongst the toddlers. Everything that was happening went against the rigid training I had had during my past twelve years as an air stewardess. When the giant shell door began to swing shut, I shall never forget the sight of Rosemary, Doreen and Ilse, standing there waving goodbye. We left not knowing if or when we would see each other again.

Our flying nursery was less than adequate and it was imposs-ible to care for the children properly. Fortunately, our first stopover would be Manila. Movement was hazardous with so many small bodies lying on the floor. The older children slumped over in their makeshift seats in an exhausted doze. Susan and Mary looked after the tiny babies in the aft section of the plane. The LeGall girls gave water to the older children. We ran out of water one hour out of Saigon.

Our arrival at Clark Air Force Base, the Philippines, was like stepping into heaven. There was one baby-sitter assigned to care for each child. Each child was given a medical examination and a number preceded by the code 'purple' to denote FFAC. The system worked fairly well. Susan and I spent the first few nights with the children, getting very little sleep, then relocated our bedroom/office in a quieter spot under a nearby shelter.

Susan co-ordinated the onward departure of the children on several C-141 aircraft bound for the States via Honolulu. Le, Chinh, and I checked to make sure all the children were properly tagged and visited the hospital to keep a close watch on the children who had been admitted.

We were glued to the hourly news reports coming out of Saigon. The news that the city had been heavily shelled was upsetting; but the reports of the final helicopter evacuation of Saigon left us numb. We had no way of knowing if Rosemary, Doreen and Ilse had gotten out. It was two weeks before we had any news of them.

We stayed on to close up the houses and generally clear up anything we still could. There were several dozen children from Sacred Heart Orphanage, Danang, and St Paul's, Qui Nhon, whose adoptions were completed but who at the last moment were unable to reach Saigon. Families in France, Germany, USA and Canada who had been awaiting children for many months, were grief-stricken when finally their children were unable to join them. These children, though already legally bearing the name of their adoptive families, were detained in Vietnam. The new government did not honour the adoption contracts of the previous government.

Mary-Nelle Gage, in America, awaiting further evacuations: In Denver, the Grant family home had been swallowed up by adoption workers, round-the-clock secretaries (organized by Madeline Porter, the secretary at FFAC), volunteers opening mail and sorting out the Presidio papers, who first filled the office, then overflowed into the dining room, and so into the living room ... Mail was delivered by the trayful. Even though several new phone lines had been installed, there was rarely a spare phone. European convoys had to be arranged with Pierre Lauritson of Air France; Minnie Gallozzi in Paris; Margarita Hugoson in Stockholm; Terre des Hommes in Germany, France and Switzerland; Charlotte Spire in Montreal; families in England and Belgium; and John Wetterer in New York and Connie Boll in Connecticut; not to mention the various consulates.

But the flurry of activity never dispelled the deep anxiety about what was still happening in Saigon. One evening, Susan McDonald phoned from Saigon, and we discussed the status of evacuation negotiations and the increasing numbers of children moving from the orphanages and refilling the nurseries. When asked if Michelangelo, who was in hospital since the C-5A crash, would be able to come with them, Susan replied in a tone that brought home to me forcibly the terrible precariousness of the situation – that they would bring him if they were allowed to stop at the Adventist Hospital and that would depend on the urgency of the departure. (Michelangelo *was* brought to his family in America.)

On about 24 April, a small group of FFAC children arrived on the last Pan Am flight out of Saigon; John Carr brought Genesis, Lamentation, Mark and Rosemary in the first-class lounge. The flight had made a dramatic impression on Al Topping, the Saigon Director of Pan Am. The regular flight attendants had brought spare uniforms to Saigon to be worn by other Pan Am employees wishing to leave on that last plane. There were in all seventy-five passengers beyond the normal maximum, and the ground crew had climbed up through the baggage hold after the cabin doors had been shut, leaving the embarkation stairs standing on the tarmac.

The reception plans were prepared, but the arrival location for each agency's children was uncertain. Once the reception staff dashed to Los Angeles and began to organize ourselves there, when word came that the first C-141 would arrive at Travis, near San Francisco. Back we went in time to compose a plan: each team of two, equipped with cards, would be assigned a room in the Presidio in which to receive and examine all FFAC children, noting down pertinent details.

Mary Cusack, Kim Tien and her mother escorted the first plane to arrive. Our cards could quickly be checked against the lists Mary had with her. Thanks to John Wetterer's organizational ability the plan worked and within half an hour of their arrival we knew which children were which, and where they were to go. The next flight, accompanied by Le, was equally successful. Two more planes, escorted by Ruth and Susan, would arrive at McCord Base near Seattle, in the Fort Lewis area.

However, as the children, who had been only briefly in the Saigon nurseries arrived, we knew less about them. There were frequent 'crises', whipped up by over-zealous volunteers, involving 'cruel, ignorant, careless' separation of brothers and sisters. Even army personnel were alerted and required us to show proof from documents and lists that the children in question were not siblings. In fact [as Wende Grant points out] there were only two cases of missing children or of mistaken identity, despite the confusion of the Presidio arrivals; and FFAC were accountable for neither. (Both cases were also solved.) Three cross-referenced index cards were now made of each child, so that he or she was filed by Vietnamese name, nursery name and by adoptive family name.

We were joined by the agency representatives from abroad: Doris Schildkamp from Terre des Hommes Germany; Minnie Gallozzi from 'Les Amis des Enfants'; the Italians and the Finns, who checked out the children destined for their countries and arranged their onward transportation.

In the midst of this work, late one afternoon I was called to the phone. A US government attorney indicated that a lawsuit was being filed, protesting the babylift. He asked me, as someone who had worked both in Saigon and at the Presidio, whether I would be willing to testify. I became quite certain that I would not be happy to testify when he revealed to me that, after the hearing, the plaintiffs might decide to name me in their lawsuit. That night we got together to discuss the pros and cons of testifying. We gathered that the group bringing the lawsuit were sophisticated, well-informed and well-prepared, and it didn't seem wise to testify voluntarily without legal counsel. Wende was confident that she could dismiss the case by providing accurate data. She called George Carnie to ask his opinion and he recommended that we should not become involved without local legal counsel.

The next morning at the Presidio Lani had just managed to attract my attention to tell me that the attorney had been calling again to see if we were going to testify voluntarily, when the Army officer of the day advised us to work fast if we had any children to move, since there was probably going to be a restraining order put on the Presidio to hold the children there. At this point Wende rushed up and without waiting to explain hustled us into the car. As we sped away, she told us that the US Marshals were on their way to serve us subpoenas requiring us to testify. We had to leave San Francisco. On the way to the airport we decided that Wende should return to Colorado; I would join our third reception group at Fort Lewis. There were local flights almost immediately for Denver and Sea Tac; we had evaded the Marshals in less than two hours.

The Fort Lewis operation was human and manageable. As the children, arriving with Susan and Ruth, were processed to families or to Denver, our team dispersed, leaving Mary Cusack, John Carr and me to meet the final medivac flight, see to the last arrivals, complete French convoys with Minnie, and make the last onward arrangements for the Europe-bound children.

But our worries did not cease. There was no news of Rosemary, Doreen, and Ilse. George Miles (who had given so much practical help in the nurseries), accompanied John and me to the midnight arrival of the medivac plane, hoping and sure that Rosemary would have made it to the Clark Air Force Base in the Philippines, and would be accompanying the last of her children. We stood at the foot of the plane ready to welcome her, but she did not come.

[M-NG]

Chapter 17

FINAL DEPARTURE
26 April–6 May 1975

As THE PLANE moved away with the last of our children, I felt only an immense sense of relief and of freedom, such as I'd never before experienced. The burden of all those children for so many years had been weighing intolerably. Now we were alone and the children in other hands. Ilse, Doreen and I returned to Rathaven, sat on the floor and drank gallons of Tang. Then Doreen went over to To Am to close up the house and I headed for Newhaven, where looting had already started. I asked the LeGalls to move into Newhaven and try to distribute what remained to Phu My and other orphanages. The details of the next two days are somewhat hazy; I mostly pottered around with no sense of urgency, sorting out bits and pieces.

With the children gone, my mind was free to wander over the untidy edges and loose ends. It bothered me to leave things in this way. I became absorbed sorting through the remaining files, choosing which to keep, which to destroy, and which I could usefully leave with the Sisters at Phu My. I did the same with the contents of my wardrobe, dividing my clothes and other trivial possessions between the various boxes designated for the teenage girls who slept next door, for the Sisters to dispose of, or for the family of Duc, my cyclo-driver.

Sr Rose Marie left Phu My on Sunday the 27th, with Sr Raymond and Sr Odile, the only French Sisters remaining. Sr Rose had been in Vietnam for over twenty-four years, and for the last ten as Superior of Phu My. She had been due to return finally to Europe the previous year, but had prolonged her stay to the very last moment, supporting the community through this difficult period. As the

Sisters left for the airport on Sunday evening they were seen off by a weeping throng of children and adults – the 1,500 inmates of Phu My for whom Sr Rose was only a little less than God. It was indeed the end of an era. There were tears in my own eyes as I bade them goodbye. Sr Rose had been a friend to me for the past eight years; she not only gave me my food and lodging but precious moral support. I don't know how I could have continued in Vietnam with such a project had it not been for the special relation I had with Phu My and the co-operation of Sr Rose. She was a pragmatist with her feet firmly planted in reality. She knew just how much credence to give to eloquent theorizing and glowing promises; which opinions deserved attention and which were best ignored. She would report to us any negative rumours or criticisms she heard concerning our work (and there were some that were quite bizarre) and from the wisdom of her own experience advised us how to deal with them. She was outspoken in support of our integrity and stood by us loyally when more pusillanimous spirits would have nothing to do with us.

I lingered at Phu My, and probably would have been sitting there long after the take-over had it not been for Doreen and Ilse in Rathaven, and the awareness that I ought to be in the USA sharing the heavy responsibility of identifying the children and placing them. One of the Vietnamese Sisters asked me when I would be leaving. I said that I wasn't sure, but I had the distinct feeling that her question carried another message – that my presence as the only remaining Caucasian was becoming an embarrassment to them, and that I ought to leave soon for the good of the Sisters. Without Sr Rose to provide a fearless bastion between them and the government, they were afraid. Sr Rose had been a woman of the greatest moral strength and intelligence. She knew her rights and would not suffer them to be violated. She had fed, clothed and protected the inmates of Phu My literally by the strength of her own personality, and woe betide any government official who might try to cheat her or cut back on the welfare support she was supposed to receive. Nothing escaped her vigilance, from the pig farm and vegetable garden, to the beautifully equipped new polio unit with its hundred children. Her presence kept all services functioning and improving. With her departure Phu My had lost an incomparable leader – a loss felt so much more keenly in the present crisis.

On Monday, the 28th, I checked with Air France – the only line that I had assumed was still operating – and only then did my mind wake up to the fact that commercial planes would be non-operational at any moment. Unless we took immediate steps to leave, we would be forced to stay indefinitely because of lack of transportation. This provoked me to a state of more useful activity. I immediately reserved four seats (the fourth was for Ilse's adoptive daughter Ulla) for Wednesday, the last scheduled flight. (Sr Rose told me later that the passengers aboard the plane on the 27th were told theirs was Air France's last flight from Saigon.) In the afternoon a friend at Air France advised us to try for the scheduled UTA flight at midnight the same day. We changed our reservations. At about 6 p.m. Air France phoned us that the UTA flight was cancelled; we were rescheduled back to the Air France Wednesday flight.

That night I didn't return to Phu My, but slept with Doreen and Ilse at Rathaven. I never did get back to Phu My to say goodbye, but left the key of my room with Lucienne LeGall who was living then at Newhaven. I was full of apologies, and felt ashamed because I hadn't been able to sweep my room after the complete demolition job I had done on it. That this trivial omission continued to worry me shows the way in which the mind seems to focus on certain unimportant details as touchstones of reality when the underlying reality is too far-reaching to consider.

On Tuesday, the 29th, I sorted through bundles of Allambie photos at Rathaven, picking out some that I wanted to send later to the adoptive parents, but scrapping most of them as I knew that, however we left Vietnam, our luggage would be restricted. Antici-pating a normal commercial flight I had already prepared a case of clothes and a briefcase of documents and items I did not want to trust to the suitcase. We had each prepared an overnight shoulder bag with a change of clothing and a few necessities. We had learnt by experience this was the safest way to travel; it was a fortunate prevision.

There was a twenty-four-hour curfew that day, I think. We were all in the living room at Rathaven, listening to the news on the radio, talking to Mr Uyen (our works manager and guardian) and his family and wondering what we should do next. Doreen offered to walk the several blocks to USAID in quest of information. Half an hour later she returned: the USAID office was empty. She had walked to a nearby USAID apartment block: empty, too. Someone suggested we should all go to the US Embassy.

We changed into long trousers (a lucky instinct) and we were ready to go. Mr Uyen drove us to the Embassy, dropping us on crowded Hong Thap Tu Street. We walked round the corner to the Mac Dinh Chi gate. Impossible to enter. We dragged our luggage back to the Hong Thap Tu gate and stood in the crowd. It seemed useless. We thought we might as well go back to Rathaven. But then a Marine guard saw us and beckoned us over to a peep hole in the gate. He told us to go into Fr McVeigh's yard adjoining the Embassy and the Marines would pull back the barbed wire and haul us over the side wall. We walked down near Fr McVeigh's gate and sat on our luggage discussing how we would manage to get over without causing a stampede. Very suddenly, we threw the luggage over, scaled the gate and dropped to the other side, then ran down the driveway. The Marines were there peering over the jagged glass on top of the wall and pulling back the barbed wire. We were told to drop our cases, hop on to the parked car and from there they would pull us over. We abandoned our suitcases as instructed, threw the briefcases over the wall, and kept our shoulder bags strapped on. Ilse cut herself on the jagged glass and I was almost strangled by my bag straps, but we were over.

It was about 4.30 or 5 p.m. The Embassy grounds were swarming with Vietnamese refugees, some Caucasians, and the US Marines, who were behaving with great restraint and courage in a situation of panic. The buildings were empty with the desolate aspect of a hasty abandonment. Litter was strewn everywhere – a shockingly dramatic change in a compound that had always been kept in such perfect order and sacrosanct privacy.

We were not clear what we were doing in this crowd. After scouting around for a while we detected some sort of slow movement around the swimming pool and through the side gate that led to the Main Embassy building and the helipads. Helicopters were landing every so often on the roof pad and on the hastily made ground pad (the tree had been chopped down only that morning), loading up with refugees and taking off for we did not know where. The sky was filled with a haze of bright purple smoke which was obviously a signal to the helicopters. I presumed they were going to the airport a few miles away. We were too conscious of the present moment to explore even the immediate future. Time was heavy, and opaque, and my imagination at least ceased to function.

We progressed slowly around the swimming pool and occasionally went to find some drinking water. Some kind Vietnamese had a bag of melted ice and an empty soft drink can. He was sharing his water with anyone, and we were grateful for a mouthful. We saw Fr McVeigh and alerted him that Sr Mary Hayden and one of the other Good Shepherd Sisters were still outside in the street. We hoped he would find some way to get them inside. Later, we saw them both in the compound.

Probably about an hour and a half elapsed before we found ourselves at the gate. Just as we were about to go through, Ilse realized that she had lost her small shoulder bag carrying identity documents for herself and her daughter. Our first reaction was to forget about the documents and pass through, but Ilse maybe foresaw the problems she would face without identification, especially for her daughter, and in great distress returned to the last place we had been sitting. The bag was there – on the ground – no small miracle! As we waited for her to return to the gate, I overheard a Marine say that third-country-nationals were supposed to be leaving in the helicopters landing on the Embassy roof and not from the ground pad. We verified this. The Marine directed us to the door of the Main Embassy building, then up six flights of stairs to the roof pad. We were the last four to be numbered on the helicopter just arriving. With heads bent low, and pushing our way against the powerful air-currents, we bundled into the back of the chopper. In all we were about sixteen passengers. From the camera equipment, I guessed a few of the others were journalists.

By this time it was past sunset and visibility was poor. The back of the helicopter was left open and we peered out of the gaping hole at the darkening landscape as we headed out towards the sea. There were no lights inside and the high noise level of the engine and rotors made any conversation impossible. We sat tensely, watched and waited. The trip seemed very short to me but by later calculations and our combined impressions we must have been in the air for almost an hour.

We were by now far out at sea. I was positioned up front of the aircraft, near a Marine who was anxiously straining to see through the window. I could discern his movements only very dimly in the darkness. He threw me a life jacket which I put on; then I helped the man next to me who was having difficulty with his. I presumed that everyone was similarly equipped, but it was impossible to see in the dark, and later Doreen said that further back they had no life jackets.

Through a window I could see the roughness of the sea; we were obviously very low over the water. I wasn't aware of any ship nearby. The Marine was studying the situation with great intentness, and when I saw him take off his boots I slipped off my sandals, accepting that this was all part of the procedure – for what, I wasn't sure, but deduced we were going to get wet. Doreen's feet were already in the water, so the tail end of the helicopter was already submerged. I was trying to work out how I could possibly hold on to my briefcase of documents in the choppy seas, as I am a weak swimmer.

At no time did I experience any emotion resembling fear, as far as I can recall. The whole level of emotional living became inaccessible. There was only instinctive reaction and habit built up from experience. As I had no preconception of what awaited us at the end of the chopper ride, I lived from second to second, and was prepared to accept any procedure as normal.

The next thing I remember was the chopper lowering itself on to the deck of a ship. We climbed out and headed for the reception area, where our bags were examined – and Ilse's pocket knife was confiscated as an unauthorized weapon. It was by now about 7.30 p.m. and we were on board the *US Blue Ridge*, communication centre of the 7th Fleet. We were treated with great kindness and cordiality. The boat was immense, and the facilities very comfortable.

We learnt later from the crew that our chopper had almost gone into the sea. It had arrived unexpectedly and was too low in fuel to circle while a landing-space was cleared on the cluttered deck. We were actually hitting the water when the pilot switched to another fuel tank and found just enough power to raise the machine and slide it on to the side of the deck.

At about 6 a.m. the next morning, the 30th, the American Ambassador, Martin, himself came aboard, and another contingent of Marines went back on the helicopter to cover the retreat of their comrades now marooned in the Saigon Embassy. The helicopters flown by the Vietnamese Air Force made one-way trips only and, because of limited deck space, were shoved overboard as soon as the passengers and pilot had jumped out. At a million dollars apiece, we saw some twelve million dollars being fed to the fishes.

While Vice-President Ky and the high-ranking Vietnamese officers stayed in their cabins below deck, the US Marines flew back and forth in a harrowing rescue operation. The entire 7th Fleet was in the area. We could count sixteen ships within our immediate range of vision, and there were many others just beyond the horizon.

After two nights on board the *Blue Ridge*, on Thursday 1 May we were told that all non-American passengers without a visa for the Philippines had to transfer to another ship going directly to Guam. We were very unhappy at the idea of another transfer in mid-ocean, but the facts that our own travel documents were in order, and that we could take normal commercial transportation beyond the Philippines were to no avail. Our arguments and even by now my tears went unheeded. We were transferred by landing craft to a decrepit cargo vessel, the *Green Port*, that was jampacked with refugees taking up every square inch of deck space, and also crowded into the lower holds. For five days and nights we were crammed with 4,551 evacuees aboard the cargo ship. We managed to find ourselves a small space on top of the hatch cover. Solid steel, painted black, it was like a giant grill in the fierce noon-day sun. But we were happy enough with this position, nevertheless, as it was elevated a little, and as far as we could get from the make-shift latrines that lined the sides of the upper deck. We shared the tiny space with a group of the helicopter pilots of the Vietnamese Air Force who had fled without their families. There were other third-country nationals aboard, too, and we soon met up with Dr André Noë, from the IRC Clinic, who had stayed in Saigon until the last minute.

We tore up Ilse's nightdress and strung it up as a shelter, but it was too thin to offer any shade, so next day we pinned it to Doreen's raincoat. Boxes of combat-rations were distributed each day, and once we were given fresh carrots. Drinking water was strictly rationed. The ship remained stationary for a couple of days, presumably waiting to rescue more evacuees. Eventually we formed a committee to try to persuade the captain to allow us to disembark in the Philippines, since we were calling there anyway for more supplies. The captain was in a predicament, since he had been contracted by the Navy to take human cargo in an emergency, and he could only sit and wait until he received instructions. He took pains to explain the situation to us, and convoked us several times to his cabin where he showed us copies of the radio instructions he had received. He allowed us to use the telecommunication system, and we cabled FFAC in Colorado, the Australian and German Embassies in Manila, Ilse's mother in Germany, the Australian Prime Minister, and the Pentagon. All we wanted was the possibility of disembarking in the Philippines and proceeding independently on our own way.

On Saturday night there was warning of a typhoon in the area. We were advised to take shelter in the lower holds should the typhoon hit, but we vowed to stay out on top come what may: death in the open seemed preferable to death enclosed. We packaged up our passports and a few valuables in plastic and attached them to our persons, then lay down and waited for trouble. For some hours a naval boat ran parallel to us, and we guessed it was there to pick up the bodies our ship would discharge as it spun like a catherine wheel in gale-force waters . . . but in fact we missed the typhoon and were never in any real danger.

We reached Subic Bay in the Philippines at about 2 p.m. on Sunday 4 May, and were told to pack up and be ready to disembark and change boat for the continuation to Guam. We packed up and shared out what little supplies we had left (Doreen's towel, some leftover C-rations, string, pins) and sat for hours in the intense heat. In the evening we were told that we would not disembark for at least twenty-four hours; it rained that night, and we lay there singing and reciting our limited repertoire of songs and poems. All this time Ilse's daughter, Ulla, was remarkably good and adaptable; she endured the heat, the boredom, the inactivity, and the limited water ration like the rest of us, and never complained.

Eventually third-country nationals left the ship at 16.30 on Tuesday 6 May. A remarkably helpful representative of the Australian Embassy met us in the processing area and smoothed the transit operation. The Embassy even provided us with transport and checked us into a hotel that seemed – and probably was – amazingly luxurious. We spent the evening bathing and washing all our clothes. Next day Ilse and Ulla flew to Australia, where they met with our families and friends to give them the news. Doreen and I flew first to Japan, and then on to Colorado to help in any way we could with all that was left to be done.

PART TWO

Chapter 18

ABANDONMENT OF CHILDREN —

Their Origins and the Orphanages

So many questions were raised at the time and will, it seems, be raised as long as children from foreign countries are adopted into different cultures, that it is essential to explain the background to the plight of orphans in Vietnam, before and during the war, and our own, almost instinctive, belief that we should seek homes for them, if necessary, abroad.

Most of the children coming into the nurseries had been abandoned at birth or in early infancy; some had spent years in an orphanage, while others came directly from the maternities. They were abandoned for a great variety of reasons: illegitimacy; poverty; homelessness (where large numbers of displaced persons congregated in the city slums, a woman bunking down on a few square feet of stall in the market place could not provide adequately for the babies that kept coming); unfavourable omens attending the birth of a child (even the wealthy might abandon a legitimate child whose birth was ill-omened); children born prematurely, with congenital defects, or serious health problems. The babies were unwanted from the start. Birth control, or termination of pregnancies, were not possibilities.

Years of war, with its concomitant social upheaval, obviously aggravated the situation. With the mighty concentration of foreign and local military, children were lightly conceived and born to be abandoned by one parent or both. Perhaps 20 per cent of our orphans seemed to be of mixed parentage. In these circumstances, it was very easy to abandon a new baby. Even the biological bond existing between a mother and child could rapidly be overwhelmed by an even more basic drive – that of self-preservation, especially if a woman had already given birth to several unwanted babies. Nor were there social or legal pressures on a woman to keep her baby. The child could be left in a maternity, or given away to a neighbour or orphanage with no formalities, no legal transfer of custody, no court case, no publicity, and no hounding by the press. A child was easily disposed of with total impunity, and there was no possibility of tracing the parents of a child if they did not wish to be traced. And nobody really cared. Why waste effort fruitlessly searching for the missing mother of one abandoned baby when there were eighty more babies in the same orphanage with missing mothers, and tens of thousands throughout the country? Moreover, no one could force the mother to care for a child she did not want. Too many babies were being born, abandoned, and dying-off in an insignificant subcycle of life that lay somewhere in the shadowy region of the not-quite-human.

People who have lived all their lives in a modern society find it curiously hard to grasp these facts. They are unable to comprehend that with so many abandoned babies, the question of identity, for instance, was fatuous. A child had no name, and the name of the mother did not really matter, since she had no intention of identifying herself or reclaiming the child. Such gross misunderstandings of the situation became crucial to us, when we had to defend our actions, later, in the American courts. When Western observers want to make some profound remark on child-abandonment, they often say that orphanages did not exist before Western (i.e. Christian) influence contaminated the East, and caused a breakdown of the ideal indigenous traditions. They conclude that child-abandonment had not existed before, and that orphans were lovingly cared for by the 'extended family'.

This is absolutely false reasoning. The orphanages did not exist. The children were instead abandoned and sacrificed to appease angry gods; infanticide was practised; children who were malformed and who would only be an economic liability, were left to die; the extended family, spoken of so reverently by our sociologists, might sometimes take in a poor relation as a cheap way of acquiring a servant. The whole idea of a devoted extended family is now propagated by the well-to-do expatriates who naturally wish to stress the noblest practices of their society. The Sisters, equally citizens of Vietnam with deep cultural roots, who live amongst the refuse of society, tell a different story. But it doesn't satisfy the inverted-racists of the Western world who want to believe that all oriental customs are always best for the East and that Asiatics should stay at home and live by the old traditions. Their desire to idealize traditions of the East that flagrantly oppose all traditions of the West is pure hypocrisy, an opting-out.

Missionaries may have come from Europe initially, with their own ideas of the worth of the individual regardless of his social status or the beauty of his physiognomy. Instead of letting the children die, they gathered up the rejects in orphanages that were naturally a blot on any society. There were a few Buddhist orphanages and other sectarian orphanages in Vietnam, but the majority were run by Christian nuns. Orphanages may not be an original Asian concept; they may have been imposed by Western philosophy, in which to be poor and untouchable cannot be seen as destiny. Christianity certainly believed that it was right to free men from the menaces of hostile gods and an enslavement to fate, and uphold the unique preciousness of each human being. Even the most deformed person is worthy of respect and capable of beauty; in practice, the orphanages often ill-succeeded in protecting the unique worth of each individual child, but their child-care workers did their best according to their lights and the means available to them.

The Sisters received into the orphanages large numbers of babies abandoned for the most part in the maternities. 'Maternity' is a euphemism which conjures up visions of sterile linen, spotless corridors, and quiet order. In fact they were sometimes grimy huts furnished with plank beds, with no amenities whatsoever. Even the large Saigon maternity, Tu Du, which was a model of organization and had a beautifully kept nursery, had several women to a bed in the charity wards. How easy it was for anyone to walk out, leaving a baby behind.

The babies would accumulate in the maternities, and eventually be taken to a nearby orphanage. Others would be found in the streets or on rubbish heaps bundled in newspapers. Some would be brought by the mothers to the orphanages; others brought by people saying they were neighbours or family members, and that the mother had died or had given them the baby, and they could no longer look after it. Since there was no birth certificate, there was no way of knowing whose baby it was. The important issue at this point was to give the child a new chance in life after such a traumatic beginning.

As the babies poured into the orphanages, the Sisters had even less time to consider questions of ancestry, occupied as they were with keeping the children alive and burying the many who died. The orphanages would have become impossibly over-crowded within a few months had not a balance been maintained by death claiming large numbers. Deaths were not declared to the civil authorities, since the birth had probably not yet been registered.

Some orphanages saw another way out of the dilemma and a way of breaking out of this tragically narrow birth–death cycle. They tried to send some of the babies abroad, to families who were eager to welcome another child. This would be the only possible chance many of these babies would have for life and development.

Before the child could be involved in an adoptive process, its existence had first to be officially acknowledged. The orphanage would give each child a name: a name would be the symbol denoting the existence of a person. This name would be ratified when a birth certificate was issued by the local office of vital statistics. In some provinces, court procedure was necessary before the child could have a document to prove it existed. Once that was obtained, he or she could be a participant in the legal process of adoption, and could be issued with a passport.

In the opinion of certain crusaders and self-styled moralists, inter-country adoption was not – and is not – an acceptable solution to the problem of child abandonment. Frequently, we were called upon to justify our actions and to answer arguments that were at best specious, only thinly disguising an underlying racism. Ironically, we never had to justify our lack of action in the case of those children we did *not* care for.

The first argument we faced was rather fundamental and attacked the child's very existence. If a child did not have the usual birth certificate, with at least the name of a mother, then the child had no legal existence. When we, or the orphanage, gave the child a name and registered its existence on a birth document, then, it was claimed, this document was fraudulent and any legal procedure based on this document, such as an adoption, was fraudulent, too. The child could not, therefore, legally be adopted since the child had no acceptable identity. We believed that a nameless child had an independent right to some identity confirming the inescapable fact of its existence, and this right preceded all consideration of parental or cultural affiliation.

The favourite cliché used against our efforts to have children adopted abroad, was that there was no such thing as an 'abandoned' child, since Vietnamese women loved their offspring and had a strong sense of family. From this, were we to understand by inference that American or European women did not usually love their children? Women of every race may cherish their offspring or reject them in various ways before or after birth, depending on a multitude of factors. In areas of peace, prosperity and advanced medicine, societies cope with the problem of unwanted children in the privacy of the home or abortion clinic. In areas of extreme poverty and upheaval a mother may be forced by circumstances to grant hospitality to the newcomer at least *in utero* until it may, if it can, survive independently, even if in an orphanage.

Then there was the frequently-voiced protest that children should not be removed from their culture – that a child with sallow skin and slant eyes belonged to a certain pattern of life and could only be comfortable with oriental gods. The culture of the Asian orphanage and the culture of the poverty-stricken, which is considered best for nurturing the Asian orphan, may consist of disease, discomfort, minimal educational opportunities, and a despair and feeling of worthlessness that frequently leads to adolescent delinquency. What makes anyone so smugly sure that these children would not profit from parental love and support; from a healthy diet; from adequate medical care; and from good education opportunities?

In sending orphan children abroad, we were even accused of depriving developing countries of their resources. Children are, of course, something more than resources for their society and if that society is not providing them with the minimum they need for human development, they surely have the right to seek it elsewhere. To answer the argument at its most literal: the exodus of a few thousand orphans could never seriously deplete the intellectual forces of any country, nor dry up its supply of cheap labour.

The opponents of inter-country adoption say it is an inadequate solution to the total problem of child abandonment since it can help only a few children. Certainly, adoption helps just one child at a time and that is surely the best way to help children, one by one. While children are still statistics they cannot be helped in more than a purely abstract way. We can read of '20,000' homeless children in this country or '1,000' babies abandoned each month in that country. At a safe distance, we imagine an anonymous horde of little people, and we can weep over intellectual symbols of suffering childhood, or maybe toss an easy coin in a collection box. But up close the crowd dissolves and there is only one child standing before us and the only way we can alleviate the misery of the suffering millions is to comfort that one child. Handing out bowls of donated rice certainly recognizes and sustains animal existence, but to protect the human personality, I must look into the eyes of one child and love him.

Finally, there is the argument of the identity crisis of a child in a foreign culture. But would an orphanage better equip an adolescent to face the question of his identity? At least if he is nurtured in an adoptive family he will have learnt the self-esteem that comes only from the security of being loved and accepted by others. He may never know the name of his biological parents, but he will have learnt a new name for himself and his own value as a human being.

All these arguments become irrelevant to someone personally acquainted with the practical human dimensions of the problem. Life itself must take precedence over questions of colour, culture, legal documentation, national image, or possible adolescent confusion.

No one is suggesting that a Western family has any child-raising talent superior to that of an Asian family, nor that it is better to grow up in the West than in the Far East. Surely, let a child grow up with his biological parents in his own country, if the option exists. But for abandoned children, such an option does not exist. To continue confronting a real and immediate problem with an ideal and hypothetical solution is unintelligent. It can only be an attempt to cover up the shallowness of one's concern and one's inability to accommodate a solution that might require a greater personal commitment. It is so much more convenient for the conscience to believe that the child should stay in his country of birth. It absolves everyone from the guilt of personal uninvolvement.

We had varying degrees of contact with forty different orphanages and maternities throughout Vietnam. Never in our association with them was any pressure put on a mother to give up her child. On the contrary, sometimes a woman had to track around to several orphanages or agencies before anyone would be willing to accept another child. The Friends For All Children nurseries in Saigon were always filled beyond capacity, and we were simply unable to cope with all the babies from the orphanages we visited. We certainly had no need to snatch children from reluctant mothers to fill the nursery cribs; nor were we searching for children to satisfy the 'baby market' in the Western world – as the more wild accusations levelled against us have suggested. We were inviting applications from parents who would make themselves available to receive a child, because the child was already there and waiting. Thousands of children did not survive the wait. And those who did survive were not always everyone's usual choice of 'ideal' child. They included crippled victims of polio; the blind or half-blind; children born with congenital defects – cleft palates, hare lips, encephaloceles, clubbed feet, heart problems; children grossly retarded in their physical and psychological development; children who risked always having difficulty relating to others because they had not learnt to form strong emotional attachments at a critical period in their lives; brain-damaged children with related behavioural disorders. FFAC also wanted parents for these children.

Before May 1974 we never accepted any direct relinquishment from a mother. All the children in the nurseries had been abandoned in orphanages and maternities. In May 1974, FFAC obtained power of custody and was expected by the Ministry of Welfare to offer complete child care services. Thereafter, a small number, less than 2 per cent of the total number of children received, were by direct relinquishment. The mother was counselled by one of our Vietnamese social workers, and always offered material assistance if it would enable her to keep her baby. If the child were sick, we offered to care for it temporarily until it was well enough for the mother to reclaim it; or if a mother showed any sign of emotional distress, FFAC offered to care for the child until she felt able to resume custody. If it were, above all, a matter of her needing employment, FFAC would try to make a job for her in one of the nurseries, or send her and the child to Phu My, where Sr Rose would make room for both and give the mother some work.

When the mothers came back to reclaim a child in our temporary care, there was never any question of payment due; on the contrary, FFAC paid the mother, made sure she had the wherewithal to care for her baby, provided her with travel expenses if she had come from a distance, and supplied her with useful items, depending on what was available. There were, however, some local crèches run as businesses by local people, where the mother committed herself to pay for the child's board. These crèches would sometimes retain possession of a child until the mother could pay her debt. Occasionally, mothers would come to FFAC for help in redeeming their children, and we would give the money needed. (One mother had her ID card confiscated by the hospital because she had been unable to pay for a blood transfusion: FFAC promptly gave her the money needed to redeem the card.)

It was made known to the Vietnamese staff in our nurseries that we would help them in any sickness to themselves or their children. Sometimes, the children came to the nursery for temporary care or would be hospitalized at FFAC expense. Never at any time was a relinquishment of a child accepted from a staff member, directly or indirectly. If a mother had problems, we helped her as much as possible by salary increments and by a special family allowance for each dependent child. If a not totally indigent mother wanted to give up her child only because she thought the child would have greater material advantages and great possibilities of an education abroad, we would not even consider accepting the child, but would try to impress the mother with the fact that her child already had so much more than the abandoned children in the nurseries.

Duc, my cyclo-driver (one of the four or five pedicabs we regularly employed on a full-time basis), overhearing us discuss the case of a child in a state of severe malnutrition, mentioned in great distress that his own baby was even worse, after what seemed to be the same kind of prolonged illness. There was an epidemic that may have been typhoid in Saigon at the time, only a few days before the evacuation of the children in our custody. We sent Duc, immediately, to bring back his daughter and she was admitted to Hy Vong, where she was found to be not only extremely debilitated, but also had secondary TB. Duc said he had not wanted to bother FFAC again since just a short time before we had rushed two of his older children to a private hospital and assumed all financial responsibility. The children pulled through from their attacks of typhoid and went home. Duc, slaving to support his family, with pride and dignity, symbolized for me all that was noblest in his race.

It was, then, in the orphanages that we found the children we could best help. It is not possible to give here a detailed description of all the orphanages with which we were in contact. But we can say that we placed more than a thousand children from the orphanages run by the Sisters of St Paul de Chartres: Phu My, St Paul's-Bien Hoa, St Paul's-My Tho, St Paul's-Vinh Long, St Enfance-Vinh Binh, Viet-Hoa-Cholon, St Paul's-Qui Nhon, Sacred Heart-Danang and Hoi An. Over a thousand children came from orphanages run by the Sisters of Providence in Soctrang, Cantho, Baclieu, Sadec, Culao Gieng, and Rach Gia. About sixty-five children came from the Good Shepherd Sisters in Vinh Long, 180 from Fr Olivier's orphanages, and fifty from Tan Mai Orphanage, run by the Dominican Sisters. The remaining children came in smaller numbers from Hoi Duc Anh, Caritas, Regina Pacis, Xom Chieu, and the Tu Du maternity in Saigon; Sancta Maria, Go Vap, Thong Thien Hoc in Gia Dinh; Hoc Mon; Dong Ha and Khe Sat in Ho Nai (Bien Hoa); Sao Mai and Tan Binh in Cam Ranh; Nha Trang; China Beach and Vung Tau Christian Home.

Caritas Nutrition Centre, Regina Pacis Polio Centre, and the Good Shepherd Home at Vinh Long were establishments giving the highest quality care and not to be considered in the same category as the orphanages. Of the large orphanages, Phu My was surely unique due to its predominantly adult population and for the relative normality of the life there. Over the years the orphanage section of Phu My underwent many improvements, made possible by civic-action assistance from the US military, donations from in-country and foreign groups and individuals. The toddlers were moved into their own specially equipped section, while the older children stayed with the babies to help feed and care for them. An air-conditioned room was eventually set up for the tiniest babies, through the efforts of a French Red-Cross doctor who not only raised the finances necessary, but continued with a regular programme of supervision. Because of the European help she received,

Sr Rose was able, in 1972, to build a new polio centre which offered complete therapy and rehabilitation services. The six polio children of 1967 increased to eighty as soon as the accommodation became available. This was a much-needed service since the polio centre run by the Sisters of St Vincent de Paul was already crowded.

Phu My was exceptional in that the babies were all held for feeding and did not have the bottle propped in the bed. This was made possible by the participation of the older children: from six years up, each child would have his own baby to feed. The normal children walked to the local school (run by the Sisters) while the polio children, unable to negotiate the staircases in the regular schools, were bused each day to a special school in Saigon.

Sponsorship programmes organized in France, Switzerland, Germany and Australia helped with the upkeep and education not only of the children in the orphanage, but also children of a few poor families of the neighbourhood. Phu My had its own small farm – pig and rabbit breeding – and a vegetable garden which provided a little food and income. It also had its own church, cemetery, and resident priest. Though Catholic in its religious direction, it was totally non-denominational in its admission policy, and the many non-Christians were free to worship and be buried according to the rite of their choice. The adult inmates participated in all the chores, food preparation, laundry, gardening, cleaning, guard duty and nursing. A few, who were able, also plied some small handicraft trades, making toys and novelties which they themselves sold for a little pocket money.

If a child in the orphanage appeared grossly retarded or abnormal, he would be moved from the children's section and given into the care of one of the adult inmates. It was a moving experience to see with what devotion some destitute and maybe handicapped old man or woman would tend to the needs of a grossly malformed and totally helpless youngster. This is what made Phu My a unique experience in human concern.

At the other end of the scale was Go Vap, the national orphanage and the largest in Vietnam. In April 1968, I had started adoption formalities for ten Go Vap babies, but when I returned a few weeks later, after escorting a group of children to Europe, five of the ten were dead. It was not surprising: if the babies were not drowned by the formula gushing out of the slashed teats as the bottles were propped in the beds, they would die of starvation as they lay there soaking in their malodorous, sodden cribs, skin raw and crusty from the cumulative adhesion of soured milk, unable to fend for themselves. Or they would sink into a severe depression and simply stop living. Elaine Moir spoke of her visit to Go Vap Orphanage in 1966:

> There was a child of about two years, sitting in a basket next to a stone pillar on the verandah. He was beating his head with slow deliberation against the stone pillar in a trance-like movement. I rushed to move him away from the pillar as his forehead was swollen and absolutely black with bruises, but the girl in charge moved him back and I was told that he liked to hit his head. I still feel sick at the memory.

And of a visit in 1972 she wrote:

> I saw a group of toddlers on the verandah, some handicapped. A Sister came with a bucket of water and a few tin cups. The children swarmed over her, grabbing at the cups of water and pushing each other and making a tremendous noise. When the bucket was empty the Sister picked it up, collected the cups, and left. I tried to tell her that many of the children did not get any water. Some could not walk and were left behind. Others were just too weak and got pushed aside. She did not seem to understand. She did not come back with more water. A child-care worker had another group of toddlers lined up in a passage. I assumed it was their 'out of cot' time – for a play or something. She made them all sit against the wall. She had a very long thin stick next to her and whenever a child moved she whacked him with the stick. The saddest thing was that most of them just sat there, immobile. A couple dared to move and were instantly whacked. They settled back against the wall. They did not cry even though she hit them hard.

Celia Barclay, an English woman who had been involved with Vietnamese orphans for some years while her husband Gordon, an orthopaedic surgeon, worked at Nhi Dong Children's Hospital, visited Go Vap Orphanage regularly and tried to provide stimulation for the children. Eventually, she organized a special team to visit several Saigon orphanages daily, conducting a supervised play-period for the children. To provide equipment for the playgroups, Celia set up a toy-making project with local Buddhist monks. The toys were transported to the orphanages each day in the team van. (They could not be left overnight at the orphanages or they would disappear without trace.)

Over the years, efforts were made to brighten up the rooms and provide a little more activity for the children. Catholic Relief sent a team to the orphanage for a certain period and care improved.

But while the buildings became much less sordid and some young trained Sisters provided better nursing care, the basic problem remained untouched: too many children together. There were over 300 confined to a small courtyard and some narrow verandahs. The children had no possibility of expressing any individuality – they were herded together, regimented and slapped into submission; they were supervised by immature and uncaring adults, often by emotionally disturbed adolescents – who controlled the children by yelling and thumping. The children could be really hurting each other while the supervisors registered only uninterest or amusement. It was a brutal scene. The children were being 'trained', not nurtured in a human fashion. Unless they adapted to their environment and responded to the training, they had little chance of survival.

Go Vap was the orphanage where on one occasion the higher Superior, Sr Agathe, told me she would rather see the babies die there than go abroad for adoption because they all 'died in the good God'.

We were involved in only a few dozen adoptions from Go Vap and in the last years made no direct placements from this orphanage. I have described it in some detail only because it epitomizes all that was most sordid in the orphanages of Vietnam. Most were better than Go Vap if only because they had fewer children, and more attention could be given to the individual.

Chapter 19

THE AFTERMATH –
THE CLASS ACTION LAWSUIT
San Francisco

RUMOURS THAT the airlift children were not orphans were circulating within a week of the children's arrival at the Presidio. The Viet Cong were reported in news stories on 6 April 1975 as accusing the Americans of killing and kidnapping thousands of Vietnamese children. Officials of the American Friends Service Committee and the International Children's Fund took instant opposition to the airlift, and seemed convinced that they knew all there was to be known about Vietnam.

During the last week of April, airlift flights of orphans resumed and two additional centres were set up in Fort Lewis, Washington and at Long Beach Naval Support Activity in California. With fewer arrivals at the Presidio in San Francisco, the processing of children became less difficult. Volunteers found time to discuss a threatened lawsuit designed to return non-orphaned children to Vietnam. A USAID official and an attorney in the US Army explained the lawsuit to Sr Mary-Nelle and Wende Grant on 28 April: an unidentified group was filing a class (that is, 'category') action suit on behalf of all airlift children said to be removed illegally from Vietnam. On 29 April 1975, at the District Court in San Francisco, a Complaint for Declaratory and Injunctive Relief was filed. Nearly a year later, the class action would be dismissed; it took until September 1976 for the only named plaintiffs – three Vietnamese children – also to be withdrawn.

Friends For All Children were invited to testify on a voluntary basis, and warned that we could possibly be named as co-defendants. We departed San Francisco at once, feeling that we would be distinctly out of place amongst the august persons named as defendants, but also convinced that the class action suit was incredible and that no court would hear it. Nothing changed our opinion, but the court heard it nonetheless.

The defendants named in the case were James Schlesinger (US Secretary of Defense); Edward Levi (US Attorney General); Henry Kissinger (US Secretary of State); Colonel Robert V. Kane, C.O. at the Presidio; Colonel Jasper Horn (Director of the 'Baby Airlift'); and Mario Obledo (Secretary of Health and Welfare in California). They were being sued in their official and individual capacities as jointly responsible for illegally removing hundreds of children from Vietnam against the will of their parents, 'in order to prevent their being raised under a form of government of which the defendants disapprove, and to impose upon them the defendants' culture and government which are alien to their own'.

The Court Case

Nguyen da Yen, Nguyen da Tuyen and Nguyen da Vuong were the named plaintiffs, two sisters and a brother who had been brought to the United States by the other Colorado-based agency, FCVN.[1] The children supposedly told a Vietnamese woman 'volunteer' at the Presidio that they had been separated from their parents, put in an orphanage, and evacuated. Their father had been an officer in the Vietnamese Army. They had been well-cared for by their family. Some other children from their extended family had also arrived on the airlift. No other children were ever named in the case as having parents: these three fit most of the stories of the 'numerous' children who had been 'kidnapped' from parents in Vietnam.

The Vietnamese woman who heard a part of the three children's story was Muoi McConnell. Married to an American, she shared her concern with a Vietnamese friend, Tran Tuong Nhu, who coincidentally was married to Tom Miller, a lawyer. We don't know whether Tom Miller was also at the Presidio to help the children, but he was immediately willing to file a suit on behalf of the children with the help of Nancy Sterns, an attorney from the Center for Constitutional Rights in New York and Mort Cohen, a

---

[1] The confusion between FCVN (Friends of the Children of Viet Nam), from which we had separated in the autumn of 1973, and FFAC (Friends For All Children), the re-registered agency of which Wende Grant and Rosemary Taylor were Directors, did not help matters. (It was FCVN who had sent the group of children on World Airways that FFAC had not taken.)

San Francisco attorney. Muoi McConnell was named guardian *ad litem* for the three children and for the other children of that class (or category): children who were not legally relinquished, had parents in Vietnam, and whose parents wanted their children returned.

In attempting to marshall some facts to lend substance to their many claims, the plaintiff's attorneys tried unsuccessfully to subpoena all the children's records. Wende Grant gave a deposition in answer to Nancy Sterns' questions and earnestly tried to explain the origins of FFAC's children. Sterns' ignorance about Vietnamese orphans and adoptions was total. It was frightening to think of this woman appointing herself as the saviour of our children.

Hearings on the class action continued sporadically through the spring and summer of 1975. There was testimony that no child was ever orphaned or abandoned in Vietnam; that there was always a relative to care for a child if the mother couldn't; that children were in Vietnamese orphanages only for day care while the mothers worked.

Within several months of the airlift, seven Vietnamese mothers appeared in the US as refugees. They asked for the return of children brought on the orphans' airlift in April. These children had been given to FCVN in Saigon. After an investigation by an independent social service agency determined that the mothers were fit and willing to care for their children, the American families with whom the children had been placed quietly returned them to their natural mothers. The considerable financial cost of those transfers was borne by the agency that had brought them from Vietnam. All the mothers admitted lying to the agency.

News of the return of the children to their Vietnamese mothers elicited a great outcry about the unethical actions of the agencies in accepting these children and bringing them to the United States. No one considered what would have become of the children had the agencies not accepted them. Would some public outcry have forced the refugee mothers to rejoin their abandoned offspring in Vietnam?

Meanwhile, for the remaining children, the court decided to rely on reports from immigration offices throughout the USA. Immigration investigators across the country packed up their Polaroid cameras and fingerprint kits and set out to find non-orphans. Some were sensitive; some menacing. They dutifully photographed children, examined paperwork and footprinted the children, for what purpose we could not imagine as the children had never been footprinted in Vietnam. Some investigators were thorough without having any notion of what evidence was useful. Once again, the several children who had been given the name of the nursery, Hy Vong, on the Presidio bus lists came under suspicion. In one case 'Hy Vong' had been miscopied as 'Hybong' and the child acquired the triple appellation of 'Hy Vong Hybong Susie'. When the child's birth certificate was examined, it revealed the Vietnamese name of Nguyen Thi Thu Van. The Immigration report detailed the multiplicity of names and found the child ineligible for resident status, because there was no way to determine which was the child's legal name. In the atmosphere of suspicion created by the accusations directed at the agencies during the suit in San Francisco, the investigator presumably felt unable to take the obvious step of calling the agency for an explanation. However, many other Immigration investigators did call or write, so for three months half of the office staff did little beyond sending copies of documents and giving detailed explanations to their offices. During this period, the spring and summer of 1975, we worked long hours to place children, check on the progress of the placements, and sort and send out children's documents, besides offering reassurance to anxious or irritated parents.

Another problem surfaced involving the validity of the children's birth certificates. We described to the Immigration authorities, in great detail, the acceptable procedure for obtaining birth certificates or birth judgements for the orphans in Vietnam, and made an affidavit concerning the origins of each child. Because we, or the orphanages, had often to give names to children who had no names, the certificates were judged in the USA to be fraudulent. The children with these 'false identities' were, therefore, ineligible for immigration to the USA, according to some Immigration officers. The same certificate, according to others, indicated their true orphan status and eligibility!

By October of 1975, Friends For All Children was sufficiently concerned about the one-sided presentation to the 9th District Federal Court in San Francisco that we petitioned to intervene in the class action suit. It seemed logical that as the only individuals who had specific knowledge of the children FFAC had evacuated from Vietnam that we should correct some of the misinformation presented in the case so far; our children accounted for about 25 per cent of the airlift children. But our presumption was not correct. The court replied that if FFAC had information they could give it to Immigration which was responsible for investigating the children.

It was relevant, then, when someone with experience in fitting artificial limbs on amputees in Quang Ngai gave testimony on orphanage customs and adoption procedures; it was not relevant to hear the testimony of an organization with eight years of experience specifically with Vietnamese orphanages.

Another motion to intervene was filed, and in this attempt the agency had to state that they might be sued or lose money should children be returned to Vietnam. Although a group of lawyers had been able to initiate the whole case by declaring their own concern for the children's civil rights, the agency's concern for and knowledge of the children was dismissed. Only a profession of financial interest could gain us the right to enter the case.

Hearings we attended in October of 1975 and through March 1976, followed a repetitive pattern. The plaintiffs' attorneys tried to convince Judge Spenser Williams that the Vietnamese children should be in Vietnam, where all Vietnamese children were loved and cared for, albeit in the orphanages: that there were no truly abandoned children, and therefore the agencies must have taken most of the airlift children from unwilling or fear-crazed mothers for their own financial gain, and with the tacit co-operation of the US Embassy, which envisaged a monumental reversal of public opinion in the US regarding financial and military aid for the Thieu regime in Saigon.

The testimony was compounded with absurdity upon absurdity. A physician who had been working at the Quaker Rehabilitation Center in Quang Ngai before April 1975, returned from Vietnam late in 1975. He gave his version of the peace and happiness which reigned in Danang, and in the orphanages. After he finished enlightening the court, Wende hurried after him and asked him if he would kindly give news of Sr Angela of Sacred Heart Orphanage. He looked blank. He had never visited or even heard of Sacred Heart. He admitted he had only visited some small Buddhist orphanages. Thus, the expert witness on Danang orphanages didn't know of the existence of the largest orphanage in that city, an institution known to thousands of Americans who had helped to support its many children.

In contrast, the US Attorney, defending Kissinger et al., brought Bobbie Nofflet and Laurie Peters to San Francisco to testify. Bobbie had worked with USAID in Saigon for years, visited all the orphanages registered in South Vietnam, been responsible for introducing or checking record-keeping systems in the orphanages, and knew the status of the children. She was, undoubtedly, more knowledgeable about Vietnamese orphanages than any other American in Vietnam. Laurie Peters had been Vice-Consul at the US Embassy in Saigon for two years; she had not only handled visa applications for orphans being adopted in the USA, but knew in detail about the Vietnamese adoption procedures and the validity of documentation. Neither of these experts was permitted to testify: the Court judged the information they could give as irrelevant.

The climate in the courtroom gradually changed as the hearings continued through the winter and into the spring of 1976. At each hearing more adoptive parents were in attendance. It became obvious that the plantiffs' lawyers were not proving that their case met the requirements for a class action suit. The defence attorneys made clear that each child's case was unique and would have to be heard individually, if there were any doubts about a child's status. On 13 February 1976, Judge Spenser Williams dismissed the class action, and the case was left with only the three originally named plaintiffs.

During the hearing of the case of the three named children, affidavits from six members of the children's family also evacuated to the United States in April 1975 confirmed the story as told to the court in the first days of the case in May 1975: that the three children had been sent from Vietnam with the full consent of their parents. The version of the story that had precipitated the case was either presented in ignorance by Ms McConnell, or was a deliberate falsification.

A letter supposedly written by Ms McConnell was sent to the parents of the three children at their address in Saigon, to ask them if they wished their children to be returned. Ms McConnell, thereupon, withdrew from the case in a letter to the Judge, dated 17 September 1976:

Judge Spenser Williams,
Federal District Court,
450 Golden Gate Avenue,
San Francisco,
California.

Dear Sir,
The purpose of this letter is to explain my position in the case of
the Vietnamese children, Nguyen da Yen, Nguyen da Vuong and
Nguyen da Tuyen.

In April 1975, while working as a volunteer at the Presidio, the
above-named children appealed to me to help them find their
family. As a mother, I had strong feelings for these children. I could
imagine how distressed I would be if my children were lost in
another country and no one helped reunite the family. I expressed
these feelings to people working in the Baby Lift operation, as well
as to others outside, in an attempt to clarify the identification and
disposition of these children. Everyone was very busy and things
were somewhat chaotic.

A few days later, I was approached by the lawyers currently
handling the lawsuit. They appealed to me to be the guardian *ad
litem* on behalf of Nguyen da Yen, Nguyen da Vuong and Nguyen
da Tuyen, to reunite them with their family. I was very reluctant to
become involved in a legal action as I knew nothing about legal
matters. However, since I was the only one who had talked to the
children, I agreed to participate in the lawsuit.

For the past sixteen months I have been going along with the
position of the lawyers, even though in some instances I did not
understand or agree with what was being done. Generally, I felt
that the interests of the children and their family were being lost in
the ambiguities of legal matters. I continued with the case because it
seemed the only way to reunite the children with their family. I
never imagined that this task could become so complex and drawn
out.

It is now my desire to withdraw from any further participation in
this case. The letter sent to the family in Vietnam is the reason for
my decision.

I had approved a draft of the letter. That version was altered,
translated into Vietnamese, and sent before I saw it. It is not a
matter of objecting to the wording of the letter. The entire tone and
content of the letter sent was not the same as the draft I approved.
If a letter is sent in my name, it should contain only what I want it
to contain.

That is why I refused to sign a new compromise letter. I deny
that the signature on the letter sent to Vietnam was mine and wish
to disassociate myself with the letter and its contents.

I do not wish any further involvement with people who seem to
be using me and my feelings as a mother to further their political
ambitions. Therefore, I will appreciate your official dismissal of me
as guardian *ad litem* for Nguyen da Yen, Nguyen da Vuong and
Nguyen da Tuyen.

Sincerely [signed]
Muoi McConnell

The Court dismissed the three children from the case. After
seventeen months there were no longer any named plaintiffs, there
was no guardian *ad litem* to represent the 'many' or 'most' or 'vast
majority' of the children who had been brought, according to Sterns
and Miller, illegally to the United States, and no class action suit had
been certified. The court case was over, without a single child's
future being decided in the Federal Court of San Francisco.

There have been no requests from parents in Vietnam for the return
of any children, despite the fact of mail and telegraph services being
open between Vietnam and the United States since the middle of
1975.[1] While fortunate to be represented by attorneys of the highest
calibre, Sara Jane Cohen in Colorado and Kate Freeland in California, we, nonetheless, came to view the legal system as shabby and
vulnerable. It was obvious to us that the lawyers who brought the
case cared not the least for the children. They knew nothing of our
agency, the airlift, the orphanages, or the needs of the children.
Based on their own views and a convenient child's story, they filed
the suit to make a political statement and to gain personal recognition. Their wildest charges, never substantiated, were widely
disseminated by the press, encouraging a distorted view of the airlift
that was largely accepted by the public. Yet they were never able to
present evidence of a single child being taken against the mother's
wishes.

---

[1] Only once was a case brought against Friends For All Children for the return of children to the biological
mother, by then also in America. In the last days in Saigon, exceptionally, we did accept custody of two
half-American brothers, after the mother had convinced the Saigon staff of extenuating circumstances.
After seven months of a court hearing in Connecticut, the Judge delivered his decision to leave the children
with the adoptive father, and not to return them to their biological mother [April 1976].

Over the past twelve years since the evacuation, parents have continued to seek ways of sending their children by boat out of Vietnam, and without the assistance or influence of any American agency. Many of these youngsters are to be seen in the camps of Thailand, Malaysia and Hong Kong, awaiting resettlement. Many others have been lost at sea or hideously abused by pirates off the coast of Thailand. Throughout these years it has become quite clear how much parents have calculated and sacrificed to give one or more of their children a chance to live in what they understand to be freedom. On the strength of this hope they have risked all, even the very lives of their children.

Chapter 20

LOCKHEED SETTLEMENTS

IN JUNE 1975, just two short months after the C-5A crash, Friends For All Children was contacted by the office of an internationally known attorney requesting a list of FFAC staff and children who were killed in the crash, ostensibly for a book they were writing. The lawyer said that, if the rear cargo door of the plane blew out, there had to be a fault in the design or construction of the plane and that the relatives of our dead should be compensated.

It was the first time that any such thing had occurred to us. We had been so enveloped by events following the crash, including preparations to enter the San Francisco lawsuit seeking to return the 'babylift' children to Vietnam, that we had not concentrated on the consequences of the crash for the survivors or the relatives of those who were killed.

FFAC had retained Sara Jane Cohen of the Boulder law firm of Cohen & Cohen to represent us in the San Francisco suit. We consulted her partner, Bill Cohen, about our responsibility to the relatives of the dead staff members, and our duties as Guardian of the children who were killed or injured in the C-5A crash concerning the possibility of a lawsuit against Lockheed. Cohen advised us that, if fault or negligence could be proved against Lockheed, the families of the staff members and friends who had been killed could receive monetary compensation. The several children who suffered obvious physical injuries in the crash would also be entitled to compensation. The dead children, except for two, had no identifiable heirs. It would be difficult to win a judgement in their favour unless the court would recognize the concept of equitable adoption, or accepting the children as already adopted by their prospective parents. Another possibility was that any awards for the deaths of the orphan children might ultimately go to the State in which the children were considered domiciled, possibly Colorado, the domicile of their Guardian, FFAC.

We felt strongly that Lockheed should not escape liability for any fault it had in the plane crash just because the victims were orphans. We believed those orphans' lives were valuable and should be compensated, even if the money went to Colorado or some charitable organization which could help orphans still living. We, therefore, contacted relatives of our lost staff, all foreign nationals, and explained that we would help co-ordinate a joint lawsuit for them, seeking compensation for their losses. We also decided to file suit on behalf of the dead children in our capacity as Guardian of those children.

Cohen recommended that we retain the Arlington, Virginia, law firm of Lewis, Wilson, Lewis and Jones Ltd. because it had considerable experience in aircraft crash cases and was already representing the heirs of another person, not associated with FFAC, who was killed in the crash. Later, a Birmingham, Alabama, attorney called J. Vernon Patrick joined the team of lawyers. In our first meeting with Dick Jones, one of the partners of the Lewis firm, we discussed possibilities and terms. Mr Jones also expressed concern about the likelihood of recovery on behalf of the dead children. However, he felt that the families of the dead staff should reasonably expect compensation. If the cases were won or settled, the legal expenses and the lawyers' fees would be taken out of the award. Were the cases to fail, FFAC would be responsible for expenses, but the attorneys would receive no fee. At that time the estimated expenses for the decedents were modest. For several years FFAC kept $10,000 in reserve in anticipation of the possibility that the suit might be dismissed or fail.

We proceeded with the prosecution of these cases with much uncertainty and mixed emotions in the US District Court for the District of Columbia. We stated firmly that we did not wish to take the financial risk or to spend our time on a case designed to grant large awards of money to prospective adoptive families. Although some of the families had already made considerable emotional commitment to the children who had been assigned to them, and experienced grief at their loss, others had barely learned of the child's assignment just prior to the crash. All but two families had been able to accept a replacement child within a short time, without any additional expenses. FFAC staff both in Saigon and in Colorado had suffered far greater loss over these children whom we knew personally and worked with on a day-to-day basis. We didn't relish reliving their deaths again and again in legal testimony. Nevertheless, we proceeded with those cases because we could not tolerate persons at fault killing or injuring our children without having to face responsibility for their negligence. This was our motivation, and despite the uncertainty in the matter of legal heirs, we continued to believe that awards could be designated to help children in great need, so that from the deaths of these children, other children might find life.

It took almost a year for the cases of the adults to be settled out of court. Each family received an award ranging from $55,000 to $315,000, less attorneys' fees and expenses. The compensation for our staff members, Lee Makk and Margaret Moses, both highly qualified in their respective fields and both to a great extent responsible for the support of an invalid or widowed mother, was less than half of what was to be given, eleven years later, to prospective adoptive parents who had received the name of a child a few days before the crash.

With the adult cases settled, progress for the children was sluggish. Numerous motions and appeals were filed as Lockheed argued that FFAC was not legally qualified to represent the children. They did not want the case heard in the District of Columbia. It was not until 1 May 1978 that the Court decided that it would be heard in Washington, DC, and that FFAC was qualified to bring the suit as the legal representative of the surviving and deceased children.

During the first three years of the court case, we spent endless hours copying files and documents to send to Washington. We responded repeatedly to questions about procedure, about specific children, and about our organization. Beyond the legal manoeuvring, our lawyers faced what seemed insurmountable problems. Basically, they knew that the huge cargo ramp at the rear of the C-5A had blown out, hitting an area of the plane containing the control cables and hydraulic lines and severing them. The pilot could no longer manoeuvre the plane other than by adjusting power to the engines. The plane turned back to Saigon, but crashed short of the airport. Beyond that, FFAC's lawyers had to ferret out the information that would have a bearing on the case.

Somehow, the thousands of photographs of the crash, taken by Lockheed and the US Air Force officials disappeared. Requests by our attorneys, in the process of their investigations, for reports and photographs were met by denials that such evidence existed. FFAC's lawyers continued to dig for information and to take depositions from Air Force personnel. Finally, their persistence was rewarded: an Air Force officer admitted he had been involved in destroying thousands of photos of the crash; a surviving batch of photos was opportunely unearthed in an Air Force installation. The duplicity involved in previously denying the existence of the photos caused the defendants no obvious embarrassment. It was, after all, just a legal stratagem.

A suit had also been initiated against Lockheed on behalf of all the children who survived the C-5A crash. In the course of their investigations during these first years, our lawyers had come to believe that the surviving children on the C-5A had been injured. Some medical experts suggested strongly that the explosive decompression, coupled with the loss of oxygen, had most probably caused some degree of brain damage to all of the children. There had been a study done to support that theory. We did not want to believe it. It took much evidence by our lawyers and by Dr Michael Cohen, a medical expert retained by FFAC's lawyers, to convince us that this was probably true. The litigation for the deceased children was temporarily shelved. It was obviously more urgent to assist the living children as soon as possible and to obtain awards that would help provide specialized care and education when and where it was needed.

Proceeding with the cases of the survivors, our attorneys selected a small group of the children who had survived the crash, and brought them and their families to Washington, where Dr Cohen had arranged for extensive testing by a team of specialists. The results of the tests were consistent with the theory of Minimal Brain Dysfunction. Some families were unwilling to accept that their child might have a problem. Others were greatly relieved to find a basis for their child's erratic behaviour or learning disability.

Lockheed at one point tried to divert blame to FFAC for proceeding with the adoptive placement of children who had been on the C-5A, without warning the parents of possible damage. With no previous experience of such an event, it had not occurred to us that the apparently physically intact survivors might have sustained any injury. It then came out that Lockheed had been well aware of this possibility from the first moment, had taken steps to protect themselves financially, but had felt no obligation to share their knowledge with us, so that we would be better able to help the children. This discovery made us all the more determined to pursue the litigation.

In September 1979, Lockheed agreed to a partial settlement of the surviving children's cases. Lockheed agreed to waive the question that it was liable for any injuries the children suffered and agreed to pay $5,000 per child to help cover the cost of examining the children and preparing their cases for the trial. In return, we agreed to waive the question of punitive damages against Lockheed for any injuries these children suffered. The issue of what injuries the children suffered and the compensation they should receive was to be decided in what we thought would be an expedited process.

Beginning in March 1980, the cases were heard one by one, with Lockheed pursuing what is known as a 'scorched earth' defence, arguing every single legal point; it could go on for years. The juries looked at enormous blown-up photos of the crash site and photos of the dead children. They heard engineers and other experts calculating from the photos, diagrams and other available data, the probable force of impact of the plane as it bounced to a stop in a rice paddy outside the Saigon airport, and disintegrated in the process. Medical experts testified as to the effect such an impact might have on the brain of a young child, and what might be the results of oxygen deprivation in the high altitude, and the explosive decompression that had occurred.

Lockheed countered all this testimony with that given by their own experts. One of their witnesses assured the Court that the impact would have been comparable to a hard but normal landing. The photos, however, showed the effect this so-called normal impact had had on the C-5A or what was left of it, and we had seen for ourselves the bodies of our staff and children smashed beyond recognition.

When Lockheed tried to make the point that the children were already damaged because of the deprivation they had suffered before boarding the plane and the time they had spent in orphanages and nurseries, FFAC staff members came to testify about the children and their state of health before departure. There was overwhelming evidence that the children had been well-cared for in the FFAC facilities, and their state of health and development was clearly known to our staff. A small number of special children certainly had had previously documented problems, but this did not account for the frequency of symptoms of Minimal Brain Dysfunction now being displayed by a large number of the surviving children. Neither did we consider it less culpable to injure children with problems already, than to injure children in perfect condition.

The jury weighed all the evidence, and in case after case they found that the child had suffered as a result of the accident and awarded judgements ranging from $37,000 to $1 million. Other cases were settled on the eve of trial for similar amounts. The enormous cost of this protracted litigation, the airfares for children, families, witnesses, experts and our lawyers' own travel in the process of their investigations, the hotel bills, the long-distance phone calls, the processing of mountains of documents and other material evidence, was borne by the law firms. The arrangement was that they should receive one-third of the award plus expenses, although the Court reduced the attorneys' fees awarded to less than one-third in every instance. The awards were substantial, but Lockheed appealed, and then the verdicts were overturned on a technicality. The delay in payment caused great financial distress to the law firms and to some of the families who were involved in costly therapy for their child.

Finally, in 1982, Lockheed paid $13.5 million in settlement for the final forty-five surviving children who had been adopted in the USA. Besides the $125,000 for each child, a trust fund of $2.25 million was established for the medical needs of these children in excess of the individual awards.

Even though it had already been established that the children who were aboard the C-5A, going to American families, had suffered and deserved compensation, separate litigation was required to show that the children adopted by non-American families also deserved compensation. In considering this second group of children, Lockheed noticed that a significant proportion of the children going to Europe had spent some time in transit at Phu My Orphanage. Lockheed's new ploy was then to try to discredit Phu My by implying that it had been such an unhealthy environment that any child living there must have been damaged before boarding the C-5A. Lockheed contended that any problems detected subsequent to the crash could, therefore, not be readily attributed to the crash.

When the first case of a non-American child came to trial in 1984, Rosemary, amongst others, was called as a witness. Having lived for eight years at Phu My, she was well-acquainted with details of diet, sanitation and health care. She found herself having to describe at great length the toilet habits of the Phu My inmates and the sewage disposal system, as well as the children's diet, treatment and mosquito protection. In fact, the first child in question had spent only a few days in Phu My.

Lockheed's next tactic was to try to cast doubt on the fact that the children were ever on the plane. The broken body of a dead child was more or less proof of involvement but, for a physically intact survivor, it was another matter. Nevertheless, the jury returned a verdict for the child to the amount of £665,000.

The second foreign surviving child never came to trial. Whereas the first of the non-American cases involved a child who had suffered average damage, the second case showed a child for whom there was documented proof of normal development prior to boarding the C-5A, and who thereafter became totally incapable of normal living, and who would need constant supervision or institutional care for the rest of her life. Before this indisputable case could come to trial, Lockheed considered it in its own best interest to make a settlement of $17,800,000 for all seventy-four of the foreign children, or about $84,600 for each child. Again a trust fund of $2,925,000 was established to provide medical care for any child needing it. This had taken nine years since the case was first started. Most of the FFAC staff, who had worked in Saigon, made the trip again and again to Washington to testify and to relive the shattering experience of 4 April 1975. They all participated willingly, and endured the inconvenience so that the living children might receive the help that was needed before it was too late to be useful.

In 1985, the lawyers resumed the decedent cases. The Court

dismissed the claims for seventy-four of the seventy-six dead children, citing the children's lack of relatives. Our attorneys filed an appeal and began the case of Willie Powell. Mr Powell was the natural father of Giang Thi Ngoc Diep. The child's Vietnamese mother had put the child in an orphanage. Mr Powell had been trying, with FFAC's help, to get his daughter out of Vietnam, and she left with the Allambie children aboard the C-5A and was killed in the crash. With this case, our attorneys were in a good position to seek not just compensatory damage, as in the cases of the survivors, but to claim punitive damages as well. The evidence and testimony they had to present was formidable.

It was a term of the earlier settlements for the living children that FFAC lawyers had agreed not to seek punitive damages, and Lockheed agreed not to deny its liability. Most of those cases centred on whether the child had been injured by the crash. Now our lawyers were ready to use the information they had concerning the aircraft itself. They had evidence and expert testimony to present and prove that:

1. Lockheed knowingly submitted a faulty design for the C-5A;
2. The contract (between Lockheed and the US government for the manufacture of the C-5A) called for extra hydraulic control lines and control cables spaced so that damage to one area of the plane would not damage or sever all lines and cables;
3. The contract required working and safe forward and aft cargo ramp locking systems;
4. In fact the extra hydraulic control lines and control cables were bunched together so that damage to that area could result in the total loss of control of the aircraft;
5. The forward and aft cargo ramps were poorly designed, difficult to lock properly, had failed several times prior to 4 April 1975, and the management at Lockheed had refused a request by Lockheed engineers to do a study on the ramp locking mechanisms prior to 4 April 1975;
6. The contract called for the wings to function for 30,000 flying hours. In trying to lighten the aircraft, Lockheed reduced the useful flying time of the wing structure to less than 7,000 hours;
7. Lockheed recognized the need to modify the wings of the C-5A and knew it would cost between $1.3 billion and $1.5 billion to

do that work. Lockheed wanted the government to pay for the repairs, but there was pressure in Congress to force Lockheed to pay for the changes because the original design was defective;

8. In order to gain favourable publicity for the C-5A and for the US government to pay for necessary repairs, Lockheed sought to exploit the publicity surrounding the government's decision to have a C-5A rescue some of the Vietnamese orphans that private agencies were trying to evacuate from Saigon. Although we had been promised US Air Force medivac planes, and although such planes were stationed in the Philippines only a few flying hours from Saigon and their crews already alerted for the operation, they were never used. Instead, some of the medics were suddenly reassigned to the unfamiliar C-5A, flying into Saigon with a cargo of arms and outbound with the orphans. It was only later that we learned that President Ford was scheduled to meet our C-5A flight in San Francisco.

It took years for all this information to reach us. Bit by bit, our lawyers, who searched for ten years, were able to uncover the whole story of our tragedy. Our babies had been used by the military, by government officials, and by the management of a major defence contractor as part of a public relations campaign supporting the 'military-industrial complex'. Unwittingly, we had played into their hands. They wanted the first large group of orphans to arrive on a C-5A with President Ford meeting the plane. They needed the resulting good publicity for Lockheed to persuade Congress to approve another $1.3 billion dollars from the US government to pay for Lockheed's engineering failures and oversights; the tax-payers were being orchestrated to pick up the tab for such misman-agement. There has not been the slightest shred of evidence that anyone in government or industry had even the faintest of qualms about what was done to our children, who were made the unwilling pawns in a world of high power and politics, where corporate finance eliminates personal conscience.

The trial of the Powell case began in April 1986. One of the first witnesses for this final litigation was Dr Malcolm Newman, an expert in mechanical engineering, who was prepared to testify about the grossly defective design of the plane and about its specific failures. Lockheed lawyers interrupted the proceedings to offer a settlement. The agreement was that Lockheed would pay $10 million in damages to settle the cases of all children killed in the plane crash.

The cases of seventy-four of the children had been dismissed in November 1985 on the ground that there was no legal authority for prospective adoptive parents to inherit from a prospective adoptive child. Our attorneys had appealed this ruling but had received no answer to the appeal by the April 1986 settlement date. After two out-of-Court encounters with the Judge, we felt reassured that he too did not wish to give large awards to the adoptive parents, but preferred the bulk of the money to go to a charitable organization for the benefit of children in a similar category to the deceased.

We established the Margaret Moses Memorial Foundation expressly to be a living memorial to our deceased staff and children, and considered this Foundation would be a logical recipient of any award. The Foundation was to be of service to deprived children, especially the handicapped and the orphaned in third-world countries. At the Judge's suggestion, we developed and submitted some preliminary programmes for the careful use of this money both in developing countries and in the USA. The Judge made it clear that he preferred the money to be used within the USA, since a percentage of the settlement was to be furnished by the US government, and hence was taxpayers' money. He felt, therefore, that it should provide services within the States to Southeast Asian refugee youth, for example, having needs that were unmet by existing government programmes. Mary-Nelle Gage, current President of Friends For All Children and a Director of the Margaret Moses Memorial Foundation, had been working with refugees in the USA for eleven years and had detailed knowledge of their problems and needs. Rosemary, President of the Foundation, had been working in the refugee camps of Thailand for seven years. FFAC thus still maintained very close ties with Southeast Asian refugees, as well as with programmes for orphaned and handicapped children.

As is customary in certain cases, the Judge appointed an *amicus curiae* to advise him concerning possible recipient organizations. The *amicus*, having no previous knowledge of the case, nor of FFAC's role, consented to an interview and listened politely to our ideas on programmes we would initiate with any award money.

When he had heard us out, he asked us if we knew of the Edna McConnell Clark Foundation. A few weeks later he submitted his report to the Judge, proposing the Clark Foundation as the most appropriate recipient of the money. The Clark Foundation, in turn, submitted a description of their proposed refugee programmes which corresponded substantially with the proposals submitted by Mary-Nelle on behalf of the Margaret Moses Memorial Foundation. The latter was quite dumbfounded on the morning of the court hearing to read all her own ideas served up as their proposal, with one major difference: whereas the Clark Foundation, with assets of over 300 million dollars, intended to spend the expected 3–4 million in one big bash for 'maximum impact', we would have spent it over many years in ongoing programmes.

A previous contact between FFAC and the Clark Foundation then came to light. In late 1974 we had approached them for a small grant to buy some milk for our children. We still had their letter of response – a polite refusal. Rosemary felt obliged to point out to the Judge that, of all the possible worthy recipients of the award, it would be too bitterly ironic for the Clark Foundation to receive it, and thus profit from the deaths of the very children they had refused to feed.

The Judge, taking everything into consideration, felt it inappropriate to follow the advice of the *amicus* and equally inappropriate to go against it by awarding the money to another foundation. He took the obvious way out, and contrary to his previously expressed intentions, divided most of the settlement money between the forty-six adoptive families. The portion designated for the nine families who did not participate in the litigation would revert to Lockheed. The sixteen children who did not have assigned parents were not considered in any way. They were killed with impunity. There was no gesture to celebrate the value of their lives by even a token contribution to the Foundation set up to honour their memory. The court also awarded Friends For All Children $500,000 for its effort over ten years to establish justice for the unnecessary deaths of these children.

Each family received $85,671 for each child. Three families adopting two children received twice that amount. The families ranged from Ilse Eward who had lived with her daughter for many months in Saigon, and who suffered terribly at her death, to a family who had not even received the names of their two children prior to the crash, as they had been assigned only on the eve of departure. All the other families fell somewhere in between. Some had become involved with the child, writing letters and sending pictures and gifts. In a few cases, Vietnamese adoptions were complete; in many others, the Vietnamese adoption process had been initiated or was in varying stages of completion. Others knew nothing, and wrote nothing, and their involvement over all these years was simply to fill in and return a questionnaire. To see them all receive equal awards was difficult for us. It seemed a travesty of our efforts for this money to go to provide extra luxuries for middle-class families when our hope throughout had been to provide a life-giving source of help to children struggling to be recognized as part of the human race. Two or three of the families have become child-welfare organizations in their own right, with many adopted children, some severely handicapped. At least, in these few cases, we felt convinced that the money would be used appropriately. But, for the most part, the payment of approximately $9 million for the children's deaths achieved none of our intended aims. Naïvely we had also wanted Lockheed to be obliged to pay so much that this might cause the company to modify its future conduct. In fact, the award did not penalize Lockheed because its insurance companies had reserved a large sum of money for this case and the interest alone on that money, over ten years, was sufficient to cover almost all Lockheed's costs. Since the American government had itself agreed in 1975 to pay 65 per cent of Lockheed's costs, Lockheed came off very well indeed, not only financially but also politically. Its critics in Congress were effectively silenced from 1975 on. Now we understood the reason for the protracted treatment of the case, which had involved about 80,000 legal hours of work for the FFAC lawyers.

In his final opinion, the Judge strongly suggested that the families receiving this unexpected windfall contribute the punitive damages portion ($39,000) to a charitable organization. One of the participating families, at the Judge's suggestion, wrote to each of the recipient families asking them to consider donating to the Margaret Moses Memorial Foundation in their child's memory. Rosemary also wrote to each family suggesting that this money belonged to children in great distress and should not be regarded simply as a piece of private good luck to be spent on pleasures.

At the time of writing about a third of the families have sent donations ranging from 0.6 per cent to 30 per cent of their respective awards. Several families wrote to thank us for working on their behalf for eleven years to gain this money for them. One of them cheerfully described the European travel her family could now afford. The majority of the recipients simply accepted the award and as yet have not even bothered to respond.

Chapter 21

THE CHILDREN NOW

IT IS NOW nearly twenty years since we assisted in sending those earliest orphan children from Vietnam to their adoptive homes in Europe. Between 1967 and 1975 almost 4,000 children passed through our hands or our nurseries before continuing on to their adoptive families in Australia, Belgium, Canada, England, France, Finland, Germany, Italy, Luxemburg, Sweden, Switzerland and the USA, with one or two also going to Denmark, Holland, Norway, New Zealand and Spain. The youngest of these children are now entering their teens, having left Vietnam in April 1975 as newborn babies, while the oldest are already adults and even parents themselves.

Some children we did not know well, as they spent only a brief time with us in transit from other provincial orphanages; other children lived with us for a year or two or even longer and were very well-known to us. Some we received a few days after their birth, and others came to us when they were already of school age. They were of various racial mixtures: besides Vietnamese characteristics we thought we could also identify children who were in part Cambodian, Montagnard, Chinese, Korean, Filipino, Afro-American and Caucasian and beyond that it was pure conjecture. For our own amusement we would imagine the biological parents of some of the children and even in the cradle we thought we could sort out the poets and the peasants. In light-hearted moods, we would decide that a certain three-month-old baby should sell fish in the market and another was born to rule.

Because Vietnamese names are very repetitive, we gave most of the younger children a nursery name that would fix them indelibly in our memory. We named them after artists and musicians, after poets and prosewriters; philosophers and theologians; after saints and sinners. There were children named from the Bible and children from ancient mythology; there were others named after the great lovers of history and literature. There were children celebrating virtues, nature, the seasons, the cities of our birth, our personal friends and favourites; fairy-tale characters, and the mood of the moment. We had a Van Gogh, a Michelangelo and a Mozart; a Will Shakespeare, Dante and a C. S. Lewis; Socrates, Jean-Paul Sartre and Thomas Aquinas; Juliana of Norwich, Joan of Arc and Mary Magdalene. We had an Abraham, Moses and Solomon as well as a Zeus, Ulysses and Agamemnon. There was a Tristan and an Isolde; an Eloïse and an Abelard; a Julius Caesar, Marc Antony and a Cleopatra. There was Courage, Fidelity and Patience; Rainbow, Petunia, Mopoke, Epiphany and Autumn; Berlin, Melbourne and Adelaide. There was a Daniel Berrigan, Thomas Merton, and a Cinderella; also Wonder, Surprise and Desperation. Thanks to our two German nurses, there were many names from German folklore or history, and a host of more traditional names in all languages.

Some children came to us beaten and bruised and a few, like Helen of Troy and Tom, with fractured bones; others were physically unscarred but retarded in all aspects of their development. One child was cranky and miserable and vomited up a tapeworm; another child was inexplicably merry all the time and we delayed his placement for a while, trying to detect the cause for his unwarranted good humour. Some children came to us in a severely malnourished condition and had to be built up; a rare few, like Blancmange, seemed too fat and we suspected some other kind of maladjustment. There was Michelle, who may have been abandoned because she was inauspiciously born with a tooth already visible; then there was a five-year-old, Bach Mai, whose dental X-rays showed her second teeth just weren't there. There were a host of others with a mouthful of rotting stubs.

Olaf, De Profundis and Turtledove survived against great odds, while others, such as Vanessa and Joni, should never have died. There were many children who had been stricken with polio and were permanently handicapped before they came into our care, and just one child who actually contracted polio while in To Am nursery during the course of her vaccination. This shocked us exceedingly.

There were children who were totally blind, like Bich, Cuong, Tiresias and Roi; children with defective hearing and damaged ears; children with problems of co-ordination and concentration.

The children were placed through many different local agencies abroad, and so far there has been no comprehensive report on their development, nor any attempt to study their adaptation as a category, or 'class'. After twenty years I do not even have current addresses of a large number of them.

To my knowledge perhaps twenty children needed to be replaced in a second adoptive home when the first family found themselves unable to meet the needs of a certain child. More than half of these replacements involved children brought over in the airlift when the usual lengthy replacement procedures were necessarily accelerated. The second placements, after a more intense study of the child's personality and needs, were successful as far as we could judge. I know of three other cases where a family tragedy provoked a mother's complete breakdown and the adoptive children were removed in the best interests of all.

An escort visiting Vietnam had taken a fancy to our 'special' child, Ginny, and wanted to adopt her when she found that Ginny had arrived on the airlift. We were well aware of Ginny's condition and did all possible to counsel the B. family against this adoption as we could easily foresee the disruption Ginny would surely cause in a family of small children. Meanwhile we had placed her in an ideal foster family and she was doing well. But Mrs B. did not appreciate FFAC's concern, and threatened us with a lawsuit if we did not comply. Finally, FFAC was forced against its better judgement to hand over Ginny to the B. family. Not long after, we heard that the parents had divorced and that Ginny was still in the custody of Mrs B. We have had no news of her for many years.

I have, however, managed to keep in close contact with a few children in different countries and have watched them grow up. Other families have been faithful in sending photographs and reports at least once a year. Karine (Marie-Rose), one of my twelve haphazardly acquired godchildren, whom I knew as a baby in 1968 at Phu My, is now nineteen and a qualified children's nurse in France. I have received news of her from her parents at least ten times a year for eighteen years; never has any godmother been kept better informed.

A number of children with whom I had never had any contact since their departure from Vietnam, have suddenly tracked me down years later and written to me themselves. Some have asked me about their past, while others have just wanted to express their gratitude for being where they are and to share with me some news about themselves. I have been very touched to receive these letters so unexpectedly, mostly from older teenage girls. Only one of these letters so far has expressed a great need to know about her biological parents – 'I can't live with this empty feeling for the rest of my life' – though she does not want her adoptive parents to suspect such feelings in her. All the other letters have expressed a sense of total belonging with no trace of anxiety about their origins. The children know that they came from Vietnam but for the most part they do not identify themselves as Vietnamese but as American, or French, or Australian, and so on – as belonging to the country where they have grown up.

Marita in France, for instance, wrote to me spontaneously after a twelve-year silence: 'The little girl Marita hasn't forgotten you. She is fourteen now, in third form. My parents are well and I am very happy.' Marita is now nineteen, in her second year at the University of Lille. Her short letter out of the blue has been followed by regular donations to be used for our work in Thailand.

Although I have seen Nathalie several times in Belgium over the years, she wrote to me herself when she was fifteen, while she was attending school for a year in the USA, just wanting to express her satisfaction with her life and thank me for the part I had played in making it possible. In Belgium since she was a year old, Nathalie assured me that she had 'grown up like any Belgian on this earth'. Now at eighteen she is studying Economics at the University of Brussels.

I first met Karine (Kim Lien), Nathalie's older sister, in Phu My in 1967 (see p. 14), and have followed her progress over the years and visited her from time to time: 'I feel more like a Belgian than a Vietnamese though I am not rejecting my origins; I am proud to have been born in Saigon. I swear to myself to visit Vietnam as soon as I can. I enjoy life very much and at school everything is working well. Now I am studying Translation and Interpreting in English and Spanish. Next year I'll spend six months in Spain and six in England just to practise the languages.'

A few months after she wrote this letter, just when her life had never been brighter, Karine fell suddenly. and inexplicably ill, was kept comatose for several weeks by the hospital, and now her memory is so severely impaired there is little hope she will ever be able to resume her studies or continue with a normal life. At the moment, she is attending re-education therapy but the prognosis is not encouraging.

Theresa, our first baby for England, delivered at Christmas 1968, made history again by being the first of our children to return as a grown-up on a visit to her country of birth. Her schoolfriend's father was British Ambassador in Hanoi and Theresa had been invited to spend the school vacation with them. Her visa, obtained with some difficulty, did not, however, permit her to leave Hanoi or continue on to her actual birthplace in the south. En route to Hanoi, Theresa spent a few days with me at our FFAC nursery in Bangkok. She caused a sensation amongst the local staff with her mildly punk haircut and trendy outfit, very familiar modes in England but not so in Thailand. My mind boggled at the thought of a confrontation between the Ambassador and this vision, but Theresa assured me that his daughter's get-up was a match for her own. It seems that the Vietnamese in Hanoi did not quite know what to make of Theresa. They didn't imagine she was Vietnamese and somehow suspected she could not be Russian. But the visit made a deep impression on her and gave her some insights into her past and into the present plight of the Vietnamese people.

In January 1985 I attended a reunion of twenty-two Vietnamese children who had been adopted by families in and around Cologne. Some of these children I had seen occasionally in the intervening years, but there were others with whom I had had no contact since their departure from Vietnam. They ranged in age from ten to twenty. I was told that the children had not been dragged forcibly to the meeting but had actually wanted to come and meet someone connected with their early life. It was a delight for me to see some of To Am's well-known residents after a lapse of twelve or thirteen years. The children were not all known to each other and introduced themselves to the assembly, giving their current names and their nursery names. When the twins Andreas and Matthias gave their nursery names as 'Marcus' and 'Aurelius' all present burst into spontaneous applause.

Torge was amongst the youngsters who attended. Coming from St Paul's Orphanage, Bien Hoa, in April 1969, Torge is now nineteen and completing his secondary studies. He is very interested and involved in the work of Terre des Hommes, the organization responsible for his adoption in Germany, and proposes to start a group within TdH of the adopted young people themselves. He plans a career in the field of social work and is particularly drawn to working with the mentally handicapped, with whom he has already done volunteer work.

Philip also came from St Paul's, Bien Hoa. I met him in Berlin in January 1986 and was very moved as this gentle twenty-year-old discussed with me, in excellent English, his plans for a future also in the field of social service. I remembered him as a placid child who was still unable to stand up when we delivered him to his parents, aged just over two years, in December 1968. Until then he had spent his entire life in his crib.

The majority of the children are now adolescents – not a moment when one wants to make any summing-up of their progress or set a seal upon their development, but certainly a time when some curiosity about identity and the past may surface in them for the first time. To a great extent the child's interest in his past will depend on how this subject has been treated over the years by his family. But from my contact with a certain number of the children, directly or indirectly, I can say that they are not leading lives in any way different from their home-made counterparts. It is amusing, but quite as one would expect, to find them reflecting some of the attitudes and characteristics of their adoptive parents. Margarita, whom we baptized in Saigon in 1969 (p. 31), is now eighteen. I met her in 1984, and was delighted to note how much she resembles her adoptive mother Barbara, whom we had known so well, particularly in her social grace, her thoughtfulness and concern for others. I enjoyed a long conversation with Margarita on that visit and she wrote to me soon after: 'the one thing I have learned this past year is never to waste my life away ... I have to admit that I love school and have made tons of friends that I hope I can keep for the rest of my life ... I like to make goals in my life.' Two years later, Margarita is Senior Class President.

Cecilia's early history is mentioned in Chapter 2. Now nineteen and in France, she has completed her secondary schooling after many interruptions due to hospitalization for corrective surgery on her lower trunk and legs; she is at the moment working in her family's florist business: 'I arrived 22 December at the Nice airport where my mother was waiting for me. For her it was a very touching moment. I was a sort of long-awaited Christmas gift. I arrived in France with some severe health problems but despite that my family accepted me just as I was. They have brought me much in life, and above all they taught me to fight in any circumstances. And so, during all my childhood, I fought with them, against my handicap. They were always there during the most difficult periods, and encouraged me to believe and hope.' Cecilia's brother, Hugues, also from Providence Sadec, has finished his studies in audio-visual technology and is working as a radio technician.

Tham, in Canada, was stricken with polio at an early age in the Delta region. When I contacted her family last year, she was abroad participating in the Special Olympics. Tham has so many adoptive siblings that I have lost count of them; at least three of them came from FFAC.

Tia also suffered extensive damage in her legs due to polio. She is now at college in the US, but finding some of the conditions discouraging. She was obliged to take a sports subject, though there are few possibilities for someone whose legs are not strong. Then, struggling to pay her tuition, it was the last straw one day when her special handicap-parking place was taken up and she was fined for parking elsewhere in an emergency. A little later half her newly purchased text books were stolen from outside her dormitory as she went back to her car to fetch a second load. Tia has bravely changed campus and is pursuing her studies. Her sister Thi is already married, while Lara is a Senior in high school.

Jean-François (Nang) lived at Phu My for more than eight years before going to France in April 1975. Ever since I first met Nang in 1967, I've had a soft spot for him, and have followed his progress over the years. Recently we went together to Chartres to visit Sr Rose, former Superior of Phu My, and Jean-François reminisced with her of their days together. He had a vivid memory of the watchdog Youka, a vicious cur that bit me once when I made a too-rapid get-away on my motorbike. He remembered, too, Sr Rose's discipline and vigilance; she would haul him over to the convent building and personally supervise his homework because she thought he was making insufficient effort. That Sr Rose, responsible for 1,500 inmates at Phu My and for the supervision of every department, took such time over one nine-year-old she considered 'lazy', gives a clear indication of the woman and the operation she ran. Jean-François admitted he was lazy in Vietnam because he lacked any incentive to work. Now, at twenty-one, he has completed his technical studies in micro-mechanics and was proudly eager to show Sr Rose the model precision instruments he had made, and to show her that her effort had indeed borne fruit. He is a very earnest young man with a keen sense of duty that is a bit unexpected in one of his years. He has seven siblings, including two younger sisters from Vietnam.

Pami was about three years old and a picture of misery when she came to Newhaven nursery in April 1975. She was given the nursery name of 'Joy' as an incentive and an expression of optimism; it seemed the least we could do for her in the time that remained. She was evacuated to the USA on 26 April and her parents came from Finland to fetch her:

We found her sitting glassy-eyed in the corner of her crib in a Denver hospital, and rattling the bars. She had a big belly and a skin rash. Her legs were too weak to support her. In the beginning communication was difficult and Pami just wanted to sit and cry. But she had a good appetite and dark rye bread and pea soup were her favourites. If we tried to stop her from overeating, she responded vigorously by spitting on us and whistling like a street boy.

After a few months' steady progress, Pami had to be hospitalized for tuberculosis. Unwilling to adapt to her new surroundings, she simply climbed out of the window and was later found chasing birds in a nearby park.

As Pami learnt to express herself in Finnish, her story came out: her father was killed. Long-haired soldiers came down from the sky and shot everyone. 'I hid under the house. Why do they always come down when it is cloudy?' she asked. 'I fled with my sister to the river where the boats go. A crocodile attacked one of the children but was shot by the soldiers. There were also bananas in the trees but we didn't tell anybody.'

Despite her inelegant beginnings, Pami is now a graceful adolescent, who, while still in school, has taken up fashion modelling at her own insistence. She maintains her original strong streak of independence and stubbornness. She had four Finnish-born siblings on arrival in Finland, and has since acquired five more Asian siblings, from India, Bangladesh and Hong Kong.

Odile arrived in France in 1969 and it would be difficult to guess at her Vietnamese past. She was one of the few children we were ever able to remove from Go Vap Orphanage. At eighteen, Odile has just completed a course in carpentry at a technical school, undaunted by the fact that she was the only girl in the class, and is now working as a cabinet-maker. Besides five French-born siblings, Odile has two adoptive brothers from Vietnam and a married sister, Lucie. All three came from Providence orphanages in the Delta.

An Italian engineer, on a trip to Vietnam in late 1970, succeeded in obtaining the release of one more child from Go Vap Orphanage. Nga-Francesca then spent a year at To Am nursery before joining her adoptive parents and older sister Sylvie in Milan, in October 1971. She was our first child for Italy. For many years I received photos of the two girls growing up together and obviously enjoying each other's company and affection. I visited them once in Milan. Now aged sixteen, Francesca is contented and independent-spirited, completing her high school studies, and at the same time studying music at the Milan Conservatorium. She is a gifted pianist and violinist.

Misha has shown her own fighting spirit right from the beginning. Apparently enjoying herself vastly at Newhaven nursery, she was not ready for any indiscriminate change of allegiance when her parents came to Saigon to fetch her in 1974. It took days for her to accept these two new adults in her life, despite their gentle attempts to win her over. Back in England, Misha finally relaxed at the sight of the other three children in the family. At fourteen Misha is a joyful and self-confident child, particularly gifted athletically. She has her blue belt in judo, and a room filled with trophies, including a gold medal from Holland. She attends the French *Lycée*, and is bilingual.

Victoria spent her first year in Allambie before going to join her family in England. From the beginning she was determined to compete with her two older brothers and girlish things were out.

She played football and excelled in athletics and running. Vicky has won many trophies over the years despite a minor heart defect and a series of operations on her perforated eardrums. At fifteen she has given up competitive sports to concentrate on her O-Levels in French, Latin and Greek.

In late 1974, when Mia's adoption was completed and her application was with the Ministry of the Interior, Sweden happened to express a political bias against the government of South Vietnam. Consequently, the government decided it would issue no more exit visas for Sweden. Mia's father, together with a delegation of adoptive families, came to Vietnam to discuss the issue. They succeeded in unblocking the impasse within a short time, and Mia was able to join her family in Sweden in January 1975. Now, at thirteen, Mia is very much part of the teenage scene in Sweden, with a variety of sporting and cultural interests. She is fluent in several languages, and is probably our only child now speaking Estonian.

Evelyn (Florence Nightingale) has had more of an Asian cultural diet than most; her parents are in the US Foreign Service, and since she joined them in 1974 they have lived in Vietnam, Thailand, Washington and now Pakistan. 'School for her is less an educational experience than an elaborate social minuet,' according to her mother. She loves to talk and to write, and has a deep husky voice that admits no contradiction and quite belies her diminutive size.

Luke (nursery name Hymn – also an act of faith) came to To Am in February 1975 in a pathetically malnourished condition. Unfit to travel on 4 April, he was evacuated to Australia later that month and spent six weeks in hospital before being allowed to join his family. The tenacity needed to survive his first months lingers on in his irrepressibility and his unbounded enthusiasm for non-academic life. His social skills are well-developed; he has an evident concern for others as well as a strong sense of responsibility for his family. Luke has a passion for sport, pop music, and animals, especially elephants.

Sanh was already afflicted with a debilitating and degenerative illness when he went to live with his family in Canada at the end of 1971 (see p. 49). Over the years he has submitted uncomplainingly to regular blood transfusions and to the increasing discomfort and weakness of his condition. He is a gentle young man, uncalculating, generous and helpful with his siblings, five home-grown, and five or six interracial. He is a good cook and is proudly employed in a restaurant. His dream is to own his own restaurant one day, though he understands he would need help in managing it.

Kim (Little Bear) won her first battle in league with her parents against the Australian Welfare and Immigration bureaucracy in 1972. Ever since then she has been strongly standing up for herself and for her family. Now aged fifteen, she is in her fourth year of high school and is a talented student in English and mathematics. She is often very earnest, expresses her ideas with great conviction, and though deprecating about her own abilities, has a lot of self-respect. She has been known to respond to racial insults with physical violence or easy tolerance, depending on their source. Her two sisters and younger brother describe her as pushy, friendly, kind, loyal, and paranoid. Kim is also my godchild.

Benjamin, now twelve and in the USA, is a serene and dignified child, who likes peace and quiet and amusing himself creatively. He has recently joined the local Chinese school and is learning calligraphy. Before he was four-years-old, he began Suzuki violin lessons, and later the piano. In 1984 when his father was on assignment in Adelaide, Australia, he met up with four other young Vietnamese musicians in the local Suzuki music classes, the four members of the McGowran family (see below), from our nurseries.

Paul (Chopin) came from Fr Olivier's orphanage to To Am in 1971, at a time when we were paying tribute to musicians. He then spent a few months in a Dutch Embassy foster home before joining his adoptive parents in England in 1972. He was joined by a sister Safi (Elaine) in May 1975. Safi had survived the crash of the C-5A on 4 April but had sustained physical injuries and was transported out of Vietnam in a medivac plane. Paul at sixteen is a well-adjusted young man with a great sense of humour. He enjoys school life and is especially keen on mathematics. He spends hours at home working on his computer and his current ambition is to be a forensic scientist. Safi at thirteen is a cheerful and active child with a mind of her own. She enjoys most aspects of school life except mathematics, and sings and plays classical guitar. She is a 'super cook' according to her parents and prefers such practical activities.

Emma (nursery name Clodine) is the same age as Safi and also survived the C-5A crash. She is at present in England, but is probably the only child from our nurseries who has lived in South

Africa and the remote island of Tristan da Cunha where she must have been a significant percentage of the population. Emma's mother Anne was Director of Allambie nursery in 1973, and her father Gerry, who worked in the British Foreign Service, was also one of our foster parents. Emma is also numbered amongst my godchildren.

Tobias (nursery name Jean-Paul Sartre) and Maria (Amanda) both survived the crash of the C-5A and then easily adapted themselves to the rigours of an arctic climate when they joined their adoptive families in Sweden. Tobias at fifteen has many friends and much determination. He also has three interracially adopted siblings. Maria is naturally cheerful, bright at school and has many extra-curricular interests and hobbies; she has one older brother.

Anna Tiffany (Turtledove) was only a few weeks old when she left Vietnam on 26 April 1975. She spent the next two months in intensive care in a Denver hospital, fighting for her tiny, fragile life. Her adoptive parents phoned repeatedly from London for news of her progress. There was none. On several occasions I fled the FFAC office before the expected call from London as it became increasingly difficult to confront the parents each day with the same depressing news. I didn't want them to come to the USA themselves, as I was afraid Turtledove would die anyhow. Then we asked Sr Rayneld, formerly of To Am nursery, to fly to Denver from New York and personally nurse Turtledove, stay by her bedside and hold her as much as possible. This human contact provided the critical ingredient and the baby's health improved steadily; by July she was ready for the trans-Atlantic flight to London. I escorted her myself; it was a long time since I had travelled with a single child and I felt distinctly underemployed during that trip. Turtledove weighed all of 6 lb when I handed her to her nervous and expectant parents. Now Anna Tiffany, Ti for short, is aged twelve, and possessed of a strong survival instinct. Her parents describe her *joie de vivre* as a real celebration of life.

At four-years of age, Ulla accompanied her adoptive mother, Ilse Ewald, Doreen Beckett and myself when we were evacuated by helicopter to a refugee ship on 29 April 1975. During that entire week-long ordeal, little Ulla behaved stoically, adapted to the confined conditions and never once complained or caused anxiety. After landing in the Philippines, Ulla travelled with her mother to

Children Then and Now.

66, 67 Little Bear – now Kim – held by Agnes at
To Am, Christmas 1971, and in Australia,
aged 15 (August 1986).

66

67

68, 69 Margarita (see also no. 18) dressed as a mascot, and now in the USA, aged 17 (1986).
70, 71 Sanh in his Cub Scout cap, To Am 1971, and now in Canada, a member of the Bronstein family (back row, 2nd from left).
72,73 Francesca hugging her sister Sophie in Italy in 1978, first seen in To Am in 1971.

74,75 Thu Van, now Tia, at Providence Orphanage, Soctrang in 1971, and in America, 1985.
76,77,78 Reunion of some children adopted in Germa Cologne 1984. Torge, in 1968 at St Paul's Bien Hoa in no. 77, is third from left, in the back row of the group. Marcus and Aurelius, twins at To Am in 1972, in no. 78, are standing together, now

called Matthias and Andreas, middle row, fourth
and fifth from right, in the German group.
,80 Turtledove, now Anna Tiffany, in Colorado
General Hospital, July 1975, is now in England.
Seen with her little sister, Josephine, in 1986.
,82 Jacqueline, now Jade, first in Rach Gia with Lola d'Orazio,
the day she arrived at Allambie, and later in the USA, aged 13.

Children of Several Nationalities.

83 In Australia, Fiona, Heidi, Lisi,
   and Rosi (1986).
84 In France, Cecilia, aged 11 in 1979.
85 In England, Sati, aged 12 in 1986.
   She was a survivor of the crash.
86 In Germany, Kim (Brian), aged 18.
87 In Finland, Pami (Joy), aged 14.
88 In America, Benjie, and Chad, members
   of different families.

Australia before returning to Germany where she met her adopted Vietnamese sister, Susan, then aged six. As a tiny baby, Susan had been found wounded and orphaned in a northern province and had been rescued and treated on the German ship, the *Helgoland*, anchored at Danang. Ilse nursed the child, who had lost a lung, and subsequently adopted her before making contact with our operation in Saigon. While Ilse worked in our nurseries, Susan was cared for by her grandmother in Germany. Ilse visited her regularly when she went to Europe escorting convoys, and several times brought Susan back to stay with us at To Am. I have met the two girls many times in the intervening years. Now Susan at eighteen and Ulla at sixteen are well-balanced young women, who have acquired some of their adoptive mother's practical competency, artistic talent and sense of hospitality and concern for others. They have expressed no anxieties about their past, and are very much at home in Germany. It is a pleasure to see how well the two girls get along together.

Fiona, Heidi, Elizabeth (Lisi) and Rosemary (Rosi), although unrelated by blood, are now all sisters in their adoptive home in Australia. They joined their parents between 1972 and 1975, Fiona coming from Phu My; Heidi from Fr Olivier's; Lisi from Providence, Soctrang; and Rosi from St Paul's Vinh Long.

My first contact with Dr Brian and Susi McGowran was in early 1971 during a home visit in Adelaide. I made it clear over the telephone that I was quite unwilling to embark on any more adoptions in Australia, since my limited experience with the local Welfare and Immigration authorities had been negative. I was also unwilling to subject the children to Australia's 'yellow peril' racism, which was even then finding expression at high levels. Dr and Mrs McGowran refused to be put off by my discouraging attitude and insisted on a personal meeting with me. I reluctantly agreed, convinced that it would be fruitless. Before the end of that meeting, I found myself firmly committed to finding them a child as soon as I returned to Saigon. Brian himself came to Saigon to collect Fiona in 1971; and we were soon looking for her sister. Vanessa died. Then Heidi was ready to be collected. Lisi went next. Finally in 1974, when I was carrying 'Moira' in my arms all the way back from Vinh Long to Saigon I knew she had to be McGowran number four: this was Rosi.

The children, a year between each of them, are now all in high school. Their academic performance is exceptionally good, but their musical education is especially interesting. All four have been playing the violin by Suzuki method and also the piano for many years, and while still in primary school they all played in, or eventually led, both the Primary Schools' String Orchestra and the Festival Orchestra. In January 1987, I was there when they played in the Senior Strings Ensemble at the Second Pan-Pacific Suzuki Conference in Adelaide, held in the presence of Dr and Mrs Suzuki themselves. The four so impressed Dr Suzuki that he strongly urged them to attend the International Conference to be held in Berlin later in 1987.

It would surely seem too much of a coincidence if four randomly chosen children should turn out to possess some mysterious essence that made them particularly musical. The parents insist (as does Suzuki philosophy) that such talent is latent in most normal children, and only needs the right encouragement and parental commitment to bring it out. The McGowrans have also found music a good way to involve the children in the activities of the growing Vietnamese community in Adelaide.

Of course, such dedication and exhilaration has to be paid for: every morning, for instance, beginning at 5.30 a.m., when the four children individually practise four instruments in a three-bedroom house! Because these girls are almost my neighbours in Adelaide, I have followed their progress through the years and loved them as any proud aunt. I am delighted to have been able to watch closely, at least in this one case, the creation of a family, in which to some extent I participated. Parents have found children with whom they can share the richness of their own love and lives, and themselves be enriched in the process. Four unrelated orphans are no longer alone, having found not only parents, but each other. This was a family formed against the odds stacked by governments, bureaucracies, and prejudices, and if I have written about them at some length, it is with a certain sense of irony in that I too almost refused to help make this family a reality.

The children I have described, and thousands of others, left Vietnam at various ages and stages of emotional development. Some of them arrived in their new families while still tiny babies and adapted easily; others had already spent years in an orphanage without the possibility of developing a relationship with any parent figure. Thus, retarded in their emotional development, a few had difficulties in forming deep bonds with their new family. Without a deep parent–child bonding there was no proper framework for healthy moral and emotional development. Some parents seemed to know instinctively how to handle difficult behaviour and worked through it with firmness and patience until the child finally understood that he was not alone and that his life had to touch and be touched by others who love him, and that this imposed obligations that went both ways. Other families needed, and sought, professional help to solve the difficulties. The instances of irremediable problems were, thank God, few. The miracle is that so many of the children have succeeded, with the help of their adoptive families, in rising above their inauspicious beginnings and in some cases years of deprivation. For the most part the children are now growing up to face an adolescence and maturity that has been built on years of security in a loving family environment.

POSTSCRIPT

FRIENDS FOR ALL CHILDREN began operating in Thailand in 1976. FFAC Thailand is now a completely indigenous Foundation, involved in a variety of child welfare activities. Besides administering a sponsorship programme for the education of more than 4,000 poor children, it runs a small nursery, conducts pre-school and family health and welfare programmes in many city slums and assists in the government home for handicapped orphans.

Although there are large numbers of abandoned children in the orphanages, there are relatively few adoptions taking place. FFAC is officially permitted eight inter-country adoptions a year, but, in fact, the Department of Public Welfare has never processed more than six of the submitted files in any one year. Last year it managed to process only four of the submitted files, and the remaining four will be subtracted from this year's quota. It is a heartbreaking situation for those who are living with the children and for the parents who are waiting years to receive them, and who are missing out on their children's most precious formative years.

It is strangely illogical that a child can languish unloved and unnoticed in an orphanage, but the moment he has the chance to become a beloved son in some family abroad, he becomes an important commodity that cannot be disposed of without endless bureaucratic procedures that are totally unrelated to his welfare. Various government departments and committees, and legions of office-workers are called upon as arbiters to determine the future of a child in whom they have no personal interest whatsoever. The child is rarely seen by the arbiters during the years of decision-making, at least not by those making the decisions. Instead, they leisurely apply themselves to a consideration of the adoption application and feel no sense of urgency in seeking clarification where they judge it to be needed; the file will sit around for months with no action being taken. They are not watching the children wasting their childhood in an institution; they feel no personal responsibility about depriving the child for so many years of parental love. They leave the office in the afternoon and return to the comfort of their own families. The tragic sadness is that these office-workers may be convinced they are rendering some essential service in the process of earning their living. They may think they are protecting the child from abuse while they are labouring such questions as diplomatic relations with Lichtenstein ('Where is it?' they ask), and what this could mean to the child's future if an adoptive father, resident and working in Switzerland, happens to have been born in Lichtenstein . . . Or, if a child has some imperfection or handicap, they will not believe that the agency, which they themselves have registered, has acted responsibly in informing the adoptive parents of the problem, because in fact they cannot believe that anyone would want an imperfect child. And again, another six months is wasted before the Welfare authorities accept that the agency has spoken the truth and that the parents indeed know about the child, and still wish to care for him. Because they are not personally involved, they cannot conceive that others amongst their own compatriots love the child and can be trusted to act in his best interest. Their mistrust is illogical and counter-productive.

The adoption process, therefore, instead of protecting the interests of the child, often becomes one more obstacle imposed between the orphan child and the family that could bring him the happiness he deserves. It is a bureaucratic procedure whose main value is to provide justification for the government department involved. A long drawn-out procedure with many months of inactivity is meant to imply a thorough investigation, as country X tries to tell the world that it takes its abandoned children seriously, and does not lightly let them seek their happiness elsewhere.

How can we measure the success of an adoption, or how can we even define success in the life of any child or adult? I would dare to speak of success in general terms as an appreciation of one's own essential worth and loveableness. In Vietnam we conducted what

Margaret Moses, in one of her unforgettable phrases, called a 'salvage operation'. It was a limited exercise in a time of great instability. But if this book is to achieve any purpose in describing the prospects then, and the new lives now, of abandoned and orphaned children, I hope it may show how in peaceful times we are bound even more to regard a child's right to life and adequate nurturing as the most fundamental of human rights, outweighing any consideration of religion, race or politics. And though a few years ago, an authority in the Thai Welfare Department informed us quite condescendingly that our ideas on child development were *passé* – that the latest theories held that children had no need of nurturing, but only of 'power models' – I am sure that no one who has ever loved a child or ever been loved as a child would agree with this woman. Children certainly do need models from whom they can learn love, trust, mutual acceptance and responsibility. Those lessons will best prepare a child to face life with confidence, and they are lessons best learnt not in an orphanage, but within the commitment of family life.

Principal Foreign Helpers in the Nurseries

Rosemary Taylor (Australia) February 1967–April 1975
Rosa Tintore (Spain) May 1968–January 1970
Anne de Stoexhe (Belgium) January 1970–early 1971
Yvette Charamont (France) March 1970–April 1971
Margaret Moses (Australia) April 1971–April 1975
Ilse Ewald (Germany) April 1971–April 1975
Carmel Curtain (Australia) May 1971–April 1972
Judy Seward (Australia) June 1971–June 1972
Tim Seward (Australia) 1972
Wendy Burdon (England) August 1971–1972
Anne Dolan (m. McCrudden) (England) 1972–July 1973
Christie Leivermann (USA) June 1972–1974; 1974–April 1975
Linda Mayers (USA) January 1972–January 1973
Brigitte Tison (France) November 1972–May 1973
Avis Roskilly (England) June 1972–May 1973
Birgit Blank (Germany) February 1973–April 1975
Jo Russell (Australia) 1974
Sr Susan McDonald (USA) May 1973–April 1975
Peggy Hammond (USA) July 1973–June 1974
Sr Mary-Nelle Gage (USA) August 1973–April 1975
Elaine Norris (USA) August 1973–April 1975
Carol Lambert (USA) January 1974–July 1974
Sr Doreen Beckett (Australia) July 1973–April 1975
Julie Chinberg (USA) August 1973–April 1975
Edie de Chadenedes (USA) November 1973–April 1974
Mary Cusack (Australia) March 1974–April 1975

Anne Barry (Australia) February 1974–February 1975
Sr Mary Rayneld (USA) September 1974–April 1975
Mrs Margaret Moses (Australia) December 1974–April 1975
May Cope (Australia) December 1974–April 1975
Kathleen Garland (USA) January 1975–April 1975
Lee Makk (Australia) February 1975–April 1975
Pat Zirk (USA) January 1975–April 1975
Debbie Chambers (USA) September 1974–April 1975
Michelle Boutagh (USA) January 1975–April 1975
Diane Bennett (Australia) 1975

Part-time

Lydia Brackney (USA)
Theodora (Dolly) Bui (Vietnam). Bui van To, Dolly's Vietnamese
husband , was an engineer, and helped us throughout with building
and administration
Br John Carr SJ (USA)
Lucienne LeGall (Vietnam)

I have listed here only the 'long-term' foreign staff – those who
stayed for at least five or six months. There were many other aides
and short-term specialists, particularly in the last two years. I also
could not list the more than 400 local Vietnamese staff, without
whose vital services the orphanages would not have been able to
function. Each nursery director could furnish a list of those deserv-
ing special mention, including Thi Ba, Marie-Nga, Agnes, and Kim-
Cuc from To Am's early days; Huy and Hien, whom Ilse first met on
the *Helgoland* in Danang, and who became her most trusted
colleagues; Sang, supporting Susan at Newhaven since its opening;
Kim Tien, our staff instructor who roused us to new endeavours
with her high-powered enthusiasm and professional expertise. But,
particularly, I must mention the general secretary, Luu My Le, a
person on whom I personally depended so much and in whose
competence and dedication we all had absolute confidence. Le left
with the final evacuation flight of 26 April.